WAʀ
after
Ukraine

First published 2024

Published under licence by Brown Dog Books and The Self-Publishing Partnership Ltd, 10b Greenway Farm, Bath Rd, Wick, nr. Bath BS30 5RL, UK

www.selfpublishingpartnership.co.uk

ISBN printed book: 978-1-83952-826-2
ISBN e-book: 978-1-83952-827-9

Cover design by Kevin Rylands
Internal design by Andrew Easton

Printed and bound in the UK

This book is printed on FSC® certified paper

WAR
after
Ukraine

Making Sense of War

Christopher K Pike

BROWN
DOG
BOOKS

Also by Christopher K Pike:
About War
War in Context

All three books can be purchased
through the website:
makingsenseofwar.com

Which has links to Brown Dog Books:
www.browndogbooks.uk

and
Amazon/Kindle

To the memory of...

Lawrence de Villamil Wragg
1943 to 2022
Friend and colleague; polymath and wit:
sadly missed

WAR AFTER UKRAINE: PREFACE

This is the third and final book in the trilogy *Making Sense of War*, the first volume being *About War* and the second *War in Context*.

The concept behind this trilogy is to recognise war as a political act and in those terms comprehend the provenance, progress and resolution of any war. Strategy is key. Any nation-state's approach to war must be multifunctional, integrating overall strategy with domestic and foreign policy, civil servants, think tanks, and, most of all, senior military officers. When discussing strategy, our definition is: *strategy is everything about the future.*

As this trilogy was being drafted, the world was shocked by the Russian invasion of Ukraine on 24 February 2022. This has prompted a shift of attention to an analysis of Russia's use of force to achieve political change, whether czarist, Soviet, post-Soviet or under Putin's regime. We take no comfort in Pyotr Stolypin's (Russian diplomat, 1906–1911) assertion that 'In Russia, every 10 years everything changes, and nothing changes in 200 years …'

Without wishing to detract from the original objective, an analysis of Russia and its use of force provides the first part of this book. Parts Two to Five stick to the original concept but take note of Russian actions and put them into context.

The complete canon of deliberations about war and its causes is vast. A lifetime of research would hardly scratch the surface. Artificial Intelligence might help in identifying some of the parameters but only leave the scholar with tricky problems of interpretation. The vastness of the war canon, with its link to and influence from almost every aspect of human endeavour, may daunt the uninitiated, but war concerns every citizen. Few people live in countries that have not experienced war in one way or another at some stage. As Trotsky said famously: '... you may not be interested in war, but war may be interested in you.'

The analysis is focussed on the future for war, but also takes an historical perspective. The main guide to the future is the past. In *War in Context* we explored a categorisation of war, yet every war is different in its own way: different in its provenance, its process and its resolution.

That said, many wars end, to every party's relief, but leave unresolved questions. Hitler's exploitation of the 'November criminals' (the Stab-in-the-back myth) and the harsh provisions of the Treaty of Versailles led to one of the greatest calamities the world has seen: the Second World War.

Many treatises on the causes of war betray their political inclinations and the era in which they were written. Most make respected reference to long dead political philosophers, damning them with faint praise or dismissing them completely. Kant was too much of an idealist (none the worse for that), Marx a dangerous Soviet philosopher (he wasn't) and then there was the Woodrow Wilson's fourteen principles (okay, but it didn't work did it?). This trilogy has not concerned itself with political dogma. There is little difference in propensity to wage war between what are described as autocratic or dictatorial regimes and democratic, left-wing or even socialist regimes.

There's an oft-repeated statement that no democracy has ever gone to war with another. How true is that and where might it fit?

There have been many attempts to solve this age-old puzzle: what causes war? Suggestions have ranged from man's violent nature through to the structure of the international environment. We are no closer to a real answer. Geoffrey Blainey in his classic *The Causes of War* (1973) suggests that a whole combination of factors cause wars. So does Robert Gilpin, American political scientist at Princeton (*War and Change in*

World Politics, 1981), who focussed on the issues of power dynamics and the well-worn concept of the balance of power.

John J Mearsheimer is an American political scientist and international relations scholar who is an advocate of realist school of thought. He is a Professor at the University of Chicago and has been described as the most influential realist of his generation: the realist's realist. In his *The Tragedy of Great Power Politics* (2001), he emphasises the anarchic nature of the international system, suggesting that nation-states are driven almost exclusively by the pursuit of power and security. Mearsheimer dismisses the idea of alliances, and also of democracies and international institutions, which he considers will not eliminate the competitive nature of international relations.

But the extraordinary thing about war is that given the wide range of the causes of war, the variety of ways in which any war progresses and the way that, ultimately, differences are resolved – or quite frequently not – the manifestation of the quarrel is armed conflict with the corresponding cost in blood and treasure. And quite often those at the front line who fight and die are no wiser than their forefathers about the rationale for that war. (See Simon Tisdall's comment in Chapter 17.)

There is relatively less attention on the subject of peace. Geoffrey Blainey observes that for every thousand words written on the causes of war, there is fewer than one on the causes of peace. Indeed, Michael Howard, the doyen of war writing in the United Kingdom and the first Professor of War Studies at King's College London War Studies department wrote *The Invention of Peace* in 2001. It is an intriguing thesis. He asserts that prior to Napoleon nobody thought war particularly unusual. Dynasties and empires waged war on other dynasties and empires using resources – men, munitions, logistical support, that were not necessarily subject to any democratic control. Summer was the time for campaigning, although the troops had to be home in time for the harvest, and winter was the time for hunting, largely to keep the aristocracy occupied and to exercise the horses. Napoleon, despite still being honoured in France, was responsible for the change and it was he who suborned the whole of the new French state to his purposes.

One other short article is worth quoting, and that is *Victory, Peace and Justice* by Beatrice Heuser (Professor of International Relation at Glasgow), which she subtitles *The Neglected Trinity*. The best summary of this article is to mention her sub-subtitle with a quote from Sir Maurice Hankey (1877–1963, a British civil servant who made the unusual transition from the civil service to ministerial office):

The first aim in war is to win, the second is to prevent defeat, the third is to shorten it, and the fourth and most important, which must never be lost to sight, is to make a just and durable peace.

Quite so.

Tragically there will always be bad people. As Euripides said in his play *Orestes*: 'when one with honeyed words but evil mind persuades the mob great woes befall the state.'

The parameters for the next war can be guessed but are unknown. Inexperienced – at least in war – politicians will be faced with new situations, new problems. Armed forces' generals will provide the best advice they can, but cannot tell what will happen when they hit the ground, or take to the air, or set sail. What we can say is that in considering war we should recall that wars seldom turn out the way you expect. The causes of war are an interplay of domestic considerations, the sovereign nation–state and international relations. More particularly the leader or leaders of those states play a dominant role.

This book integrates these many factors and, with appropriate caveats, looks at the future of war. It is divided into five parts:

Part One: The Russian invasion of Ukraine, 2022. In this part we consider Russia's use of armed force and find that there is very little difference between the czarist, Soviet, post-Soviet and Putin eras. It does not bode well for the future of European security.

Part Two: The Nation, the State and the Nation-State; the Nation-State and War. About 80 per cent of current wars are intrastate. That is to say an established and accepted state is having to cope with an insurgency, a revolt or even a civil or secessionist war. In this part we explore the exact nature of the nation, the state and the nation-state as a basis for thinking about peace. We also consider whether the nation-state will endure.

Part Three: European Security Architecture, NATO and Ukraine. No individual European state, whether a member of NATO, member of the European Union or a member of neither can defend itself against a coordinated attack from a third-party such as the Russian armed forces. However, many EU members are NATO members and rely on NATO for defence. Although NATO has performed well during the Russia-Ukraine war, its future is precarious, and it may not survive if the United States withdraws support.

Part Four: Past decisions, future questions: the prospects for nuclear weapons. The accepted wisdom is that for nuclear matters, deterrence is the answer, which means CASD (continuous at sea deterrent) for the United Kingdom. This part of the book suggests that this may be an overhang from decisions made about nuclear weapons at the dawn of the nuclear age. Are they still valid?

Part Five: War after Ukraine. We review the ten main concepts advanced during the trilogy and explore what we have learned from the Russian invasion of Ukraine. After some observations, we advance seven perspectives on war as a basis for thinking about and achieving peace.

CAVEAT

This section on the Russian-Ukrainian War is concerned only with that calamitous and disastrous conflict. This is not to make light of other current wars in the western hemisphere, tragic for those affected. Examples include:

Syria, a civil war that started in 2011, with more than 200,000 casualties (includes both killed and wounded);
Yemen, a civil war that started in 2014, with casualties around 400,000;
Ethiopia, a civil war involving Tigrayan secession, starting in 2018 with around 700,000 casualties.

There are also conflicts that could be defined as civil war, secessionist violence or insurgency in Libya, the Democratic Republic of Congo, the Central African Republic, Iraq, Mali, Nigeria, Myanmar, Sudan and many others.

CONTENTS

Part One: Russia

INTRODUCTION: THE RUSSIAN INVASION OF UKRAINE

The Russian Federation's invasion of Ukraine in February 2022 was the greatest calamity of the 21st century, greater than the 9/11 attacks and greater than the 2008 financial meltdown.

It marked a turning point in European history, the end of countless illusions, and heightened security concerns for many countries, particularly those contiguous to the two protagonists. It called into question the value of the United Nations, provided a revitalisation of NATO and, paradoxically, furthered the move away from oil and gas to renewable energy sources. It confirmed that Europe, however configured, could not stand on its own with regard to security and confirmed the United States as, in Madeleine Albright's words, the 'indispensable nation'. President Macron's 'strategic autonomy' is now, if not a lost cause, certainly delayed for several years.

The Russian-Ukrainian war demonstrates that there are many more dimensions to security than the simply physical, satisfied by either adequate military resources or through alliances and treaties. Security is absolutely a political matter.

It might be asserted that much progress has been made over the past few years and that a security architecture has been outlined or formed, but coming second in any war is losing, not a consolation prize. For liberal, democratic countries to lose a war against an authoritarian and dictatorial regime could have far-reaching and serious consequences. That applies as much to Europe as it does to Ukraine.

Let us emphasise this: the United States, NATO and Europe, however formed, may well facilitate Ukraine's triumph over Russia, but the fact that the war started in the first place is a failure of Western international diplomacy stretching back to the dissolution of the Soviet Union in 1991. Yes, the war was absolutely Putin's responsibility, but the West has agency for creating the circumstances.

And, as if to confirm the bad news, there are many second-order issues to consider: the war represents the end of illusions about living with and accommodating authoritarian regimes, the end of any thoughts that reliance could be placed in treaties and international agreements in what is, to the realist, an anarchic international system (see the first volume in this series: *About War*).

It has shown in stark contrast the difficulty of achieving any consensus amongst European states. Although the EU and Europe as a whole have reacted well and generously to Ukraine's predicament, there are growing divergencies amongst the countries as to how to continue, and particularly what the final resolution, insofar that such exists at all, might look like. The good news is that it has jolted Europe out of its complacent slumber and demonstrated to its leaders that Europe, as one of the world's largest economic and trading blocks, involves political responsibilities – the unrealised as well as the accepted.

The word *strategy* is usually thrown about with casual abandon in commentaries about war, but real strategy (long-term, competitive, contingent and multi-functional) has been and will always be a complex undertaking, beset by intelligence contradictions, lack of agreed protocols and difficulties of implementation – all the more challenging where a consensus has to be reached amongst sovereign allies. Resolving this current conflict will require formidable diplomatic skills, billions of dollars and persistence and stamina for the long haul. It will need many countries and institutions to provide security guarantees, to both Ukraine and the Russian Federation.

There was an element of triumphalism in the west, and particularly in the United States, at the collapse of the Soviet system. Many saw the Soviet Union and communism as indivisible. Perhaps they were. But nostalgia for the old Soviet Union persists in Russia. Bitterness at its demise defines its current leader, the ex-KGB agent, Vladimir Vladimirovich Putin. It would be tragic if similar triumphalism prevailed should Russia demonstrably fail in this war. At the end of the Second World War, any triumphalism at Germany's defeat was tempered by the distinction made between Nazis and Germans.

There have been two great surprises in this war, one a reflection of the other. Prior to the start and in the early stages, some European countries were reluctant to provide arms and to support Ukraine on the basis that it would prolong the conflict and extend the agony. It was believed that the Russian armed forces were well equipped, well led and had a sound logistics capability and a good technological base. On the other hand, it was assumed that the Ukrainian Armed Forces, especially having had a hard time in Donbas, were poorly equipped and generally not up to the task. How wrong people were! We explore this in depth below but, in short, the Ukrainian army performed extraordinarily well and this encouraged other European countries, particularly the United States, to supply more and better munitions. The Russian army performed very poorly on every front, demonstrating appalling intelligence failures. Our spies seriously underestimated Ukraine and overestimated Russia.

And this is where the war will have global consequences. Russia's poor military and political performance may encourage other countries such as Belarus and Kazakhstan to distance themselves from the Russian Federation. It might also encourage China to acquire disputed territories in northern Manchuria. Ukraine's heroic performance, and particularly the generous provision of munitions from the United States, might just deter China from thinking about acquiring Taiwan for the time being.

This war has been widely reported by the usual news media, but also – a notable feature for this war – by almost all think tanks such as

Carnegie, Brookings, Chatham House, RUSI and King's College London War Studies Department. It might also be described as the first internet war. Properly edited and cross-referenced, social media has provided invaluable data to organisations such as The Institute for the Study of War and Bellingcat, who have skilfully turned raw data into useful information. There are also internal social media groups within Ukraine that have kept up Ukrainian morale. A cheeky virtual group called the North Atlantic Fella Organisation §harangues Ukraine's enemies on social media and raises funds for the defenders, thus supporting Ukraine's efforts.

On the Radio 4 programme *Today* on Thursday 29 December 2022, Jeremy Fleming, the head of the UK's GCHQ, interviewed Avril Haynes, the US Director of National Intelligence. There was but little we did not know already, but comments were revealing. Haynes admitted that we cannot manage threats without partners and allies (hardly a revelation), that we were facing a battle of narratives between Russia and the West (yes!) and that the task was to counter Russian propaganda (yes!). As we consider in the first chapter, there was no hint that Russia might have some justification. This is not to admit any culpability on behalf of the West, but it is vital to understand Russian grievances and Russian motivation for the attack when the inevitable negotiations start.

Neither was there any admission that the intelligence agencies – including military intelligence as well – had seriously overestimated the capabilities of the Russian Federation's army. The numerical advantage over the Ukrainians was well-known and is publicly available, but what we – and Ukraine – needed to know was just how well the Russians would fight on the ground. We could easily understand that this represented the most challenging aspect for the intelligence agencies but, given that there are sixteen agencies of the United States Intelligence Community, with over 100,000 employees and a combined budget of (according to the *Washington Post*) over $50 billion, might not the American taxpayer have expected something more? Incidentally, according to some ten-year-old figures, some 70 per cent of this budget goes to private companies. The UK equivalent seems to be around £3 billion, but the same criterion applies: what were the intelligence agencies doing? In the appendix to the second volume in our series, *War in Context*, were laid out some twenty possible security risks on Europe's fringes. How prepared are Western agencies and leaders for such exigencies?

1 THE STORY SO FAR

In order to present a complete and coherent account, there is some overlap here with the supplement in *War in Context: The Russian Attack on Ukraine*.

On Thursday 24 February 2022, Russian armed forces crossed the border with neighbouring Ukraine and attacked the country from the north, the north-east and the east. Surely the most spectacular attack, and most permanent to date, was from the south: from Crimea and the southeast into Kherson and Zaporizhzhia – possibly betrayed by some of Ukraine's senior armed forces personnel. There was 'previous' for this: after the Russian takeover of Crimea in 2014, the acting commander of the Ukrainian Navy, Sergei Yeliseyev, defected to Russia, followed by Denis Berezovskyis, a rear admiral, who is now the Russian Black Sea Fleet deputy commander.

It was the day after the Olympic Winter Games ended in China.

Despite the enormous military build-up and a warning from the Pentagon, the world was shocked. President Putin's plan to reclaim what he considered to be Russian territory had been signalled on many occasions previously, but using brutal physical force to achieve this came as a surprise. If Putin's plan was to incorporate over 40 million people into the Russian Federation, then bombing and killing civilians was exactly the wrong way to go about it.

Both Putin and the world expected that Russian Federation's forces would take Kyiv and Kharkiv in three days, and use the eastern oblasts (regions) making up the Donbas to launch a takeover of the whole country. Russian troops were told they would be welcomed as liberators from Ukraine's 'drug-raddled', 'Nazi' leadership and that they should bring dress uniforms for their victory parade through Kyiv. The Russian plan was that the Ukrainian army would be quickly destroyed, Kyiv taken, its president, Volodymyr Zelensky, captured (and probably shot) and an interim government, subservient to the Kremlin, set up.

The meme that 'Ukraine will not be able to resist the Russian onslaught' may need some unpicking. On the one hand, the conventional wisdom was that the Russian army was well equipped, well trained and had a workable and modern set of doctrines for the operation. On the other hand, although the Ukrainian army had not fared well in Donbass in the early days of Russian incursions, they had learned quickly and were then a formidable fighting force, albeit much smaller than the opposing Russians. Maybe this was one of the oldest lessons in military history for the Russians: never underestimate the enemy and never overestimate your own capabilities. Mainly though, Ukraine's performance reflected the way that, since the Soviet yoke had been lifted, they had come together as a nation. Despite the fact that nationalism is sometimes used in a pejorative sense, here, it really worked for Ukrainians.

The consensus then and now is that the attack was and remains wrong from every point of view: political, legal, moral and, from Russia's point of view, it was completely unrealistic. Responsibility rested entirely with one man: President Vladimir Vladimirovich Putin.

As we now know, things did not quite go to plan. The oldest lesson in military history, don't underestimate the enemy or overestimate your own capabilities, operated with a vengeance, and the brave and capable Ukrainian Armed Forces repelled Russian attacks in the north and held them in the east, despite suffering terrible and gratuitous shelling of civilian targets.

Russian Federation forces also attacked southwest from Donbas towards Mariupol, Zaporizhzhia and the Kherson region, and the city of Mariupol, which they captured, having devastated it with artillery shells and missiles. Many civilians, in addition to Ukrainian troops, were killed.

Putin claimed victory, but the world was appalled by the carnage. The Russians also sent missiles into Odesa, one of two important ports for Ukrainian exports that remained in Ukrainian hands. The first seventy-two hours were critical; Putin failed and that phase of the war was won by Ukraine. Critically – apart from a failure to take-out, capture or silence Zelensky – was the failure to hold Hostomel Airport, which was intended to be the Russian bridgehead for seizing the capital. Without that, the convoy of tanks and other vehicles coming out of Belarus had nowhere to go and became sitting ducks.

Only one month after the invasion, at the end of March, Russian Federation forces, having had no success in reaching Kyiv, were obliged to withdraw, claiming that the offensive against that Kyiv was diversionary and that they would now concentrate on Donbas, where they had been fighting since 2016 in support of the two breakaway regions of Donetsk and Luhansk, recognised by Vladimir Putin as republics just before the Russian invasion. It was a pathetic excuse for a botched invasion. If the intent really had been diversionary, it was ineffective. The bulk of Ukraine's armed forces – and certainly the most experienced – remained in the east, and in fact the Russians advanced very little from the east in the first months of the war except for territory around Kharkiv (taken back spectacularly in the autumn of 2022). Most Russian gains in the east – e.g. Severodonetsk and Lysychansk – weren't taken until the summer of 2022. Russia's big territorial gains were in the south – advancing north out of Crimea. Hardly a surprise, but it indicated the lies and misinformation that would accompany all Russian announcements from there on in.

The Russian Federation's biggest and swiftest gains were in the south of Ukraine, where they succeeded in establishing a land bridge to Crimea and so controlled (after a long and bitter siege) the port of Mariupol and the whole coast of the Sea of Azov, as well as the rite of passage through the sea itself.

In April, as the Russian Federation forces fell back, mass graves were found in Bucha, near Kyiv. There is also evidence of summary execution, torture and theft. In November, mass graves were also found in Mariupol, the uncertainty of not knowing of the fates of relatives causing further agony to civilians who had lost touch with their families.

Perhaps in retaliation, on 14 April, a Ukrainian missile (unconfirmed) sank the Russian Federation's Black Sea Fleet's flagship, the *Moskva*. Russian propaganda, unable to concede Ukrainian competence, pretended that an accidental on-board fire was the cause.

President Biden has not permitted Ukraine to attack any targets within Russia (ignoring a few on arms dumps), particularly with American supplied weapons, for fear of it being seen as a US–Russian conflict.

This changed at the end of May 2024: Biden has now given Ukraine permission to use American-supplied weapons to strike targets in Russia, but only near the Kharkiv region.

Early on in the war, a no-fly zone was proposed for over Ukraine, enforced by NATO aircraft, but this too was not sanctioned. Neither the USA nor NATO could risk an open war with Russia, which still hold thousands of nuclear warheads with a triad of delivery systems: intercontinental ballistic missile systems (ICBMs), ballistic missile submarines (SSBMs) and aircraft. It is thought that the Russians have no inhibitions about using tactical nuclear weapons, regarding them simply as an extension of artillery capability. Their reluctance to use them so far may well be related to American and NATO warnings about how they will respond, which have not made public.

The consequences of the Russian invasion of Ukraine are many, multidimensional and will last for at least a generation. They are also unknowable: Russia could be distracted by a Chinese land grab in the east, by a palace coup or – perhaps a bigger danger for Putin – a popular uprising. Such are only of interest to the West if they affect the West's security, as they might well.

Sanctions on Russia were introduced after its illegal occupation of Crimea in 2014. These were reinforced and widely extended after the February 2022 invasion, taking the form of sanctions on banking, trade and on oligarchs and other individuals, such as members of the Duma, Russia's parliament. Early on, there was some disappointment, indeed anger, that Germany refused to stop buying Russian gas, with the accusation that the nearly €1 billion they were sending nearly every day to Russia for gas was being used to kill Ukrainians.

Considering the devastation Germany caused in the last century, many of the fellow Europeans thought that they should be prepared to suffer a small hit on their GDP for the sake of peace in Europe. We might also mention the devastation caused in Ukraine itself in 1943: a long time ago, but still a small part of Ukrainian popular memory. Also, like much of Europe, West Germany benefited from the Marshall plan in 1948 and were also largely spared the considerable expense of defending themselves throughout the Cold War, courtesy of Anglo-American forces and a much higher military spending of some of their NATO allies. The issue of contribution to NATO is still a sore subject between the Americans and, barring a few high contributors, the rest of NATO.

The German reply was that they would wean themselves off Russian gas eventually, and they have made enormous progress towards this between then and when this book was written. However, it should be mentioned that, despite having some 'Greens' in the new coalition government, they are still burning lignite. Maybe the Greens have redeemed themselves in other ways: they have been conspicuously amongst the most militarily hawkish of political parties in Germany regarding the war in Ukraine, and seemed to be genuinely and stridently pro-Ukraine – not just capitalising on an opportunity to burn less gas.

A later delegation to China, led by the chancellor, Olaf Schulz, demonstrated their focus on a mercantilist approach rather than European security. Only towards the end of January 2023, and under intense international pressure, did the Germans agree to send Leopard tanks and allow other European countries to do the same. Fortunately for Ukraine, the debate moved on after that to consider, and eventually approve and supply F16 aircraft, Swedish Gripens, ATCMS and cluster bombs. At the time, these tanks were considered vital in repulsing what was expected to be a major Russian offensive in the spring. The Germans still insisted on political cover, with the Americans also agreeing to send Abram tanks. All very well, but it may be a step too far: the Abram tanks are powered by gas turbines with different maintenance requirements. And Abrams are complex, and heavy on gas and maintenance. In the event, and fortunate for Ukraine, the early 2023 Russian offensive was poorly planned and prosecuted and this, to some extent, let Ukraine off the hook.

The international community has been impressed by the Ukrainian Armed Forces and also by the courage and leadership of President Volodymyr Zelensky. The memorable early comment from him when asked by the Americans whether he wanted to be exfiltrated, that he wanted 'ammunition, not a ride' will inevitably become a required component of every future history of the war. He continues to address the Ukrainian people every night on television, giving an honest and factual account of the war, and is seen walking round the centre of Kyiv in his now traditional khaki army issue T-shirt. His defiance, and the performance of the Ukrainian Armed Forces, have encouraged supporting countries to step up their contributions in terms of both quantity and quality. If Putin's hit squads had found him in the early days of the war, the war might have ended. He was as key to Ukraine's survival as Churchill was to Britain in 1940.

There has been an enormous, unprecedented effort by the United Kingdom, the European Union, other Western allied states across the world and, most particularly, by the United States in sending arms and ammunition to the Ukrainian army. The United States contribution to the Ukrainians has been impressive.

However, supply has been somewhat restricted, partly by the problems of depleting NATO stocks, partly by manufacturing the appropriate weapons and partly by the problems of training Ukrainian soldiers to use what are sophisticated, electronic detection and firing systems. In some instances, this can take three week's training or more to master. The United States also provides lavish intelligence in the form of satellite reports, and counter cyber-attack facilities.

In December 2022, following Zelenskyy's visit to Washington to meet Biden, the US agreed to supply the Patriot anti-missile system to Ukraine. One unit was dispatched, but these cost about $1 billion each and require about 90 soldiers to operate them. As of early 2023, the United States has supplied one other system. And, as an indication of Germany's new awareness, having already supplied one Patriot system themselves (July 2023), they announced that they are sending two more.

TANKS FOR UKRAINE!

To achieve superiority on the modern battlefield, a whole range of complex and expensive equipment is required; even a partial list would be lengthy. One key war machine is the tank, an armoured fighting vehicle providing a combination of heavy firepower, strong armour to protect the crew and mobility. Tanks usually have a powerful engine, and are driven by tracks rather than wheels. They are not to be confused with Armoured Personnel Carriers (APCs) which can be wheeled or (mainly) tracked and deliver infantry to the battlefield, or self-propelled guns, which would have a much larger artillery piece than the usual tank.

There has been much discussion in the military press of late about whether the tank is obsolete (it isn't), and even some discussion about what a tank actually is. *The Economist* ran an article on exactly that subject. The layman's answer is that it would be pretty obvious if one was bearing down on you!

Ukraine's President, Volodomyr Zelensky, repeatedly asked his Western allies to provide tanks for defence and to push the Russians back to the pre-war border, but there was much reluctance amongst allies to meet this demand. Eventually, Germany became the biggest supplier of tanks to Ukraine and, by a significant margin, the most munificent supporter after the US in terms of military aid.

There may have been, amongst some German commercial and political quarters, a yearning not only for the war to end but for things to be back as they were. Their fears may have been more to do with the prospects for business should Russia totally collapse or descend into civil war. This may be a characteristic of the new post-Merkel government in Germany or some concern about escalating the Ukrainian war or a feeling that, as the aggressor in two world wars, the Germans feel responsibility for the Russians' casualties – which ran to millions – on the eastern front during First and Second World Wars. The treaty of Brest Litovsk was particularly harsh on the Russians; Russia lost control of Ukraine, Poland, Belarus, its Baltic provinces (now Lithuania, Latvia and Estonia) and its Caucasus provinces of Kars and Batum.

But, for Germany and the rest of the Western allies, the charge of *too little, too late* will stick. Perhaps whilst not being *too* late, opportunities were missed to counter the Russian advance and before they had an opportunity to dig in, particularly in the south. With regard to the United Kingdom itself, in an article in August 2023, Dr Jack Watling of RUSI wrote:

For all the UK's boasting of its 'Fusion Doctrine' and cross-government working, the war in Ukraine has seen more interdepartmental feuding than collaboration across Whitehall.

Germany is important because it produces the majority of tanks for European use: over 2,000 of their Leopard 2 tanks, which are generally considered to be a good combination of weight, economy and firepower. It is also reckoned to be easier to maintain and has a better fuel efficiency than most other Western tanks.

It was not really until after the Ukraine Defence Contact Group meeting in Ramstein on 20 January 2023 that it was agreed to send some Leopard 2A6 tanks, an advanced variant. Despite hopes that this would stimulate donations from other countries who operate the Leopard, the promise has been more parsimonious. Initially, Ukraine received just two battalions of these Leopards (a Ukrainian tank battalion is thirty-one tanks). Between Denmark, Germany and the Netherlands, Ukraine later received a hundred older refurbished Leopards, making up another three battalions. Other allies have sent tanks: Britain sent a company of fourteen Challenger II; the United States sent thirty-one M1 A2 Abrams, its most advanced tank, which arrived in October of 2023. Poland had already sent about 250 Soviet era T-72 tanks plus some more modernised versions of these.

However, tanks are not the only thing that Ukraine needs, and the media reports of the Ramstein meeting may have eclipsed the other crucial equipment that was promised for Ukraine: ammunition and 'soft' military equipment (e.g. boots). The statistics on this are illuminating: some 40 per cent of the US equipment supplied to Ukraine, at a cost of some $8 billion, arrived in the three months between December 2022 and the end of February 2023, and the military aid agreed in Ramstein amounts to something like two thirds of the total sent to Ukraine between March 2022 and the end of February 2023.

To say that Ukraine's army is being transformed may be something of an exaggeration – the bulk of its hardware is still Soviet-era stuff – but something like a third of Ukraine's army will have equipment which is well up to NATO standard.

In Chapter Seven: The Strategic Consequences for the West, we pose the question of whether NATO's contribution to Ukraine, and by implication the West's in general, has been parsimonious or a surge. Given the forgoing commentary, this may look like a substantial contribution, but this has come only after a year of agonising, and agony for Ukraine. Volodymyr Zelenskyy has on several occasions said that, had they had the munitions they were requesting in the middle of 2022, they could have chased the Russians out of Ukraine already. Still... better late than never.

WARPLANES FOR UKRAINE!

Zelensky repeatedly asked his Western allies to provide warplanes as well as tanks. There is no doubt that warplanes would be of enormous help to Ukraine in its struggle against Russia. There was some comment in various media about the West supplying warplanes to Ukraine based on the tank precedent. The US were very reluctant to send any of their planes because they did not want to engage with Russian planes and risk an escalation, perhaps as far as a nuclear weapon being used.

The supply of tanks was great step forward in terms of logistics and maintenance and training crews, but the supply of warplanes would be a radical new dimension. They require hardened runways and an enormous amount of maintenance but, most of all, the pilots need considerable battle training to even fly them, and of course there is no substitute for combat experience. The supply of warplanes demonstrates a real prevarication amongst the Western allies. Indeed, the Ukrainian summer 2023 offensive was, in some military strategists' opinion, foolish and risky without adequate air cover. We can accept that that might have been difficult to provide but it was, and remains, an important factor in this war.

2 PUTIN'S POINT OF VIEW AND THE WESTERN POSITION

Nothing can excuse, justify or condone Russian actions. The invasion was malicious, inhuman and cruel, and an action contrary to international law from one of the Permanent Five members of the United Nations Security Council, a body set up to:

> *... save succeeding generations from the scourge of war, which twice in our lifetime has brought untold sorrow to mankind, and to reaffirm faith in fundamental human rights, in the dignity and worth of the human person, in the equal rights of men and women and of nations large and small, and to establish conditions under which justice and respect for the obligations arising from treaties and other sources of international law can be maintained, and to promote social progress and better standards of life in larger freedom ...*

By any standard, Russia should resign from the Security Council forthwith, and possibly from the United Nations itself.

It is clear that there are many echoes of Soviet thinking about this war, and war in general, but one in particular stands out: an obsession that 'the collective West' – one monolithic West – is out to 'get' Russia, and to destroy it. How on earth do they imagine that any other country or any other coalition of countries could take over such an enormous land area with 140 million people? It is quite clear that this is a case of the tail wagging the dog, of political leaders using external threats to divert attention from their own internal failings. Certainly, many could be attributed to Putin.

Perhaps the most apposite comment was made many years ago by President Ronald Reagan (US president from 1981 to 1989), quoted from his memoir:

Three years had taught me something surprising about the Russians: Many people at the top of the Soviet hierarchy were genuinely afraid of America and Americans. Perhaps this shouldn't have surprised me, but it did. In fact, I had difficulty accepting my own conclusion at first.

He went on:

... the more experience I had with the Soviet leaders and other heads of state who knew them, the more I began to realize that many Soviet officials feared us not only as adversaries but as potential aggressors who might hurl nuclear weapons at them in a first strike; because of this, and perhaps because of a sense of insecurity and paranoia with roots reaching back to the invasions of Russia by Napoleon and Hitler, they had aimed a huge arsenal of nuclear weapons at us ...

He then made a droll diary entry in 1983:

... without being in any way soft on them, we ought to tell them no one here has any intention of doing anything like that. What the hell have they got that anyone would want?

... which rather ignores Russia's oil and gas, rare earths and minerals, including platinum, palladium and, amongst others, titanium, but the point is made.

Nevertheless, we might examine what Putin considered to be his case for the invasion and thereby ponder whether the West's diplomatic and military intelligence services were meeting the challenge or providing a good basis for foreign policy decision-making.

JOHN J MEARSHEIMER, REALISM, POST-RATIONALISATION AND THE PERFORMATIVE

John Mearsheimer is an American political scientist who belongs to the 'realist' school of thought. He is a Professor at the University of Chicago, and has been described as the most influential realist of his generation. His theory of 'offensive realism' describes the interaction between great powers as being primarily driven by a rational aspiration to achieve regional hegemony in an anarchic international system. He is also well known for arguing that that the Israeli lobby exerts disproportionate influence over US foreign policy.

Realism in this context sees international politics as driven mainly by the pursuit of power and interests of states as the main actors. He defines power as factors like military strength, economic might, population size and technological advancement. Realism assumes that sovereign states are fundamentally self-interested, always seeking to ensure their security and ultimately their survival. Realism therefore sees international relations characterised by competition and conflict, rather than cooperation.

For reference, the antithesis of realism in international affairs is often considered to be idealism or liberalism. The focus here is on moral, ethical and ideological values, with cooperation, international institutions and global norms. Liberalism, a parallel to idealism, sees the role of international organisations, trade and diplomacy as promoting peace and mutual benefits among states. Both liberalism and idealism contrast with realism's emphasis on power and national interests.

Caution: *realism* is a theoretical framework with its own priests and disciples, such as Mearsheimer. It needs to be distinguished from *realistic* as in 'Let's be realistic ...' although there is a parallel. The words are quite often used together. Then there is the time dimension. Whatever the path advocated by *realism*, we then need to be *realistic* in devising any strategy going forward. Lexical problems aside, it is no good bleating about Putin's invasion of Ukraine and quoting realism ('I told you so...'); we need to be realistic about resolving the situation.

Conventional wisdom holds that Putin's attack on Ukraine is nothing other than *waging aggressive war*. Should Putin find himself in the dock – admittedly a vanishingly small possibility – this is one of the charges which would be brought against him. It was one of the charges brought against the Nazi leadership during the Nuremberg trials during 1945 and 1946. One of the Nazi defences was that waging aggressive war was not an international crime when they started. This was dismissed by the court. Putin, of course has always claimed that Ukraine is, and always has been part of Russia, but see comments about Kievan Rus later in this chapter. Perhaps those histories were purged in Russia at some stage.

There is however a divergent realist view, supported by Mearsheimer that 'the West', mainly NATO, and led by the Americans, goaded Putin into attacking Ukraine and that their actions were deliberate in the full knowledge of what they were doing and the likely consequential effect on Putin and the Russian Federation. Certainly, the motivations behind Putin's invasion of Ukraine involve a combination of security concerns, geopolitical ambitions, historical ties and internal politics. Putin has long been wary of NATO's eastward expansion. The prospect of Ukraine joining NATO was seen by Russia as a direct threat to its national security and sphere of influence. Russia perceives NATO's presence near its borders as encroachment and a strategic threat. Putin has a similar reaction to the European Union's expansion.

Looking at it from his point of view, Putin has a point: since the collapse of the Soviet Union, which he lamented, the Czech Republic, Hungary, Poland, Bulgaria, Estonia, Latvia, Lithuania, Romania, Slovakia, Slovenia, Albania, Croatia, Montenegro, North Macedonia and Finland have joined NATO. The published rationale for NATO expansion was that any country could apply to join (in the early days it was even mooted that Russia itself might join NATO). It is also a condition of membership that every existing NATO member has to agree to the new country joining. Sweden is joining NATO after the application had been delayed by Turkey's withholding approval.

Putin's voiced grievance is that three of these countries have contiguous borders with Russia, five if you count the Lithuanian and Polish borders with Kaliningrad, and six if you count Poland's border with Belarus, a Russian client state, and seven if you count Romania and Bulgaria who have littorals on the Black Sea, which Putin sees as Russia's sea.

Further, since the collapse of the Soviet Union, Austria, Finland, Sweden, Cyprus, the Czech Republic, Estonia, Hungary, Latvia, Lithuania, Malta, Poland, Slovakia, Slovenia, Bulgaria, Romania and Croatia have all joined the European Union.

NATO and EU leaders were smugly satisfied, quite rightly in many people's opinion, that their system (variously described, but 'liberal democracy' will serve) had won and had vanquished the detested Soviet interpretation of socialism: communism.

In the September/October 2014 edition of *Foreign Affairs*, Mearsheimer published an article: *Why the Ukraine Crisis Is the West's Fault: The Liberal Delusions That Provoked Putin*. This was *after* Putin had appropriated Crimea, but *before* the full-scale invasion in February 2022. In it, Mearsheimer appears to make a convincing case for *not* expanding NATO and, by implication, the EU.

He mentions several actions taken by the US which has had a part in provoking Putin. First, President Clinton's push for NATO to expand in the mid-90s. Second, that the United States between 1991 and 2013 invested about $5 billion to give Ukraine 'the future it deserves'. Regarding Crimea, he suggests that the majority of Crimeans wanted out of Ukraine. He does not provide any reference for that statistic, although he recognises that Crimea is 60 per cent ethnically Russian.

Mearsheimer claims that Putin's actions should be easy to understand from the point of view of security: Napoleonic France, Imperial Germany and Nazi Germany have all attacked Russia across the North European plain, echoing Tim Marshall's comment in his seminal book *Prisoners of Geography*. Mearsheimer also claims that US and EU officials tried hard to assuage Russian fears and that Moscow should understand that NATO has no designs on Russia. In retrospect, this is completely disingenuous, and seems to negate the whole idea of realism in international relations. If the Russians believed that, as Oscar Wilde would have said, they'd believe anything.

So, does Mearsheimer's and other realists' approach have any value in analysing or comprehending Putin's actions, or the West's reaction to him? It's quite clear that realism is essentially descriptive and not prescriptive. Although often described as a theory, it falls short on that front. To qualify as a theory, and so to have any utility, a theory must provide a systematic explanation for observable empirical evidence; there must be an element of prediction; there should be some consistency insofar as, more often than not, the theory is validated. We might even invoke Occam's Razor, where William (of Occam) suggests that contributory factors should not be dependent on other factors. And if they are, use the ordinally first factor or assumption. It is often shortened to 'the simplest explanation is often most likely to be correct', but this is insufficient and ignores the possible interdependency of the various factors.

Finally, of course, any theory of international relations, even if it doesn't quite pass muster as a theory, needs to be useful and have some practical application in advising and guiding practice in international relations.

It is here that Mearsheimer's realism falls down. The attitude of the United States to the fall of the Soviet system was smug satisfaction and, as some diplomats said at the time, Russia had to 'eat their greens ', meaning they would have to suffer to catch up with the West.

The Washington consensus was offered as the only model, with dire consequences. Whereas in the business world the whole idea of change models is taken very seriously, recognising the disruption within the corporation and the timeframe involved, it seems to have been assumed that slapping a Western economic plan on Russia's desk was all that was required.

There is no general model of war and therefore no model, however sophisticated, can predict war (see chapter in *War in Context*) and, for pity's sake, please let's not invoke Artificial Intelligence!

There are two enormous holes in Mearsheimer's reasoning. Not expanding NATO further towards Russia would make the newly independent and sovereign 'frontline' states: Estonia, Latvia, Lithuania, Poland, Slovakia, Hungary and Romania virtually 'buffer states' for the West against Russian aggression. Putin conveniently forgot that Kaliningrad, a Russian exclave, which nestles neatly between Poland and Lithuania, and with direct access to the Baltic could be considered a threat to the West. It's unlikely that these seven states would have accepted this situation, with hard to imagine consequences for their own, and Europe's security.

One wonders whether any of this came up in any of the internal NATO, European or EU discussions, or whether this was ever put to Putin.

Second, who are the actors? One of the confusions in international relations is to identify who the actors are and what polities are relevant. Hitherto, the standard approach has been to see the sovereign state, sometimes known as the nation-state, as the accepted and main actor in international affairs and with agency. With an increase in national consciousness (witness so many intrastate wars), it's time to identify nations within the multi-nation-state as being actors in their own right. Realism might ignore this. And rather than competing, individual nations, whether they even achieve statehood or not, may simply be more interested in freedom from oppression than a realist agenda.

The idea of secession is now heard much more frequently, not yet in the Russian federation, but the UK, Canada and many other countries are facing this conundrum. Even in the United States secession is now discussed frequently, particularly in California, and especially if President Trump is elected again. And, as one American friend said, 'We'd really like to get rid of Texas ...'. It cuts both ways of course. Texas is full of vehicle bumper stickers proclaiming: *We're Leaving.*

Let's not dismiss realism; it's often portrayed as having been validated by previous experiences. It may be a useful analytical historical tool, but it is not predictive. Realism is pessimistic, appealing to the lowest and base instincts of mankind. It eschews trust, and forgets FDR's maxim that the best way to engender trust ... is to trust people. Even Lawrence Freedman, one of the doyens of modern writing about war admits that, even in the context of dealing with Russia, that there has to be an element of trust somewhere.

The Joint Comprehensive Plan of Action (aka 'The Iran Deal', 2015/2016) started with a lot of mutual mistrust. During months of painstaking negotiation, at the end there was a sufficient element of trust between the United States and the other parties (China, France, Russia, United Kingdom, Germany and the EU) and Iran to sign the final declaration. It is a tragedy that this deal was repudiated by Donald Trump and, as of 2024, we are now paying the price. The building of trust is also demonstrated by the Northern Ireland peace deal, the Good Friday Agreement. This was negotiation was patiently chaired by one George J Mitchell, a US Senator.

Realism is pessimistic, unimaginative and lacking in aspiration. If France and Germany had taken a view based on realism at the end of the Second World War, perhaps the European Union would never have come into existence. The European Union may now be slow and ponderous, but is essentially going in the right direction. The EU alone is enough to repudiate the application of Mearsheimer's cogent but outdated realist theories. Always remember Churchill's dictum: 'In War: Resolution, in Defeat: Defiance, in Victory: Magnanimity in Peace: Good Will.'

Finally, on a cynical note, it may be that proclamations of realism, especially from tenured professors, might have a whiff of the performative. And, of course, the danger of ideology drifting into dogma. It is possible, for example, that some UK privatisations suffered from this, although much could be laid at the door of politicians and civil servants inexperienced in the ways of business. See *Late Soviet Britain* by Abby Innes, at LSE.

HOW STRONG IS PUTIN'S CASE?

Let us repeat: there is no doubt that the responsibility for this attack lies entirely with Putin. However, to learn lessons (as politicians are always keen to emphasise, though the results never quite live up to the initial promise) we need to understand what went before this invasion. There are six factors of which we should be aware: established history, the collapse of the Soviet Union, the Budapest agreements, the Founding Act, Minsk I and Minsk II.

HISTORICAL WISDOMS

Might there be some justification for Putin's claim that Ukraine is 'part of Russia'? It means going back many hundreds of years and would be rather like Rome claiming suzerainty over the Iberian Peninsula or England claiming Aquitaine. In the 10th and 11th centuries, 'Kievan

Rus' became a large and powerful state in Europe, known as its Golden Age. Catherine the Great incorporated Central Ukraine into the Russian Empire between 1764 and 1781 and Novorossiya, literally 'New Russia' – much of eastern and southern Ukraine – was settled by Russians, establishing a policy of Russification. Russia claimed Crimea in 1783. Putin's use of the term *Novorossiya* harks back to these times. There would be as much sense in saying that Russia was part of Ukraine, though a reverse takeover might not be appropriate just now.

There was a resurgence of Ukrainian nationalism in the 19th century, but during the Polish-Soviet war of 1920, Poland took control of western Ukraine, while the Soviets took control of the eastern part. In more modern times, it was often said that the western part of Ukraine was Ukrainian and the eastern part Russian. The dividing line was roughly the course of the Dnieper River. The Poles treated the western Ukrainians badly, whilst the Soviet Ukraine, became a founding republic of the Soviet Union. But for the Ukrainians, all this fell apart after Stalin's 'Great Break' of 1928 to 1929. This included collectivisation and central control from Moscow. The Ukrainian peasantry suffered appallingly, with millions starving to death in a famine that became known in Ukraine as the Holodomor. This hardly endeared the Ukrainians to Russian control.

Following the collapse of the Soviet Union, the Russian Federation was proclaimed in December 1991. Outright independence for Ukraine had been proclaimed in August 1991. It did not go well. Between 1991 and 1999, Ukraine lost 60 per cent of its GDP and then suffered hyperinflation in 1993. This was also accompanied by widespread corruption and mismanagement.

Ukraine also had its own colour revolution, a name given to a series of protest movements that also included Georgia in 2003, Kyrgyzstan in 2005 and Lebanon in 2005. The Ukrainian movement was called the

Orange Revolution and occurred between late November 2004 to January 2005, the root causes being massive corruption, voter intimidation and electoral fraud.

In 2014, there was the 'Revolution of Dignity', also known as the pro-EU 'Maidan Revolution'. This culminated in the resignation and flight of the elected president, Viktor Yanukovych, who had been trying to trade off benefits from closer alignment with the European Union with a closer alliance with the Russian Federation. But there was still strong Russian influence and some pro-Russian movements, particularly in the east and south.

Following the 2014 Ukrainian revolution, several people were killed in Odesa in clashes between pro-Maidan and anti-Maidan movements. In January 2015, the Russians launched a rocket attack on the city of Mariupol, on the coast of the Sea of Azov, killing thirty people. In 2016, NATO and Ukraine signed a comprehensive, assistance package and, a year later, the Ukrainian parliament voted to restore the aim of NATO membership as the country's strategic foreign policy objective. Earlier, Ukrainian President Yanukovych had ordered the suspension of talks with the European Union, and was considering turning east, towards Russia. He had been threatened by Putin and, some suggested, bribed.

Given the abuses visited on the Ukrainian people during the last century, it is understandable why the population would want to throw off the Soviet (now Russian Federation) yoke. We could, at a stretch and reluctantly, see a shred of justification for Putin, imagining that Ukraine was 'lost' to the Russian Federation. After all, if one of the states wished to secede from the United States, this would not go down in well in Washington.

What is impossible to imagine is that Putin thinks he can abuse and murder hundreds of thousands of people and then talk about 'our people' and, astonishingly, 'amity'. Putin seems unaware that, whereas the Soviet

Union lasted three quarters of a century at the most, the United States, despite one bitter civil war, has kept itself together for the last two and a half centuries. The USA got something right; the Soviet Union didn't.

SECESSION

In the second book in this trilogy, *War in Context*, we offered several categories of war, one of which was secession, which is where a polity within a larger sovereign state attempts to break away and form a new sovereign state in its own right. The breakaway polity is almost always geographically contiguous.

Sovereign states are generally reluctant to lose territory and the two sides frequently descend into civil war. As a rare exception to this, the Czech Republic and the Slovakian Republic managed to part without acrimony or violence in 1993, in what became known as the Velvet Revolution.

There are many examples of secession around the world, such as Portugal, Bangladesh seceding from Spain Pakistan in 1971, Northern Ireland in its desire to be independent of the United Kingdom (which really meant England), and we cover the secession of East Pakistan, now Bangladesh, below. It seems that all wars of succession are particularly bloody, even if they are designated as civil wars. But perhaps the best example of secession is the desire of the southern states within the United States to secede from the union.

The US was obliged to launch and wage what was the one of the bloodiest civil wars in history and the bloodiest war, in terms of American casualties, that the US has ever engaged in, with some 700,000 dead on both sides. Often described as a war about slavery, and although it certainly would not have occurred without the divisive issue of slavery, it became a war of secession. Indeed Abraham Lincoln was on record as saying that he would be prepared to keep slavery if it maintained the union. In this particular case, there followed half a century of bitterness and economic deprivation in the south. Divisions were only overcome at the cost of turning a blind eye to the South's Jim Crow laws and through the conscious cultural and historical rehabilitation of the South. The US is thus hardly an exemplar of national unity, maybe even the contrary.

It's even conceivable that Putin could argue that he is taking his lesson from Lincoln – that waging a ruthless war is indeed justified to keep a nation – Greater Russia – together. After taking Atlanta, Sherman, a general in the Union army, followed a 'scorched earth' campaign, destroying military targets as well as industry, infrastructure and civilian property. The operation debilitated the Confederacy and helped lead to its eventual surrender. Putin's actions in Ukraine echo Sherman's in 1864.

Putin might well see himself in a similar position, subjecting 'Greater Russia' to four years of slaughter followed by fifty plus years of bitterness if that grants him the accolades of Russian posterity. There are precedents for this in Russia: Ivan Grozhny, Peter the Great and Stalin were hardly squeamish when it came to inflicting pain to secure what they saw as long-term ends, largely for themselves rather than the people.

Another puzzle to the Western mind is why Putin hasn't exploited the vast resources that he has. Though oil and gas are going out of fashion, with some sensible investment in industry he might have found prestige and power returning. He seems unaware that tiny countries such as Estonia (with a population of only 1.3 million) have managed their transition to freedom and sovereignty extremely well.

THE COLLAPSE OF THE SOVIET UNION

Many and mighty tomes have been written on this subject, but all we need to recognise here is Putin's famous statement in a 2005 speech to the Russian people. There are variations depending on the translation:

... above all, we should acknowledge that the collapse of the Soviet Union was the major geopolitical disaster of the century. As for the Russian nation, it became a genuine drama. Tens of millions of our co-citizens and co-patriots found themselves outside Russian territory. Moreover, the epidemic of disintegration infected Russia itself ...

Some translations use the word *catastrophe* for disaster, but the sentiment is the same.

THE BUDAPEST MEMORANDUM ON SECURITY ASSURANCES

This included three more or less identical political agreements signed in Budapest in December 1994. It provided security arrangements through the inclusion of Belarus, Kazakhstan and Ukraine to the Treaty on the Non-Proliferation of Nuclear Weapons (NPT). The memoranda were signed by the Russian Federation, the United Kingdom and the United States, being three nuclear powers. In effect, the three former Soviet countries, now recognised as sovereign nations, abandoned their nuclear arsenal and gave them up to the Russian Federation. Previously, Soviet nuclear weapons had been located in Ukraine. The terms were as one might expect:

... the signatories independence and sovereignty in the existing borders ... they undertook not to threaten or use force against the signatory, or to use economic coercion ...

Also, to seek UN Security Council action to provide assistance to the signatory if they:

... should become a victim of an act of aggression or (and here is an important clause) *the threat of aggression in which nuclear weapons are used ...*

And, of course:

... to refrain from the use of nuclear arms against the signatory ...

THE 1997 FOUNDING ACT

This was signed in Paris and concerned *Mutual Relations, Cooperation and Security between NATO and the Russian Federation.* Here is an edited version of the first couple of paragraphs:

... NATO and the Russian Federation ... based on an enduring political commitment ... will build together a lasting and inclusive peace in the Euro-Atlantic area on the principles of democracy and cooperative security ... NATO and Russia do not consider each other as adversaries. They share the goal of overcoming the vestiges of earlier confrontation and competition and of strengthening mutual trust and cooperation. The present Act reaffirms the determination of NATO and Russia to give concrete substance to their shared commitment to build a stable, peaceful and undivided Europe, whole and free, to the benefit of all its peoples ... marks the beginning of a fundamentally new relationship between NATO and Russia. They intend to develop, on the basis of common interest, reciprocity and transparency a strong, stable and enduring partnership ...

The bathos of all this is obvious.

MINSK AGREEMENTS I & II

Donbas is a cultural and economic region in eastern Ukraine. It comprises the Donetsk and Luhansk oblasts and is bounded to the east by the Russian Federation border. In March 2014, immediately following the Euromaidan protests and the Revolution of Dignity, protests by pro-Russian groups, led by a former (Russian) Federal Security Service (FSB) thug and Russian army veteran known as Igor Girkin (he has other names and aliases), started demonstrations against the Poroshenko-led Ukrainian government. Girkin and his cronies proclaimed the Luhansk and Donetsk People's Republics. It is not clear to what extent he was under the instructions of the Russian government or whether he was operating independently. Certainly Russian-backed groups seized government buildings throughout Donbas. All this was happening at about the same time as Russia's seizure of Crimea, and it was part of wider pro-Russian protests in southern and eastern Ukraine.

The Ukrainian government countered this with its regular army, but it was a scrappy and bloody conflict with little progress on either side. Two things should be noted here: first of all, the Ukrainian army did not make much progress, and this might have indicated to the President Putin that their capabilities were fairly limited; secondly, the four million strong population of Donetsk is roughly 38 per cent ethnically Russian; the two million population of Luhansk is 39 per cent. Note, though, that the Russian definition of 'ethnic Russian' may not be quite the same as the western meaning.

In an attempt to stabilise the situation and to seek an end to this conflict, the OSCE (Organization for Security and Co-operation in Europe), with representation from France and Germany and after much discussion, developed the first Minsk Protocol known as Minsk I, signed in Minsk, Belarus in September 2014. Representatives of Donetsk People's Republic and Luhansk People's Republic also signed, but their status was not formally recognised.

Minsk I offered some autonomy to these oblasts: protection of the Russian language and the usual stuff about prisoner exchange and the retraction of armed formations. One interesting aspect was the establishment of a buffer zone on the border, which may have been a marker for future negotiations to end the war. Though there was some compliance, Minsk I did not work. In an article in *The Economist* in October 2014, entitled *Fight Club* and subtitled *After the war that was not a war, the ceasefire that is not a ceasefire*, they quoted Serhiy Taruta, the Kiev-appointed governor of Donetsk, as saying 'the Minsk accords are just too vague'. More particularly, he opined, 'the parties do not have a mutual vision of the future of the Donbas region'. *The Economist* went on to report that Igor Plotnitsky, head honcho of the Luhansk People's Republic and also a signatory to the Minsk agreement, had told Russian media that 'sooner or later, we will become a part of the Russian Federation'.

Minsk I had failed to stop the fighting and had not provided the circumstances for a long-term settlement. One reason for this was that there were too many parties involved: the Kyiv government, the Kyiv appointed governors of those oblasts, the populations therein, the leaders of the breakaway groups and the Russians themselves. Compromise is always necessary in the circumstances but, to coin an old peacekeeping protocol, *you can't keep the peace if there is no peace to keep*. There, in Donbas, there was no peace to keep; it was stalemate. The Minsk Protocol, Minsk I, did not so much expire as peter out. Russian troops returned after some partial withdrawal and there was some bitter fighting in Donbas, particularly around Donetsk airport, which changed hands several times.

Talks in Minsk resumed in February with a new 'Package of Measures' and an improved agreement. Minsk II was signed in February 2015. The fighting decreased but never really ended. The protocols were never really fully implemented by either side. By March, it was evident that Russian forces were deployed to Donbas in greater numbers. In June 2015, it was reckoned that 6,500 people had died in the previous year, with 16,000 wounded.

By now, Putin might have realised that the separatist movements were not up to much from a military point of view and that his strategy for resolving the long-term position of Donbas, securing his borders and influencing the Kyiv government – which was always his goal – was going to have to be through overt military action by the Russian army. At that stage, no single party of the many had a strategy for bringing the conflict to a conclusion. However, the Ukrainian army was developing its skills and benefiting from the West's suggested reforms and improved training.

PUTIN'S RATIONALE

At the end of the 1980s, during the closing days of the Soviet Union, the Politburo and the US agreed in principle to German reunification. A major hurdle had been whether the new Germany would remain a member of NATO, as West Germany had been. Putin claims that assurances were given that the reunification would *not* result in NATO extending beyond the then East German border. In the event, Poland, the Czech Republic and Hungary joined in 1999, followed in the next few years by several other former Warsaw Pact countries. This continues to be Putin's bête noir, described as 'an unhealed scab'.

What Putin saw was democracy, which he abhorred, getting nearer to the Russian homeland. And not just democracy, but a free press as well. It seems strange to the Western mind that Putin cannot understand that the populations of Poland, the Czech Republic and Hungary et al. did not want to live under the Soviet yoke, even though the Russian Federation had forsaken communism. This intellectual and emotional gap continues.

It's even more surprising to the western mind that the Russian Federation pretends to have democratic elections. This applies to dictators around the world: no plebiscite would expect a percentage turnout of the electorate into the high nineties – not even in Australia, where voting is compulsory. Even then, the incumbent party getting 95 per cent support is well-nigh impossible under a truly democratic system.

Another reason that Putin would be interested in Ukraine is straightforward resources. Ukraine has 60 per cent of the world's black earth and is potentially a huge breadbasket for the Russian Federation. The more it moves into the western orbit, the less there is for Russia, although Russian agriculture has improved considerably since the end of the Soviet Union. The mineral wealth of Donbas was also very tempting.

In *About War* and *War in Context*, we suggested that, during the 20th century, the pursuit of power and glory had shifted from controlling territory to focussing on the individual citizen's wealth (and even justice) though trade, technology and, for the state, political influence.

This was before Russia attacked the Ukraine in what most people thought of as an unprovoked, unnecessary and horrifically brutal war.

Putin's mindset is that power, glory and self-regard – be that for Putin himself or for Russia – is linked to territory and visions of being a world power. However, as this chapter seeks to illuminate, geographic expansion is very much part of the Russian playbook.

Whereas the western European kingdoms sought glory on a global scale (witness the 'Scramble for Africa'), Russia expanded largely through contiguous geographic ventures. Their growth was as brutal as anything found in the Western kingdoms. It started in the 12th century with the Kievan Rus, who eventually came under the control of Moscow, Siberia (16th and 17th century), Ukraine, Caucasus, Central Asia (Kazakhstan, Turkmenistan, Uzbekistan, Kyrgyzstan and Tajikistan), Poland and the Baltic states, Alaska (although they sold that to America in 1867), the

Far East (including Kamchatka and the Kuril Islands) and of course, never to be forgotten, Crimea.

Britain's expansion started later, in the 16th century, but really got underway in the 17th to 19th centuries. Few British people would have thought it odd or unusual to hear that British armies were fighting local tribes, the French or the Germans in Africa at any time during the 19th century.

There are several intriguing counterpoints here. Whereas the conquered territories saw the western Europeans coming from overseas, and called them imperialist and colonists, the conquered territories across Asia, Poland and the Baltics did not quite see the Russians in the same way as they were 'next door'. The crimes, exploitation and the arrogance of the conquerors were of a similar nature.

Russia has not been through the angst that Western Europe has put itself through over the wrongs of imperial expansion, however genuine this sentiment may be. Judgements on the ills of empires vary considerably – they are not all bad. On the other hand Russia has had so little democracy over its long history that it has probably never questioned its role as an imperial power, let alone thinking of apologising for it. Putin's mindset harks back to Catherine the Great and her plans for Nova Rossiya which he often mentions. It goes further, too, of course. Expansion was well underway under Ivan the Terrible ('Grand Prince of Moscow and Sovereign of all Russia' and then 'Tsar of all Russia' from 1547 until his death in 1584) and especially under Putin's particular hero, Peter I ('Tsar of all Russia' from 1682, and the first 'Emperor of all Russia' from 1721 until his death in 1725).

Even then, this Imperial guilt might be largely amongst English-speaking nations and part of their penchant for self-flagellation.

Leaving aside the reunification wars in Germany in 1870, which incorporated Prussia, Bavaria, Saxony and Wittenberg and other princely states, the German Empire expanded into Africa, Asia and the Pacific during the late 19th and early 20th century. We might count here what is now Tanzania, Rwanda, Burundi, Namibia (where they massacred some 100,000 Herero and Nama people; the excesses of the Third Reich were not the first instance of German brutality) and Papua New Guinea.

France expanded into North Africa, and still has difficulty leaving it alone, and also Indochina. For the sake of completeness, let's not forget Spain, expanding into Latin America and the Philippines, or Portugal in Brazil. Even then, when 'liberated' from Spanish rule, by the US during the Spanish American War (1898), the hitherto grateful Filipinos were somewhat surprised that the Americans were not intending to leave. When the Filipinos rebelled against US rule, the put down was every bit as brutal as anything conducted by their previous colonial masters.

Yet remorse over empire and its accompanying violence is much greater in the English-speaking nations, particularly United Kingdom, than we find in Germany, France, Spain or Portugal. Much of this has not been lost on Putin or his supporters in the media. The term Anglo-Saxon has come to be a common pejorative term in his speeches.

Putin sees the Anglo-Saxons, which is to say the British (worst of all), the Americans, Canadians, Australians and New Zealanders as the true criminals of the world, at the heart of all Russia's problems, and he and his circle seem to have recently taken to adopting a particular hatred for them.

One wonders what Vladimir Putin would say when confronted with these facts. Probably something along the lines of: 'явное направление'[1].

But then, objective judgements were never Putin's strong point.

---

1   'Manifest Destiny' in Russian

THUCYDIDES LIVES! IS PUTIN'S RATIONALE RATIONAL?

Thucydides' aphorism that war is about *fear, honour and interest* is apparent here: *fear* of being encircled by hostile powers – of NATO coming up to Russia's borders; *interest* in terms of natural resources and access to Crimea and *honour* in terms of Putin's belief that Russia is a great state and a great empire.

The problem with understanding Putin and Russia is how to untangle truth from propaganda. We will be familiar in the West with a 'post-truth' world and 'alternative facts'. Thank goodness for a free(ish) press! But Putin has taken this further, so much so that it represents a new insight into political and social psychology.

In Peter Pomerantsev's book *Nothing is True and Everything is Possible: Adventures in Modern Russia* (2015) he documents the depths – or one might say heights – that propaganda has reached in modern Russia. It's no surprise that Putin has not ceased in his centralised accretion of power, but this is also accompanied by an attempt to rewrite history: buildings are destroyed and replaced, renamed and redecorated to form a backdrop to the current political story at what Pomerantsev says is a dizzying rate. He reports that Moscow changes so fast that individuals lose all sense of reality, so much so that they cannot recognise streets with which they were familiar.

This extends to TV and radio, where Kremlin propaganda is a mixture of show business and authoritarianism, with Putin himself being seen as a performance artist in his role as soldier, lover, bare-chested hunter, businessman, spy, star and superman. The vulgarity of it all is appalling.

Those parts of the media not already closed down already are complicit, with TV stations creating a fake world with a pretend western society for Russian viewers and subjects such as (for young women) *How to Bag a Millionaire*. Pomerantsev reports that the Kremlin's hold on society is extraordinary. Anyone who displeases the government can be picked up and put on trial for crimes with no basis in fact. The conviction rate is often 100 per cent. As we note in the following panel on Maskirovka, the problem with propaganda is the danger of coming to believe it yourself.

Very few responsible parties outside Russia agree with Putin's thesis about Ukraine. There may be countries that have abstained in UN votes, but this has more to do with hedging bets or self-interest than any sense of either reproach of or affinity with Putin.

Despite Putin's rambling 'essay' on Ukraine, the historic rationale for that country to be a part of Russia has no traction. The collapse of the Soviet Union surprised most observers – and the Russians themselves. Although the Americans and the West subscribed to a policy of 'containing the Soviet Union', the country fell apart because of its own internal contradictions, not primarily because of external pressure.

The collapse of the Budapest security assurances was a tragedy but perhaps they were too naïve to function – likewise, the 1997 Founding Act. All parties are to blame for these arrangements, but mainly the West, who saw this experience as a shame, rather than as an alarm bell.

Seen against Russian excesses in Grozny, Georgia, Syria etc., the demise of Minsk I and II were seen again more as an (inevitable?) disgrace rather than a warning. For this, almost all parties are to blame.

EDWARD LUTTWAK: 'GIVE WAR A CHANCE.' (OUTLINED IN
WAR IN CONTEXT.)
Edward Luttwak's article in *Foreign Affairs* (July / August 1999) opens with the term *Premature Peace-making*, and discourses as follows:

… an unpleasant truth often overlooked is that although war is a great evil, it does have a great virtue: it can resolve political conflicts and lead to peace. This can happen when all belligerents become exhausted or

when one wins decisively. Either way, the key is that the fighting must continue until a resolution is reached. War brings peace only after passing a culminating phase of violence. Hopes of military success must fade for accommodation to become more attractive than further combat.

Or, did none of the protagonists understand that war is first, last, and always a *political* action. Fighting bitterly over Debaltseve or over Donetsk Airport might have seemed critical at the time, but what political purpose did it serve?

Or was it all part of a devious and cunning plan by President Putin simply to establish more influence over the Kyiv government and, at the same time, achieve suzerainty over the Donbas. It must also have occurred to him that he could thereby open a shorter road route to Crimea.

And if this is a case of *giving war a chance*, as per Luttwak, then the West needs to face Putin with raw power. (See *The Teddy Roosevelt Solution* in *Diagnosis and Prognosis*.)

3 THE RUSSIAN USE OF FORCE

In the past hundred-odd years, Russia has changed its character and status several times. Prior to the First World War, Russia and its conquered territories were ruled by the Czar, who had absolute power over the government, the population and the various territories.

The Russian Revolution in 1917 changed that to the Soviet system, where power rested in the Central Politburo and the Soviet Presidium. In fact, Joseph Stalin (Communist leader 1922–1952) was an absolute dictator, with the power of life or death over anyone he took against. They didn't call him the Red Czar for nothing.

That changed again between 1989 and 1991 when the Soviet system collapsed and, after some trauma for the unfortunate population, some form of democracy prevailed – until 1999, when Vladimir Putin took over as president. There then started a long erosion of democracy, accountability and a free media (some, such as RT, was state-controlled) until the present day when Putin operates as an absolute dictator, perhaps more so than Stalin's successors.

That represents four different regimes in just over a hundred years. Yet one thing that has not changed is the use of military power to enlarge and maintain Russian territory and Russian suzerainty over other polities.

THE SOVIET UNION

In fact, and although many world empires were established by force, military power was fundamental to Russia's expansion under leaders such as Ivan the Terrible, Peter the Great, Catherine II and eventually Stalin. The legacy of territorial expansion and maintenance by military power was evident during the Soviet period (Hungary, Czechoslovakia) and is still evident today, as Putin's actions illustrate. This might be contrasted with other empires, such as the British, French or Portuguese empires which, although reliant on military force, were largely mercantilist. Putin's concept of territorial expansion is almost the opposite of this.

It is witness to Russia's crude thinking about international relations that we must go back to the early Romanovs or even the later Ruriks to examine Soviet perspectives on the use of force to meet its political objectives. (The Rurik dynasty was founded by the Varangian prince, Rurik, who established himself in Novgorod in the late 9th century. His successors established a dynasty over Kievan Rus until its disintegration in the 12th and 13th centuries, but continued to rule in many of the Rus principalities that evolved out of Kievan Rus.) Things haven't changed very much since then.

After the formation of the Soviet state in 1917, the newly formed Red Army used military power in Georgia, Chechnya and elsewhere – and further. As a result of the Molotov–Ribbentrop Pact in 1939, it was the turn of eastern Poland to be subsumed into its empire. After the outbreak of the Second World War in 1939 but before Operation Barbarossa (the German invasion of Russia in June 1941) Russia attacked Finland in what has been called the Winter War (December 1939 to March 1940). In the justification, the provocation and prosecution of that war are uncanny echoes of Putin's pretexts for invading Ukraine.

For completeness, we must record that the Soviet Red Army turned and defeated the Nazi German army, starting with the battles at Stalingrad and, ironically, eastern Ukraine, over the winter of 1942/1943, but only with support from the United States. Between 1941 and 1945, the US sent nearly $200 billion's worth (in 2023 values) of goods and services to the USSR to support their war effort. Notwithstanding involvement of the United States and the United Kingdom, there was absolutely no way that even their combined might could have defeated Nazi Germany without the Russians, despite the Red Army's phenomenal losses immediately after Barbarossa. But back to 1939 …

FINLAND: THE WINTER WAR

In the early 19th century, the Grand Duchy of Finland had been an autonomous but Russian-influenced state positioned geographically between Russia and the West, Finland having been prised away from Sweden during its wars with Russia. By the end of the 19th century, Czarist Russia had attempted to assimilate Finland into the Russian Empire by Russification, but this was overtaken by the First World War and the Soviet revolution, after which the Finns grabbed their opportunity for independence, together with the Baltic States.

Perhaps nervous of Nazi Germany's power, and notwithstanding the Molotov–Ribbentrop Pact, Soviet Russia wanted to protect the approaches to Leningrad (Saint Petersburg as was and is again), which was only 32 km from the Finnish border. To achieve this, Soviet Russia sought to trade some Russian territory for some Finnish territory, but the Finns refused and, although the Finns imagined they were still in the negotiating stage, the Red Army attacked across a broad front during December 1939.

Conditions in winter that far north were appalling. Karelia experienced record low temperatures of up to *minus* 43 °C. This was a region of deep forests with few metalled roads; most were just gravel tracks, if that. The Finns, more accustomed to the cold and the snow, fought bravely (as do the present-day Ukrainians) and were skilled at cross-country skiing and winter warfare. However, given the numerical superiority of the Red Army, the Finns were eventually overcome, and the Moscow Treaty was signed in March 1940. Although occurring some eighty years ago, there are many parallels between the Winter War and the Russian Federation's attack on Ukraine:

First, Soviet propaganda portrayed Finland's government as a 'vicious and reactionary fascist clique', a foretaste of Putin's claim that the modern-day Ukrainian government was a load of 'drug crazed Nazis'. We might expect some hyperbole in all political pronouncements but, to the Western mind, 'Nazis' is a curious approach. Why does Russian propaganda feel it has to resort to so much *obviously* dishonest hyperbole?

Second, Putin claims he is suspicious of NATO's eastern expansion. *Maybe* Russia's attack on Finland was to protect the approaches to Leningrad, but this is debateable. More likely, it was simply hegemonic.

Third, the Red Army in 1939 attacked along the entire border, some 1,340 km, although there were few passable roads. Putin's attack on Ukraine was from what is now considered to be too many axes. The Russians bombed Helsinki, but to what effect? Putin has launched many missile strikes on Kyiv, the Ukrainian capital, but this has only had the effect of strengthening Ukrainian resolve.

Fourth, overall Russian objectives were confused, and the political commissars within the military command had too much influence. Putin planned the attack on Ukraine with a small clique of cronies and without in-depth military advice. Historians are still debating whether Russia wanted to take over the whole of Finland. Did Putin really want to take over the whole of Ukraine? Could he have held it?

Fifth, is a comparison of casualties. Although the modern-day Ukrainian casualties are horrendous, during the Winter War the Red Army lost as many as 130,000 soldiers against 26,000 Finnish dead. Russian losses in the invasion of Ukraine may amount to some 200,000, but this includes both dead and injured. In February 2023, the Center for Strategic & International Studies (CSIS) estimated that more Russian soldiers had died in Ukraine than all of Moscow's wars since the Second World War, somewhere between 60,000 and 70,000. As a ratio (70,000 to 200,000), this is high. In the Second World War, it was thought that about third of casualties were fatal but, with modern treatments and with good medical practice, the current ratio may now be as low as 15 per cent fatalities to casualties. Generally unreported, Russian medical support to troops does not seem as advanced as in the western world.

Sixth concerns artillery. During the final offensive in February 1940, the Red Army fired some 300,000 shells into the Finnish front line inside twenty-four hours, presaging the Russian Federation's use of artillery and now missile attacks on Ukraine.

After the Second World War the Red Army was active in a number of theatres around the world.

THE BALTICS

Between the end of the Second World War, in 1945, and 1956, the Soviet Union suppressed a guerrilla war in the Baltic states: Estonia, Latvia and Lithuania. Eventually, the partisans were defeated, but with Baltic casualties amounting to over 27,000 and Soviet losses over 15,000. Four thousand pro-Soviet civilians were also killed.

UKRAINE

The guerrilla war in Ukraine lasted until 1953, with the partisans, the Ukrainian Insurgent Army, being defeated. The Ukrainians lost something like over 150,000 dead and the Soviet Union somewhere between 9,000 and 12,000 dead.

POLAND

Up until the mid-50s, the losses of the anti-Communist resistance in Poland amounted to nearly 9,000 killed in the fighting, about 80,000 arrested (fate unknown) and 5,000 executed. In addition, 21,000 Poles died in prison and 10,000 Polish civilians were killed.

KOREA

Russian forces were also involved in the Korean War (1950–1953), suppression of the East German uprising of 1953 and the Vietnam War, some 3,000 troops committed from 1964 to the fall of Saigon in 1975.

THE HUNGARIAN REVOLUTION

You would have to be in well into your seventies now to remember the Hungarian Revolution of 1956. Despite Soviet leader Nikita Khrushchev's pledge that there would be a retreat from the Stalinist policies and repression of the past, he sent the Red Army to suppress the Hungarian Revolution – it is often said 'with Russian tanks'. The Hungarians lost about 300 fighters with some 13,000 wounded. Some 3,000 civilians were also killed. Hungary's losses did not end there: maybe as many of a quarter of a million Hungarians sought refuge abroad, and we might imagine that many of these were scientists, engineers and intellectuals. Over 700 Russian soldiers were killed and about 1,500 wounded. Hungary remained a member of the Warsaw Pact (see *About War* for details) and remained within the Soviet sphere until the collapse of the Soviet Union in 1991.

The West was stunned by the events of 1956 but did nothing. Many Hungarians were disappointed 'the West' did so little to condemn the invasion, despite various pronouncements by American leaders that they supported the 'liberation' of 'captive peoples' in communist nations. The disaster for Hungary was, indirectly, Suez. The wholly misconceived adventure diluted the West's response to Soviet aggression. It distracted attention away from central Europe and compromised the West's moral high ground.

Nevertheless, it was a major blow to Communist Parties in the West, with many of their members leaving in disillusionment. Many prominent left-leaning UK politicians and intellectuals of the 1970s–90s traced the end of their love affair with Communism back to 1956 and the Hungarian Uprising.

CZECHOSLOVAKIA: THE PRAGUE SPRING OF 1968

What upset Moscow were the liberal reforms brought about by Alexander Dubček (1921 to 1992 – he died in a car crash, though not thought to be suspicious). He was First Secretary and de facto leader of Czechoslovakia from 1968 to 1969. In August 1968, some 200,000 Warsaw Pact troops and as many as 5,000 tanks invaded Czechoslovakia to crush the Prague Spring and re-establish Soviet control.

There were widespread demonstrations against the invasion and more than a hundred protesters were shot by Warsaw Pact troops. The overall losses were not as bad as in Hungary, but nearly a hundred Warsaw Pact soldiers were killed and about ninety wounded; and, during the exercise nearly 140 civilians and Czech soldiers were killed. Perhaps as many as 500 were seriously wounded. Again, as with Hungary, some 70,000 Czechoslovak citizens sought political refuge abroad. As a personal note, I learnt about this as I was shaving at 5 am in the morning (I was on shifts). I remember thinking to myself that the West would not do anything about it. It gives me no pleasure to recall that I was right.

AFGHANISTAN

The Soviet Union's last and most disastrous foreign war was in Afghanistan between 1979 and 1989, and is often credited with contributing to the demise of the USSR itself. Although the Soviet Politburo agonised over the decision as to whether to intervene in Afghanistan, the core of its decision was the Brezhnev doctrine, which was a Soviet foreign policy that announced that a risk to socialism and socialist rule in any state of the Soviet Bloc in Central and Eastern Europe was a threat to all of them, and therefore, it justified the intervention of fellow socialist states. That is, the Warsaw Pact countries. It was originally proclaimed to justify the Soviet-led occupation of Czechoslovakia in 1968.

In reality, 'socialism' meant control by a communist party which was loyal to the Kremlin. It was repudiated by the last Soviet leader, Mikhail Gorbachev in the late 1980s. The principles were so broad that the Soviets even used it to justify their military intervention in the communist, but non-Warsaw Pact, nation of Afghanistan in 1979. At that time the Soviet Union shared a 2,300 km border with Afghanistan.

Although known as the Soviet–Afghan War, it was largely a guerrilla war fought by insurgent groups collectively known as the Mujahideen, who were variously backed by the United States, Pakistan, Iran, Saudi Arabia, China and the United Kingdom. It was essentially a Cold War proxy war. Some of the arms, like the Stinger missiles, were still in use when the Americans invaded Afghanistan in 2001.

Casualties were horrendous. Between half a million and two million Afghans were killed and the Soviet forces lost nearly 15,000 personnel in all. Statistics are available for the losses of Soviet equipment: over 450 aircraft, nearly 150 tanks and over 1,300 IFVs/APCs (Infantry Fighting Vehicles and Armoured Personnel Carriers). Over 400 artillery guns and mortars were lost and over 11,000 cargo and fuel tankers. Millions of Afghans fled the country as political exiles. They mostly went to Pakistan and Iran and some to Turkmenistan and Tajikistan. In all, some estimates are that 10 per cent of Afghanistan's pre-war population perished and as many were displaced.

THE END OF THE SOVIET SYSTEM

Mikhail Gorbachev, the last Soviet leader, became General Secretary of the Communist Party of the Soviet Union in 1985 and famously attempted to introduced both glasnost (openness) and perestroika (restructuring) as attempts to revitalise the economic performance of the USSR. He was popular in the West. He got on well with President Ronald Reagan and Prime Minister Margaret Thatcher said he was '... a man she could do business with ...' However, what he really achieved was a revival of nationalist movements in many of the so-called independent republics (see *About War* for details), who chose to secede – or at least try to – from the Soviet Union. By 1991, the political crisis had become acute, the USSR was dissolved and the Russian Federation formed.

The above conflicts are illustrative. There were many more proxy wars in defence of regimes sympathetic to the Soviet Union and/or communism. Also, they were mostly in states and regions geographically contiguous to the USSR itself, and it is here that we find most casualties. Korea for example, shares a ten-mile border with Russia.

All in all, in the forty-six years between the end of the Second World War and the collapse of the Soviet system, the Soviet Union caused the death of some 200,000 civilians who did not want to be dominated by Soviet Russia anyway. They also lost some 50,000 of their own soldiers, though that figure may include soldiers from Warsaw Pact countries as well.

Perhaps the key question is whether all this death and destruction achieved any of Russia's, political, economic or strategic objectives? We consider this after looking at the Russian Federation's use of force.

THE RUSSIAN FEDERATION

One might imagine that the collapse of communism, and thereby the Soviet Union, would result in an aspiration for Russia to become a democratic country (let's just for the moment forget the idea that Russia might become a 'free-market liberal democracy'; with seemingly more countries becoming led by autocrats or even tyrants, this concept seems to be fading anyway) and an honoured, or at least respected, member of the international community. It is worth examining the record in this regard, not from every aspect of Russia's relationship with other peoples, but purely with their use of force.

THE CAUCASUS

In Tim Marshall's book, *Prisoners of Geography*, we are reminded of the importance of geography in determining states' outlook and security concerns. For example, Britain became a maritime nation because it was surrounded by sea, which protects against foreign invasion. As Admiral John Jervis, Earl St Vincent quipped in a letter to the Board of the Admiralty in 1801, 'I do not say, my lords, that the French will not come. I say only they will not come by sea.'

There is no way that the nascent United States could have tolerated the land west of the Mississippi remaining in the hands of the post-revolutionary French, hence the Louisiana purchase in 1803. France is neatly defined by the hexagon, and Italy similarly defined by being a peninsula. The Iberian Peninsula looks as if it might be one country, but Spain and Portugal have long been separated by a mountain range.

Whilst there is no excuse whatsoever for Putin's attack on Ukraine, Western Europeans do need to understand Russia's security concerns, even if they do not accommodate them. According to Tim Marshall, with Napoleon's assault on Russia in 1812 and the Crimean war of 1853, we might say that Russia has been fighting on the north European plain roughly every thirty-three years.

The geography of Russia is significant. To the east of Moscow are the Ural Mountains, behind which they hid much of their industry after the Germans attacked them in 1941. Then there are the vast open Asian plains over which an eastern attacker would have to travel. To the south-west are the Carpathian Mountains and, to the south, the Caucasus.

The Caucasus comprises three main countries: Armenia, Azerbaijan and Georgia. These are squeezed between the Black Sea to the west and the Caspian Sea to the east. To the north is Russia, to the south Turkey and Iran. The Caucasus mountains have historically been thought of as a natural barrier between eastern Europe and western Asia. The region is characterised by vast mountain ranges that have separated people, ethnic and religious groups, who have developed separate identities and languages over thousands of years. Incidentally, Mount Elbrus in Russia is Europe's highest mountain (5,642 m) and is situated in the western Caucasus.

The Caucasus has been fought over by Czarist Russia, the Ottoman Empire and by Persia (modern day Iran). It should not, therefore, come as a major shock to discover that Russia (note Russia, rather than Putin) takes independence movements on its southern Caucasus border very seriously. The politics of the region is complex, with some enmities going back hundreds of years. To illustrate the Russian Federation's and the Soviet Union's use of armed force in this region, we examine wars in Georgia and Chechnya, with a mention of their continuing involvement in Syria.

Even before the Soviet Union was finally put to rest and the Russian Federation declared, its constituent parts – 'independent republics' – had started to think about independence. In the Baltic in August 1989, two million people from Estonia, Latvia and Lithuania – a full third of a total population of six million combined – joined hands to form a human chain some 700 km long. Lithuania declared independence in March 1990, Estonia and Latvia in August 1991. But back to the Caucasus ...

THE GEORGIAN CIVIL WAR (1991–1993)

Georgia declared independence from Russia after a referendum in March 1991 and elected a new president. He was deposed by a military coup in December, but the country then descended into civil war, which lasted until the end of 1993. There was occasional Russian intervention, revolts and counter revolts, insurgencies and coups. The result was the de facto secession from Georgia of the 'independent republics' of Abkhazia and South Ossetia. In the process, some 300,000 Georgians were expelled from these regions. Although nominally independent, they are heavily influenced, politically and militarily, by Russia. A quick look at the map of the Caucasus would show how they would be seen as important to Russian security. The number of Russian casualties is not known but, between the various parties to the war, there were about 20,000 deaths on all sides. The war also produced nearly 260,000 refugees and IDPs.

THE FIRST CHECHEN WAR (1994–1996)

Just north of Georgia and to the east of North Ossetia lies the Russian Chechen Republic. Chechnya has suffered two appalling wars since the fall of the Soviet Union: from 1995 to 1996 and then a much longer conflict from 1999 to 2009.

After the Soviet Union fell apart in 1991, Chechnya split into two parts: the Republic of Ingushetia and the Chechen Republic. Ingushetia remains within the Russian Federation, whereas the Russian Federation waged a war against the Chechen Republic from 1995 to 1996 to prevent it from seceding. The Russians demonstrated their approach to war in devastating Grozny, the Chechen capital, with artillery. They have continued this practice to this day with similar attacks on Ukrainian towns and cities, notably, among others, Mariupol and Bakhmut. The Russians then attempted to control the mountainous areas of Chechnya, and, despite their strength, the Chechen guerrillas won the battle. Yeltsin's government declared a ceasefire in 1996, which led up to a peace treaty in 1997. This war was particularly bloody for all sides. Perhaps up to 3,000 Chechen fighters were killed, and maybe 100,000 civilians. The Russian Federation suffered between 6,000 and 14,000 soldiers killed, and somewhere between 18,000 and 52,000 injured.

THE SECOND CHECHEN WAR (1999–2009)

This began when Islamist fighters from Chechnya attempted to force the Russian Federation to relinquish their control over the Dagestan region to the east of Chechnya, bordering the Caspian Sea coast. Russian Federation forces and pro-Russian Federation Chechen paramilitary forces took the Chechen capital Grozny after a two-month siege. Russia took direct rule over Chechnya in May 2000, although the Chechen resistance inflicted a heavy toll on Russian troops. This continued for several years, and it was only in 2009 that the fighting ceased. There were atrocities on both sides, but the total casualty figure is unknown. More than 16,000 Chechen military died and about 7,300 Russians. However, a Russian NGO, The Committee of Soldiers' Mothers, claims that 14,000 Russian servicemen were killed during this deployment. Amnesty International estimate that about 30,000 civilians died.

WESTERN ATTITUDE TO THE CHECHEN WARS

Russia's abuses in Chechnya were well known at the time, but the reaction in the West was muted. Then, America's attitude seemed to be to engage with Moscow rather than to criticise. One dare not use the word 'appeasement'; we know how that ended. What influence the United States and the West could have brought to bear on Putin (then acting president) at that time is a moot point, but to Putin it may have seemed that there was little concern for Russian hegemonic moves and even their atrocities, particularly as Putin was, at the time, offering himself as a prospective ally in the 'war against terror'.

There is, of course, a contrary view: if the US or Europe had become involved in condemning Russian crimes in Chechnya, the fear was that it could have started a war between the major powers. There could possibly have been other ways of diplomatic signalling.

THE RUSSIAN-GEORGIAN WAR (2008)

Vladimir Putin was elected Russian president in 2000, but in 2003 Georgia developed a more Western perspective. Relations with Russia deteriorated, reaching a full diplomatic crisis by April 2008. The result was that Russia recognised the full independence of Abkhazia and South Ossetia from Georgia, and the Georgian government severed diplomatic relations with Russia. However, 'full independence' might mean one thing to some, but the European Court of Human Rights ruled Russia had 'direct control' over Abkhazia and South Ossetia and was also responsible for some human rights abuses. In fact, the International Criminal Court issued arrest warrants for some Russian nationals because of war crimes against ethnic Georgians. Mercifully, casualties on both sides were probably less than several hundred. Though tragic for those people and their families, this was considerably less than previous Russian involvements.

THE RUSSIAN TAKEOVER OF CRIMEA

Crimea is almost unique in terms of geography: a peninsula of about 27,000 km², nearly the size of Belgium. It is connected to mainland Ukraine by a narrow isthmus, with one narrow road going through the current (2023) checkpoint. Putin built the Kerch bridge, which was opened in 2018 and connected Crimea directly with Russia's Krasnodar Region, sticking out between the Black Sea and the Sea of Azov. It quickly overtook the Kerch Strait ferry as a preferred route of between Crimea and Russia. Other access to Crimea was by the narrow isthmus or by sea.

Crimea has a mixed topography, with some mountains and some agricultural land. Crimea is surrounded almost completely by the Black Sea and also the smaller Sea of Azoz. It has a population of 2.4 million people – far fewer than Belgium, with 11 million people, and comparable with Estonia with 1.3 million, Latvia with 1.8 million and Lithuania with 2.8 million.

Crimea has had a chequered history in terms of sovereignty. It was part of the Mongol empire for 200 years, the Ottoman Empire for 300 years and part of the Russian Czarist Empire for over 130 years. In 1921 it became part of the Soviet Union and remained so up until its dissolution in 1991. In considering the Russian invasion of Ukraine, there are four important points to make about Crimea here.

First, it was supposedly 'given' to what was then then the Soviet Republic of Ukraine by Nikita Khrushchev in 1954. This is sometimes portrayed as an act of generosity, but the reality was more based in geography (Tim Marshall's *Prisoners of Geography* is mentioned several times in this trilogy). Ukraine had suffered appallingly during the Second World War, and Crimea particularly so. By 1953, Crimea, then part of Soviet Russia, was in dire straits, producing far less grain than it had in 1940 and half the number of grapes. Khrushchev visited the peninsula in 1953 to find his car besieged by distressed settlers, who had been brought in by Stalin, demanding assistance. He quickly realised that Kyiv was in a better position to help Crimea and, by the early part of 1954, Crimea became part of Ukraine. And, with reference to the current Russian retreat to the left bank of the Dnieper River and the subsequent destruction of the Nova Kakhovka Dam, we need to recall that the North Crimean Canal was built in the 1960s, which brought up to 30 per cent of the water of the Dnieper to the peninsula, irrigating more than 6,000 km² of agricultural land and providing water to a number of its cities.

Second, before the Russian takeover, some 70 per cent of the population in Crimea was Russian, although 'ethnicity' may not be quite the same as ethnicity in other cultures. Ukrainians make up some 16 per cent of the population, Crimean Tatars about 11 per cent and the remainder are Belarusians, Armenians and Jews. So, although this may not be comfortable for the final peace negotiations – not currently on the horizon anyway – there is some validity in saying that Crimea is Russian. Crimean Tatars are a Turkic ethnic group of Sunni Muslims and native to Crimea. After Stalin's forced relocation of Tatars, there may be especial hostility towards Moscow within this group.

Third, Crimea is home to the Russian Black Sea Fleet in Sevastopol. After the dissolution of the Soviet Union, the Russians held a lease on Sebastopol, which would have run out in 2017 had Russia not seized Crimea.

Fourth, and most importantly in terms of any negotiations between Russia and Ukraine, with or without the brokerage of such as the UN or Turkey, the sea route out of Odessa, one of two vitally important Ukrainian ports in terms of export – particularly for grain – passes within 200 km of Sevastopol.

There is no specific international treaty provision referring to Maritime Exclusion Zones, but their use does have some validity under international law. Since a usual figure for exclusion zones for shipping is 300 km, this may present a stumbling block for negotiations.

Whatever the outcome of the Russian-Ukrainian war, most Western commentators do not believe that Ukraine can ever recover Crimea. In order to be seen to support Ukraine in the war, this is very rarely mentioned.

'LITTLE GREEN MEN'

Following the Maidan Revolution in Ukraine in February 2014 and the likelihood of Ukraine taking a more Western or European outlook, Vladimir Putin decided that Crimea should be 'returned' to Russia.

According to Simon Shuster of *Time* magazine: 'before dawn on Feb. 27, at least two dozen heavily armed men stormed the Crimean parliament building and the nearby headquarters of the regional government, bringing with them a cache of assault rifles and rocket propelled grenades …'

A few hours later, Sergey Aksyonov, a Russian army officer, walked into the parliament and, after a brief round of talks with the gunmen, began to gather a quorum of the chamber's members. At the same time, Russian troops ('little green men') captured strategic sites across Crimea.

In March of that year, remarkably swift for any organised and fair referendum by Western standards, a status referendum was held and, with a 90 per cent turnout, 95 per cent of the population supposedly agreed to join the Russian Federation. There was some cynicism in the West as to how this result was achieved. A pro-Russian Aksyonov government was installed. Denis Berezovsky, the head of the Ukrainian Navy, defected to Russia, later followed by about half the Ukrainian military in the region. Ukraine later charged Berezovsky with treason. Ukraine subsequently withdrew its troops and their families from Crimea, Russia was expelled from the G7, and sanctions were imposed.

WAR IN DONBAS (2014–2022)

The War in Donbas was a precursor to the wider Russian-Ukrainian War. Popular protests against the Ukrainian government's abrupt decision not to sign the European Union–Ukraine Association Agreement and instead to look east to Russia and the Eurasian Economic Union, led to large demonstrations in Maidan (Independence) Square in Kyiv.

While Russia was taking over Crimea, there were also demonstrations by pro-Russian, anti-Ukrainian, government separatists in the eastern provinces (oblasts) of Donetsk and Luhansk, together called the Donbas. The protesters declared the Donetsk and Luhansk People's Republics (DPR and LPR, respectively). Ukrainian government buildings were seized. Ukraine started an anti-terrorist operation, which had some success. In response, Russian forces invaded Donbas. Soon, the situation became involved and complex, with many ceasefires (see the Minsk Protocols I and II), all to little effect.

As is not uncommon in such messy conflicts, there were many casualties: as many as 5,000 Ukrainian soldiers killed, with some 14,000 wounded, and over 3,000 civilians killed. The Russians and insurgents also suffered: up to 7,000 soldiers killed and 16,000 wounded. On 21 February 2022, Russia recognised the Donetsk and Luhansk People's Republics, declared the Minsk Protocols repudiated and, three days later, began its large-scale invasion of Ukraine.

THE SYRIAN CIVIL WAR

The Syrian Civil War is a modern tragedy, made more intractable by there being so many factions opposing the Syrian government and, from time to time, each other. The one constant is the Syrian Arab Republic led by its president, Bashar al-Assad, who studied medicine in London and married an Ealing girl. His elder brother having died, Bashar inherited the presidency from his father, Hafez al-Assad, notorious for the Hama massacre in February 1982. His son seems to be just as cruel.

The roots of the conflict can be found in the Arab Spring protests, which cannot be called a movement as there was little coordination across the Arab world. There were calls for Bashar al-Assad's removal. Violence was at its worst in 2015 but, although the situation has stabilised to some extent, the crisis remains. There have been several attempts at peace talks, but the violence continues. Over half a million people, troops and civilians have died and it is estimated that there are over six million IDPs and refugees. Amongst the several foreign countries involved, such as Iran, Turkey and the United States, the Russians have taken a leading role.

RUSSIAN INVOLVEMENT IN THE SYRIAN CIVIL WAR

The age of empire ended during the Second World War or even earlier, though some imagined empires, notably the British, staggered on for another generation. There is little classification for empires, despite some modest academic interest in the subject. We can, though, discern two distinct types. Some empires, such as the Czarist Russia, were contiguous; some worldwide and dispersed like the British Empire.

Russia's policy since the end of the Cold War seems to have been to regain, or at least control, contiguous areas, some of which wanted to be, or thought they were, independent states. Russian–Syrian relations go back into the Soviet era, but in the present day, the Russian Federation has use of and sometimes operates several bases in Syria, including the Tartus naval base and the Khmeimim air base. They are about 50 km apart and opposite Cyprus.

Involvement in Syria was the first time since the end of the Cold War that Russia deployed and took military action outside the boundaries of the former Soviet Union. In 2015, Russian aircraft and missiles started hitting ISIL, the Army of Conquest, al-Nusra Front and the Free Syrian Army, all in support of the 'legitimate' Syrian Arab Republic.

In 2018, Russia began bombing hospitals and medical facilities, so much so that Russia's seat on the UN Human Rights Council was removed. According to Airwars, a UK organisation that tracked the air war against ISIL and other groups in Iraq, Syria and Libya, between four and six thousand civilians have been killed in the Russian military actions, which included shelling as well as air attacks and missiles. Other sources put the figure much higher, with a civilian total of about 21,000.

4 THE RUSSIAN FEDERATION'S USE OF FORCE

It is salutary to note that conclusions about the Russian Federation's use of force are almost identical to those about of the Soviet Union. There are still wars that are in defence of regimes sympathetic to the Russian Federation or regimes they wanted to influence, like Mali, Libya and the Central African Republic. Many were geographically contiguous to the Russian Federation itself, some not; both the Soviet Union and the Russian Federation has always had bases in Latakia in Syria. In the thirty-odd years since the collapse of the Soviet system, we find the same lack of political engagement, the same brute force in the form of air attacks and artillery to devastate their enemies and then to impose their will.

Civilian casualties are at a similar level. All in all, in those thirty-odd years, the Russian Federation has caused the death of some 200,000 civilians who did not want to be dominated by the Russian Federation or, indeed, the Soviet Union. The Russian Federation has also lost some 35,000 of their own soldiers. (This is prior to and excluding losses incurred in Ukraine since February 2022.)

Soviet Russia showed itself to be heedless of civilian casualties and careless of its own losses, all to maintain oppressive regimes that were not only undemocratic but failed to deliver the promised consumer paradise. It shows that, instead of political engagement, the Soviet Union used brute force in the form of air attacks and artillery to devastate their enemies and then to impose their will. The Russian Federation is the equivalent, but without the checks and balances of the admittedly heavy-handed and ponderous Soviet Politburo, which could dismiss a leader, as it did Khruschev in 1964. The Russian Federation is a danger to its constituent parts, to contiguous states, to world peace, and ultimately to itself and its population. To the Western mind, and probably even the majority of the population in Russia, it is amoral and nihilistic.

RUSSIA'S CONTEMPT

The Russian Federation has also demonstrated itself to be as careless about battlefield casualties as was ever the case with Czarist Russia, Soviet Russia and the Russian Federation, pre- and post-Putin. It sets Russia, in whatever incarnation, apart from the liberal democracies of the West. Indeed, *careless* may be too mild a word: Russia's rulers almost display contempt toward their own people, and, it must be said, towards whoever they see as the enemy.

It may be apocryphal, but some reports suggest that Zhukov claimed that the Soviet army's method for clearing minefields in the Second World War was to send infantry across them as if there were no mines. Apologists say this only applied to convicted criminals, which is an interesting precedent for the Wagner group releasing convicted criminals from prisons to fight in their battalions. Also attributed to Zhukov was the aphorism '... women will give birth to more ...', and one could easily imagine Putin saying pretty much the same thing – though somebody, somewhere, should warn Putin that, in today's interconnected world, there may soon be very few young women left in Russia ...

DID IT WORK FOR SOVIET RUSSIA? IS IT WORKING FOR THE RUSSIAN FEDERATION?

Judging by the number of young tech-savvy, people – hundreds of thousands by some accounts – who have left the country since the attack on Ukraine; considering the long queues to get out of the country when the general mobilisation was announced; judging by the fact that the population is declining rather than growing, we must conclude that

Russia, despite its vast $600 billion foreign holdings and despite its attempting to influence some African countries, has multiple problems of its own, some of which would seem intractable.

A survey was carried out by the Atlantic Council on the *Prospects for 2023*, in which they canvassed 167 foreign policy experts on what geopolitics, climate change, technological disruption, the global economy, social and political movements and other domains could look like a decade from now. Nearly two-thirds of respondents were US citizens with European citizens making up most of the balance. They conclude, among other things, that:

'... *one of the most surprising takeaways was how many respondents pointed to a potential Russian Federation collapse over the next decade – suggesting that the Kremlin's war against Ukraine could precipitate hugely consequential upheaval in a great power with the largest nuclear-weapons arsenal on the planet. Nearly half ... of respondents expect Russia to either become a failed state or break up by 2033. More than a fifth consider Russia* (the Federation) *the most likely country to become a failed state within the next ten years. Even more striking, forty percent of respondents expect Russia to break up internally by 2033 because of revolution, civil war, political disintegration or some other reason. Europeans are particularly pessimistic about Russia breaking up: half of them foresee such an event compared with one third of Americans ...*'

Dagestan, Abkhazia and South Ossetia may try and secede, and also client states – even Belarus – may find their loyalty to Russia tested. That said, one must be careful of what one wishes for (see Neal Ascherson's remarks in the London Review of Books about the *[Black] Sea of Blood*). Although Putin has made some progress in modernising Russia's economy, much of his thinking is still stuck in the old Soviet way of dealing with international relations.

For ordinary Russians, it's quite clear that nothing will change until Putin and his cronies have disappeared – and, even then, it may take a generation or more to lose its pariah status. Given the loss of confidence, amongst the population, one of Putin's fears is large-scale street protests. The 'mob' was the great fear of patrician ancient Romans. We might already be seeing a loss of morale amongst the Russian troops in Ukraine, but we must be careful not to overstate this. The Russian army still has elements of the old Red Army internal discipline. Recall that during the Second World War it executed over 150,000 of its own number, sometimes for an offence as little as not pressing an attack hard enough or for the trivial transgression of thinking unrevolutionary thoughts.

The world is often described as an 'increasingly dangerous place'. Post-Second World War this has never been truer since the Russian invasion of Ukraine, despite Korea, Cuba, Vietnam and the Gulf wars.

5 THE RUSSIAN ARMY AND ITS SHORTCOMINGS

If the Soviets and now the Russian Federation have typically resorted by default to the use of force, is the Russian army up to the job? And what are the implications for the West?

The Russian army has performed poorly in Ukraine. Contrary to expectations and even intelligence, there was fear that the Russian attack on Kyiv would take the city within a few days, consolidate its gains and then focus on the Donbas and the Kherson area. In the event, the Russians failed to reach Kyiv and were driven back into Belarus, suffering great losses and leaving behind a trail of civilian abuse and murder. And although they made significant incursions into Donbas and Kharkiv oblast of Ukraine, the Ukrainian army put up stiff resistance and, in many instances, pushed them back. It is misleading to imagine that the Russian army is therefore beaten or useless. Although they may have had similar sized armies at the beginning of the war, the Russians can call on a much larger population, although many of the conscripts would need to be trained to an appropriate standard.

Analysing the complex shortcomings of the Russian army is challenging: on the Ukrainian side there is an understandable secrecy and, on the Russian side, propaganda. Western media reports also reflect a certain schadenfreude, which may also cloud judgement. This was apparent when the world learned in early March of a forty-mile-long Russian convoy outside Ukraine's capital, unable to move because of lack of ability to travel off-road and with food and fuel running out. Whilst not denigrating the bravery and technical knowledge of journalists on the ground, it takes a real expert in military affairs, and *land warfare* at that, to appreciate the many aspects of the military machine. In some cases, the range of artillery is a determining factor; in others it might be the sheer speed with which radar can talk to a missile battery. Outside the MOD and the UK armed forces themselves, whose detailed analyses must obviously remain confidential, we are fortunate in the United Kingdom by having two experienced experts. One is Jack Watling, a senior research fellow for land warfare at RUSI; the other is Shashank Joshi, defence editor for *The Economist.*

Distilling their comments and those from other sources over the past eleven months, we can identify five main elements of weakness. But, first, it is worth citing areas where the Russians were and remain strong.

Jack Watling suggests that Russian doctrine – the set of principles by which you fight a war – is essentially sound. Their problem is that the practice rarely matches the theory. Thus, there is a compounding problem: senior generals might feel very pleased with themselves to have identified and implemented the latest doctrine, but this might get lost further down the chain, further confusing front-line troops.

Watling also suggests that Russian munitions are well designed and adequately built. But Russia lacks a competent microelectronics industry. Many components used to be imported from the West and therefore this is now of limited value to them. We know that the Russian military is largely supplied by rail, and this seems to work reasonably well. It's when materiel is transferred to road vehicles that the problems start.

There is one other area of Russian strength, and that is in terms of manpower. Russia is three and a half times as big as Ukraine in terms of population, but again there is a problem in exploiting this. The moment a major conscription exercise was announced, it was reported that hundreds of thousands of young men, and we assume some young women, left the country. Many of them were Russia's tech-savvy. So, although we might estimate that the total war losses for the Russian population was small, it represents a larger portion of that section from which they need to draw on to fight a war. Russia is short of young recruits. In *War in Context*, we looked more generally at population loss, suggesting that if Russia does not take this seriously, the population might halve in ten years.

RUSSIAN ARMY WEAKNESS: NCOs

Anyone who has any ever read a book or seen a film about an ordinary soldier's life at the front line (typically termed a 'private soldier') will know that the main focus of the front-line fighter's attention is on his immediate superior: Lance Corporal, Corporal or Sergeant – all non-commissioned officers (NCOs). 'Yes, Sarge' is the usual phrase. NCOs are known as the backbone of any army. Whereas officers can direct operations in terms of platoons, companies or brigades, it's the NCO who controls individual soldiers on the ground. It's a common meme that Russian forces do not have NCOs. They are known not to have NCOs in the Western military sense, but it's unlikely that they can operate with a big gap between offices and front-line private soldiers. It is probably true to say that the first line management of troops is undertrained and does not have very much in the way of decision-making authority, something that could also be said of junior officers below the rank of colonel.

Both the British and United States Army rely heavily on NCOs to great effect. It is often said (you might guess by whom) that the NCOs really run the battle while the offices simply issue orders (and drink tea).

According to General Mark Milley, chairman of the US Joint Chiefs of Staff, '... the Russians practice a top-down, very top-heavy directive ... with orders coming from the top, which is not necessarily the best thing to do in a dynamic battlefield...'. This is in contrast to the Ukrainian army, which not only operates with assisting NCOs but delegates authority much further down the chain of command. They also encourage up-to-date intelligence reports from civilians.

The Economist (30 April 2022) references Leon Trotsky: 'the army is a copy of society and suffers from all its diseases, usually at a higher temperature'. Does the existence of so many absurdly rich oligarchs influence the military right down to the front-line soldier?

RUSSIAN ARMY WEAKNESS: CORRUPTION

The Russian army, its officer corps and the industries that supply it are horrendously corrupt. As a nation, Russia looks pretty corrupt too. It is ranked 136 out of 180 in a table of the least corrupt nations with the UK at number 11, France at 22, the US at 27 and Italy at 42. (Out of interest, Denmark Finland and New Zealand are the least corrupt countries in the world, and coming right at the bottom are Somalia, Syria and South Sudan.)

There is also moral corruption. Jack Watling suggests that '... corruption is structurally encouraged by the Kremlin so that the civilian authorities have the threat of legal action against military commanders ...'. He goes on to write that this '... wreaks havoc on Russian logistics (and) leadership, being enforced by fear means that soldiers will doggedly implement orders even when they no longer make sense...'. Though the Western approach may be imperfect, this is a damaging aspect of Russian culture.

RUSSIAN ARMY WEAKNESS: LEADERSHIP AND EDUCATION

Leadership in the Russian army is weak. In Western armies this aspect of management is emphasised and developed. In the Russian army, leadership seems to be dictatorial, with orders being followed no matter what. It goes with lack of training. Training usually takes place in the units, which means that new recruits may not have access to professional trainers and that the training they do receive focuses on their particular function rather than on the generalities of being a soldier.

In Western armies, it is almost the opposite. It is difficult for the layman to appreciate quite how important training is. Untrained troops will find it very difficult and dangerous to move around the battleground and will sustain far more casualties than if they were properly trained. And an aspect not well advertised is that an efficient, well-trained army might cause fewer casualties amongst the enemy. During the endless Isonzo battles, the Italians would send wave after wave of soldiers against the Austrian attackers. At one point, after so many Italian casualties, the Austrians broadcast to the Italians to 'stop doing it else we'll kill you all'. They were right, but to little effect! Tragically, the Italian commander General Cadorna was so disappointed in the Italians' performance that, taking a page out of the ancient Roman generals' book, he decimated them, which really means executing one in ten. He was eventually sacked in 1917.

A seemingly contradictory observation is that Russia claims to have some nineteen military academies, including the most senior and strategic: The Military Academy of the General Staff of the Armed Forces of Russia, for lieutenant colonels and above.

RUSSIAN ARMY WEAKNESS: RELIANCE ON ARTILLERY

In terms of *warfare* (which we distinguish from *war as a political act*), there are two aspects that are inherited from the Soviet era, and maybe even going back to Peter the Great (Russian Czar from 1682 to 1725). The first is the use of artillery. This has always been Russia's 'God of War', and indeed on the Eastern Front between 1943 and 1945, the Red Army had something like 40,000 artillery pieces.

Artillery is invaluable for 'softening up' (a horrid phrase) the opposition, both in terms of their troops and infrastructure, but not if it's used as a substitute for manoeuvre and advance. Also, for uninitiated troops, artillery barrages can be terrifying. In the initial few months of Russia's advance into Ukraine, they were firing an enormous number of shells against what they claimed were Ukrainian military targets. In fact, they were civilian buildings – a war crime. Despite Russia's mighty ordnance, they still find it difficult to advance.

Massed heavy artillery has been a standard feature of Russian doctrine for centuries. Other countries in the West, such as the US, use artillery but also rely on precision airstrikes from aircraft. So, what's wrong with relying on artillery?

First, artillery is vulnerable to counter-battery fire. Modern practice requires that as soon as a battery has fired, it needs to move very quickly to avoid the response. Using an artillery piece is more than just turning it into a field, orientating it and firing. There has to be a logistical path to the battery and shells have to be unpacked. Second, unless artillery is closely controlled by advanced electronics, it is not very precise.

ESCALATION

This may come in two guises. First, the most usual comment is that fear of nuclear escalation has hamstrung prompt support from the West in supplying Ukraine with tanks, planes and long-range missiles, especially when Putin, Lavrov and Mad (rent-a-threat) Medvedev start nuclear sabre rattling. Second, it may be that the military hierarchy within Russia is terrified of any nuclear escalation as they may not have confidence in the higher political command to resist escalating. Also the thought that they might lose much of their army and equipment. There is very little commentary on what the Americans would do (it would be down to them to decide) if Putin used a nuclear weapon. If it were a strategic nuclear weapon with an ICBM, the Americans have contingency plans for every eventuality. But if Putin used a battlefield nuclear weapon, the response would be a massive conventional attack on Russian troop concentrations and assembly areas, the Russian Black Sea Fleet and also proximate Russian airfields and aircraft.

RUSSIAN ARMY WEAKNESS: CASUALTIES AND ABUSE

Following the practice of Soviet Russia, the Russia Federation shows itself to be heedless of civilian casualties and careless of its own losses. What is worse in this modern age is the rape, pillage and murder of the Ukrainian civilian population. There are several reasons why Russian troops resort to such actions.

First is the erosion of any feeling that the enemy is human. This usually happens in very long wars where the troops have seen abuses heaped on their own side. There were some instances of British and Indian troops abusing Japanese prisoners of war in the Far East during the Second World War because of the treatment meted out to British and Indian troops by the Japanese. This rationale is not available to the attacking Russian Federation troops, as there have been few instances of the Ukrainian army abusing Russian POWs.

The second factor is lack of discipline within the ranks. Research has shown that without any constraints or the possibility of discipline soldiers will tend to mistreat anyone in their care within a very short space of time: days or even hours. The lack of any NCO corps within the Russian army may have contributed to that. Another factor, rather more chilling, is that this is a deliberate policy promulgated by senior generals right down to the front line. The moral repugnance of this makes it difficult to accept.

This abuse may have contributed to a lack of morale among Russian troops. At the end of the Second World War, when the 'Allies liberated Nazi concentration camps, guards disguised themselves by wearing prison clothing. If they weren't contrite, they were at least sheepish: they knew they had done wrong.

The current autocratic regime in the Russian Federation, their propaganda machine and the suppression of independent news can only go so far in preventing and managing public opinion. This may not stop a Ukrainian court or the ICC (International Criminal Court) from pursuing justice and holding regimes and even individual officers to account.

A MAJOR CAVEAT …

The West must not be lulled into a false sense of security by Russia's failures. Russia remains a powerful country with a strong sense of itself. They see their leader, whether dictator or elected president, as the legitimate heir to the mighty Czars of the past.

Orlando Figes is a British historian and writer, known for his works on Russian history. His *A People's Tragedy* is an intriguing study of the Russian Revolution. He points out that, in Russian culture, this is a '… *form of despotism and enslavement of society that goes from the Mongols to Stalin, who was described by Bolshevik Bukharin as 'Genghis Khan with the telephone'.* He goes on to say that the very word for power in Russian (vlast) comes not from action as in Western languages, but from the term for a fiefdom, a territory owned by its ruler.

If Putin is thought of by the West as a pariah now, there is little recognition of this outside the Western and European allies. Perhaps French president Emmanuel Macron has a point in suggesting that we should not humiliate Putin, but engage with him, unsavoury as this might be. 'To Jaw-Jaw is better than to War-War,' as Churchill didn't quite say. (It actually was, 'Meeting jaw to jaw is better than war.' Churchill was not quite as inarticulate as the misquote suggests.)

Russia still celebrates the triumph over the Nazi hordes between 1943 and 1945 in the Great Patriotic War, though the cost in human life may be unknown to most. But squeamishness over the butcher's bill has never been a Russian sentiment.

The essential Western support is of course reliant on continuing public support from the West's electorates, particularly the US and, by happy coincidence, support in the form of President Joe Biden. It was particularly heartening to see him embrace Volodymyr Zelenskyy when the latter visited to Washington just before Christmas 2022.

The Russian Federation also has more nuclear weapons than anyone else, nearly 7,000 at the latest count; the United States has slightly fewer.

STRATEGIC IMPLICATIONS FOR THE RUSSIAN FEDERATION

In the introduction to this chapter, I suggest that it was no exaggeration to say that the February 2022 Russian attack on Ukraine changed the world forever. Now that the strategic implications are coming more into focus, we can see innumerable consequences: assumptions about Russia's place in the world; the use of technology in warfare; European security; American involvement in Europe; globalisation versus autarky – particularly with regard to energy supplies – and nuclear weapons. All of these are now called into question.

Putin is obsessed, like many Russians, by Russia's status in the world, and by perceived disrespect by the West. Barak Obama's comment that Russia was a great *regional* power really wounded Putin, who sees Russia as a great *world* power (see observations on the Primakov Doctrine in *War in Context*). The Kremlin repeats these resentments to this day, almost two years by the time of publication.

To attack a neighbouring country, something that has not happened in Europe since 1940, simply to incorporate that country into its own sphere, with no concern for the population of that country – and, come to think of it, little concern for your *own* troops and population, is egregious.

Putin's false sense of Russian greatness harks back to Yevgeny Primakov, who was Prime Minister of Russia between 1988 and 1989. Ironically, he was born in Kyiv and grew up in Tbilisi in Georgia. His aim, one might say doctrine, was a multipolar international system not so dominated by the United States, a concept that appealed, and still appeals, to Putin and inspires him.

But this was not simply what we might call a 'Clausewitzian' invasion, where military force is complementary to political and diplomatic moves, but one of rape and pillage, theft, torture, murder and a general abuse of the population. Indeed, it is the complete opposite of what you might expect, if it were a matter of winning hearts and minds. Perhaps that comment is witness to a Western, rather than a Russian mindset, but one that is based on decency and morality. It was, in short, a war of aggression, something that the Nazis were accused of at the Nuremberg trials, which Russians participated in as prosecutors!

In the judgment of the International Military Tribunal at Nuremberg that followed the Second World War:

War is essentially an evil thing. Its consequences are not confined to the belligerent states alone, but affect the whole world. To initiate a war of aggression, therefore, is not only an international crime; it is the supreme international crime differing only from other war crimes in that it contains within itself the accumulated evil of the whole.

Russia is a well-established country, the largest in the world by land area. It covers seven time zones, though be careful if you take the trans-Siberian Express, as it always runs on Moscow time. From a Western point of view, there are no threats to its existence or sovereignty. Putin may perceive a threat to its existence, but this may be simply for domestic consumption rather than anything he actually believes – we really don't know. It has a wealth of natural resources and also a military that can summon, however unrealistically, the success that their forebears had in turning the tide against the German army at Stalingrad, despite the cost in terms of blood and treasure.

It has already been established that Soviet thinking about security, the use of force and a casual disregard for civilian populations of other nations, or indeed their own, have carried over from Soviet Russia to the Russian Federation. It is recognised that Putin does not negotiate in good faith. This was known, but now it is absolutely confirmed. Xi Jinping, please note. Indeed, he does not negotiate at all. He has let it be known that the only terms on which he will meet President Volodymyr Zelenskyy is to receive his unconditional surrender.

Putin inhabits an intellectual and political bubble, bereft of considered advice or opposition. The theatre of consulting his Cabinet before the invasion was transparent and didn't even reach the level of a joke. His approach has echoes of Stalin. Uncle Joe became suspicious of everything and everybody, eventually becoming completely paranoid, much to the detriment of the Russian government and the Russian people, though he did come to respect his generals towards the end of the Second World War. There is no sign that Putin has widened his court of advisers. Indeed, he has retired two generals in addition to the estimated eighteen who have been killed. With perhaps as many as a hundred colonels killed in action, the advice he's getting from the military must be very thin indeed.

Russia still has vast resources sitting in overseas banks that they cannot access at the moment. These will no doubt be on the negotiation table when it comes to reparations for Ukraine. However, judging by the latest reports, Russia's economic problems are more long than short term. It still sells oil and gas to countries that have not imposed sanctions and Putin does seem to have taken some notice of the need to re-industrialise. However, he is still in need of some Western technology, such as chips and software. The consensus is that it will take several years for Western sanctions to really bite, but then the effects could be devastating for the Russian economy and its people. It remains to be seen whether the West's sanctions will stay in place for those several years.

In Ukraine, he has, single-handedly, boosted Ukraine nationalism and patriotism and made it a more coherent and respected country.

Before considering the impact that the Russian invasion of Ukraine has had on Russia, Europe and the world in general, we need to be aware of two relevant aspects: Russia's approach to *maskirovka* in the first place, and Putin's attitude to nuclear weapons in the second.

Putin has failed in his strategic objective. If it was to exert hegemony over Ukraine, he has failed. If it was to realise the Primakov doctrine, which was to establish a multipolar international system less dominated by the United States, he has failed. If it was to establish the Russian Federation as a feared, if not exactly respected, member of the international community of states, he has failed. If it was to curtail the expansion or fragment the cohesion of NATO, he has failed. If it was to demonstrate how powerful the Russian army is, as befits a powerful state, he has failed. If it was to showcase Russia as a modern technocratic state, he has failed. Nor will his natural resources, which are considerable, achieve his objectives. His threats to use nuclear weapons should be taken seriously but are also a sign of weakness.

But not only has he failed, there have been some remarkable achievements by Ukraine and the West: it is now almost impossible to see Ukraine caving in to Putin's demands or being fully occupied by Russia or abandoned by the West. Even if, by some remarkable chance, he could win the war in Ukraine, Putin would suffer an insurgency such as the world has rarely seen. His casualties would be enormous, and the Russian Federation would be even more of a pariah on the international stage.

In terms of establishing a multipolar international system, he has simply brought into being a much stronger community of democratic states, who are now absolutely determined that he should not get his way. There is now much more in the way of thinking about strategic security, and about the threat from Russia.

Strategy, as explained in *About War* and *War in Context*, is multifunctional. High-tech weapons need technically literate operatives. To enact brilliant doctrine requires a hierarchy of competent officers, particularly NCOs. Powerful weapons are only useful if you can get them to the front and keep them supplied with good logistical support.

Finally and above all, one must have faith and confidence in your military leaders. Putin and a small clique planned the invasion and then issued instructions to the military. Large-scale invasions require considerable, detailed professional preparation. Putin allowed only a few hours' notice, based on counsel from a small group of associates. D-Day was a year in the making and succeeded. Arnhem was the product of a week's planning. And failed.

6 PUTIN AND NUCLEAR WEAPONS

When Putin announced his invasion of Ukraine on 24 February 2022, he made the comment that '... an attempt to interfere with Russia's invasion of Ukraine will lead to ... consequences never encountered in your history ...' It was a clear threat to use nuclear weapons, but, in a subtle interpretation of his words, not against Ukraine; the threat was against the West in general and against Western troops, ships and planes being used against Russian forces. Putin has also been using cyber-attacks and most likely sabotaged the Nord Stream 1 and 2 gas pipelines. There is another danger: subsea cables, all 500 or so, are pivotal for a global communication infrastructure, accounting for around 95 per cent of all transatlantic data traffic. Putin could cut off Europe from the rest of the world.

There are several dynamics to take into account with an enemy who may be considering using nuclear weapons. First, though, we have to appreciate the difference between strategic and tactical weapons. Strategic weapons are large ICBMs. These are very closely monitored by the intelligence services and any launch would be instantly detectable, whether that launch was of an ICBM, an SSBM (Submerged Ship Ballistic Missile) or from an aircraft.

Tactical weapons are different in terms of yield. There is no defined technical difference between a strategic and a tactical nuclear weapon, other than the latter are smaller with less of a yield and can be carried by shorter range missiles and even artillery shells. They would probably have a capability something like the bombs that fell on Hiroshima or Nagasaki. However, the distinction between strategic and tactical is academic. The use of a tactical nuclear weapon in any field for any purpose would be treated as a major *strategic* problem.

The first dynamic is the breaking of the nuclear taboo. This is defined in detail in *War in Context* but, in short, nuclear armed countries will not threaten other countries with a nuclear strike during negotiations. It is an informal agreement, though this has been broken in spats between India and Pakistan, and Israel has also made disturbing noises with regard to Iran. We might also mention here (again, see *War in Context*) that the absence of nuclear negotiations makes the breaking of this taboo more likely.

The second dynamic is that even if the probability of a nuclear weapon being used is deemed to be a fraction of one per cent, it needs to be taken as a near certainty in terms of intelligence, preparation, contingency planning, and a non-escalation plan. Although this might be a sensible approach, the risks of a mistake being made would be heightened.

The third dynamic is that the world could cope *physically* with one tactical nuclear weapon being used, or even one strategic weapon. It is rather horrible to think about, but if escalation could be contained, the end of the world would not be nigh. Since the 1945 Hiroshima and Nagasaki bombs, there have been some 2,000 nuclear detonations in the world, some of them atmospheric, some of them underground. Spread over fifty years, this has not resulted in a nuclear winter. Of course, 2,000 nuclear detonations in a shorter time span would be a real problem. The problem with any nuclear detonation anywhere in the context of a battle is that it would cause much fear and panic amongst all parties, even those not concerned in the actual conflict.

However terrifying for civilians (and soldiers), the main concern would be with political leaders. As Lord David Richards, Chief of the Defence Staff UK from 2010 to 2013 mentioned on the radio in November 2022, following a (Russian? Ukrainian?) missile hitting a village in Poland, as most politicians nowadays have not had any experience of war, and certainly not the dangers of nuclear war, they might be advised by their military to put their military's defences on higher alert, but then that might increase the risk of an accident.

In *War in Context*, we quote the then Chief of the General Staff, General Sir Nick Carter (head of the British Army), admitting that: '... on our side, we don't have the same level of understanding that we had of each other in the Cold War, and the tried and tested systems and diplomatic instruments are not what they once were – confidence-building measures, arms reduction negotiations, public monitoring and inspection of each other's military activity, etc'. Considerably more effort – diplomatic, political and technical – should be committed to this as part of an overall strategy.

It seems that Putin has missed one of the most famous aphorisms in terms of the use of power, which came from Theodore Roosevelt in 1901. It said quite simply: 'speak softly and carry a big stick' (see *Diagnosis and Prognosis* to follow).

Putin is unlikely to resort to nuclear weapons, although he will continue to threaten. There are several reasons.

First, to fulfil his threat against the West itself, he would have to attack a Western (NATO) country. This would result in immediate and overwhelming retaliation. My conjecture is that the US president – for it would be he who decides – would not resort to a retaliatory nuclear attack for fears of escalation that would be difficult to manage. Such a retaliation would probably involve ground troops or a massive conventional missile attack. It would *not* involve attacking Russian territory, even though Putin has declared some of the pre-conflict Donbas to be Russian territory. NATO might risk an attack on Russian assembly areas just inside Russia, but we're getting into the realm of wild speculation here.

Consider a comment made by Margarita Simonyan, the editor in chief of RT, a state-controlled media channel in Russia. This is she of the 'beauty of war' comment – she obviously has not been in one. The United

Kingdom is her particular animus, as we imagine it to be for Putin. She at one stage said that the way to conclude the war with Ukraine was to 'take out' the United Kingdom. This would be achieved by detonating a nuclear bomb in the North Sea, with the resulting tidal wave destroying the country. I asked an old colleague who had worked with her, and he responded that she was very good at judging exactly what Putin would like to hear but didn't want to say himself. We might mention here that the United Kingdom survived the Storegga Slide, far worse than a nuclear bomb, although – full disclosure – this was 8,000 years ago.

This raises the possible question of how rational Putin is. After all, attacking Ukraine in the first place would not appear to be a rational move. What might a nuclear attack achieve? Attacking the West with any form of nuclear weapon would, as previously stated, invoke a massive retaliation. What options might Putin see in terms of using a nuclear weapon in Ukraine? It seems there are three possibilities:

First would be a demonstration attack with only a few casualties. An obvious choice might be Snake Island. It would seem very unlikely that this would worry either Zelensky or the West in general.

Second might be a battlefield attack, but the conventional wisdom about using tactical nuclear weapons on the battlefield is that you have to use quite a lot of them to make any difference *strategically* to the war on the ground. Such a ground would then be irradiated, and it could be that Putin's generals would resist this.

The final option is an attack on a Ukrainian centre of population or command centre, which, it is thought, would only strengthen Ukrainian resolve.

Robert Pape is a professor of political science at the University of Chicago, and an American with expertise in national and international security affairs and a particular interest in air power. In his seminal book *Bombing to Win: Air Power and Coercion in War* (1996), he considers various air power strategies, although one could argue about whether he's actually talking about strategy or tactics. At over 400 pages, it's challenging to grasp his thesis, but in essence he suggests that, rather than inciting citizens of an attacked nation to rise up against their government, bombing often backfires, resulting in a community that much more resilient and loyal.

There is also the moral angle. The cover of this book *War after Ukraine* shows the results of a British and American bombing raid on Dresden in February 1945. Whether this raid was necessary and whether it achieved any objectives is still being debated. It certainly did not make the German population rise up against Nazism, but probably just prepared them for the inevitable defeat. It is difficult to rise up against a dictator if you're dead.

Finally, Putin's use of nuclear weapons against the West or in Ukraine would be a strategic, political and diplomatic disaster, with unknowable consequences – for Russia too, and for Putin, who may find himself being replaced. It would turn all the countries who appeared to be indifferent to his invasion of Ukraine against him; it could fracture his relationships with China, and India who have to think very carefully about its relationship with Russia, particularly on weapons development. Having had the nuclear taboo broken, India and Pakistan would each be nervous about the other. Finally, there is the issue of compliance down the line. Later in life, Denis Healey claimed that, when he was UK minister for defence, he could not have pressed the button on a nuclear attack, knowing what devastation it would cause. Although we are treating Russia as a pariah at the moment, there is a reasonable chance that the instruction to launch a nuclear attack would not be followed.

There is one other piece of nonsense that needs to be dismissed. Putin claims that there are precedents for using nuclear weapons in war, citing the Hiroshima and Nagasaki bombs that the United States dropped on those cities in 1945. This is not comparable. In 1945, the United States was geared up with an immense number of troops and an enormous supply of war material to invade Japan. Before the bombs, Japan was institutionally incapable of conceding the inevitable defeat. The two bombs allowed her to accept the 'unendurable'. They actually saved lives.

ADDENDUM

MASKIROVKA

For many years and up to the current day, the Russians have practised *maskirovka* (literally disguise), generally known as Russian military deception. It was introduced in the early 20th century and developed from then on. But, as practiced, it's not just disguise or deception; it covers a whole range of actions from camouflage to denying military actions – the 'false flag' accusations that Russia levels at its enemies – misinformation and denial.

A usual military tactic is to try and fool the enemy into thinking you're going to attack one place when you're actually going to attack another. The most famous example was George Patton's Ghost Army in East Anglia, ready to attack Nazi-held France on D-Day (a ruse that was part of Operation Fortitude South). In fact, the tanks and aircraft were dummies and the whole thing was a fiction, supported by radio traffic. It fooled Hitler; he thought the coming attack was going to be in the Pas-de-Calais.

The Russians have developed maskirovka into a wholesale doctrine of political, diplomatic and media opinion to contribute to achieving their strategic objectives.

So far, so good. No country, no army, would claim that there is no hyperbole in their pronouncements.

There are though, four problems with maskirovka:

First, whoever is trying to deceive needs to coordinate their message. When the Ukrainians sunk the *Moskva* in the Black Sea, the message put out was that it was an on-board fire. In fact, it was a Ukrainian missile and could be shown to be so.

The second problem is that the deception has to be in some way credible. Donald Trump achieved notoriety for claiming that the Mexicans who were coming across the border into the United States contained murderers and rapists. Technically, he was correct: among the multitude, there must have been one or two. It played well with his audience. As with maskirovka, one needs to tailor the message to the audience.

The third problem is your own, domestic audience. Does the message chime with anecdotal or social media observation? Great victories don't look so good when the body bags come home.

Finally, there is the contingent possibility that you will fall for your own propaganda. Putin believed his army was powerful. It wasn't. Maskirovka is useful, but needs to be used carefully.

CHANGE IN RUSSIA

Pyotr Stolypin (1862–1911 – when he was assassinated by Dmitry Bogrov, a leftist revolutionary Jew) was a Russian politician and statesman and was one of the czar's ministers from 1906.

He was a famous reformer of Russian society and her economy, and his reforms facilitated an unprecedented growth phase of the Russian state. He knew of what he spoke. His most famous aphorism was:

'In Russia, every 10 years everything changes, and nothing changes in 200 years.'

7 STRATEGIC CONSEQUENCES FOR THE WEST

Let us concentrate on just five consequences of this war on Western strategic thinking:

INTELLIGENCE

Whilst diplomatic posture, trade policy, geography and any number of other factors are a basis for managing any continuing relationship, and particularly for negotiating a new treaty or agreement, intelligence, in all its forms, is the lifeblood of international relations.

Intelligence becomes vitally important for any military action against any other country – attack or defence – and particularly so when, as is often the case, it is one country on one side and an alliance on the other, as in certain phases of the Second World War, Iraq or Afghanistan.

Intelligence gathering often conjures up images of spies, covert operators and leaving microfilm in dead letterboxes. In fact, intelligence is now quite different (see the next section on OSINT).

There are many stages in the handling of intelligence, but two of them are critical: the gathering of raw data and its interpretation – so that a response, if one is necessary, can be formulated. It also has to be timely. Intelligence about an imminent attack or a ship's position is useless if delayed.

Whereas interpretation remains something of an art, the gathering of raw data has been transformed over the past few years by three remarkable technological innovations: satellites, the internet and mobile phones with video capability. Satellite data, whether through Google Maps or Google Street View can show terrain and imagery from the US technology company MAXAR, and social media posts provide a clearer picture than state-based intelligence capabilities! Mobile phone footage, uploaded to a social media platform from the front line, is invaluable for communicating to the general public how the war is going.

OSINT

Open-Source Intelligence is the latest buzzword in intelligence gathering and interpretation. There are two main sources of information about any country's military personnel and hardware: Wikipedia and the International Institute of Strategic Studies (IISS). Every country listed on Wikipedia has a page that covers their armed forces. So, for example, you might look up that the United States has about twenty stealth bombers. You might observe that Gambia has just over 1,000 troops. For a more accurate figure, you have to buy the IISS Location publication *The Military Balance*, which is published every year and has the most impressive amount of detail on almost everything military. It's also quite expensive: £402.50, but no VAT …

Satellites and OSINT really came into their own during the Russian preparations for the invasion of Ukraine and also Russian movements since then. Some authorities even suggest that it represents an entirely new chapter in the political and diplomatic use of intelligence in international affairs. The intelligence community is quite often accused of getting things wrong, particularly in warnings about strategic moves from other countries. With Ukraine, they got it right, even if there were differing interpretations between NATO allies. Another benefit of OSINT, together with the interpretive models now available, is that it is now possible for politicians, diplomats and just interested members of the public to identify and, if they wish, challenge Russia's narrative of events. In fact, by monitoring Russian movements, it was quite obvious that they were intending to invade Ukraine. What could not be anticipated – which observation of troop concentrations never can –

was Moscow's ultimate goal.

There are some gaps. However much data one might gather and however skilled the intelligence officers may be, it is still difficult to establish how effective an army will be in the field. This is amply demonstrated by the

Russian Federation Army's performance in Ukraine.

Indeed, in the few days before and after the invasion, many commentators were suggesting that the best thing that Ukraine could do would be to negotiate an immediate and realistic settlement. According to the website *euronews*, Ukraine's foreign minister at one point accused Germany of undermining unity among the country's allies and of even 'encouraging' Putin by refusing to deliver arms to Kyiv. Christine Lambrecht, the previous and hapless German Defence Minister, said that sending military aid now would not help 'defuse' the crisis. The Germans obviously thought that Ukrainians stood no chance against the Russians. So much for the German intelligence apparatus! This sentiment changed after the successes of the Ukrainian army in resisting the Russian onslaught. Then help, in the form of intelligence, military training and munitions, ramped up.

Many of the crippling weaknesses of the Russian army were suspected before this invasion, but now we can identify them with some confidence, as detailed earlier.

The strategic lessons are evident: OSINT is a great leap forward, based as it is on up-to-date satellite imagery and photographs and videos uploaded to social media. Of course, the other side will have similar access to information. But with autocratic regimes, encrypted (that is where it is not possible for the state to listen in) social media feeds are invaluable. Satellite imagery and social media are important sources of competitive advantage, particularly as much of it is in real time. OSINT is also used extensively by independent publicly funded organisations whose resources depends on private individuals. There are too many of these to list here, but one interesting example is Covert Cabal.

TECHNOLOGY, WAR AND STRATEGY

The application of technology to warfare is covered in detail in both *About War* and *War in Context*. Those volumes looked at technological developments: from primitive man discovering gut to make bowstrings and wood that bends, from bronze to iron to steel to make swords, through gunpowder, flight and electronics. They covered materials, science, drones, missiles – both cruise and strategic – AI (Artificial Intelligence) and satellite technology. In this section on the Russian-Ukrainian War, we look at some of the applications of technology, some of the strategic consequences of technological developments, and their use.

In terms of the contribution of arms from other countries, useful lists of US equipment (some of it of a practical nature, some of it hi-tech) can be found on a variety of American websites; putting the name of the weapon into the search bar can explain exactly what it is and what it does. The only caveat is that some of the information on performance might be modified to confuse a potential enemy. Other contributing countries include the European Union (Commission and Council), whose aid has been largely financial; the United Kingdom, Germany, Canada, Poland, France and Norway. The biggest contribution by value at the time of writing compared with GDP has actually come from Norway, with Lithuania, Estonia and Latvia not far behind. Germany has greatly increased its contribution in the course of 2023 and is now second only to the US in the amount of assistance provided. It supplied significant numbers of Leopard tanks to Ukraine and the United States has also contributed M1 Abram main battle tanks. Germany also agreed to waive the 'no further export' clause in the supply contract to other countries such as Poland and Finland. All in all, it is hoped that Ukraine has had nearly one hundred of these tanks in all.

Science and technology, in all its forms and manifestations, are obviously vital to the conduct of warfare and in consequence, war itself. This is irrefutable. Witness the US 2022 National Defense Strategy, which emphasises a deep need to accelerate the Pentagon's capacity to buy and deploy emerging and disruptive technologies that will be vital to securing *military superiority* over advanced adversaries such as China. All very specific! There is then some hyperbole:

> ... *newer, faster-building technologies and applications that are complicating escalation dynamics and creating new challenges for strategic stability* ...

No, neither do I ...

The United Kingdom's rather more restrained MOD Science and Technology Strategy 2020, having mentioned 'uncertain and turbulent times' (spoiler alert: 'twas ever thus), suggests that by 'excelling in Science & Technology, we can secure our future strategic advantage'. These statements are useful to clarify the military's need, and also as a briefing for manufacturers. Underlying what are clearly well-thought-out, coherent plans, we can identify several competing themes:

First is the issue of sheer cost. Military equipment inflation is generally much higher than general inflation – witness the cost of some of the weapons systems referred to, and also the missiles themselves. Military budgets compete with other calls on the public purse, such as health and education. Notwithstanding that the primary function of the state is security, politically, these other demands tend to win out. In 1940, at the start of the Second World War, a Supermarine Spitfire cost about £5,000. But then the average private soldier earned about £2 a week! £5,000 then would be worth about £350,000 now, but the latest fighter plane, the Lockheed Martin F-35 Lightning II, comes in at about

$120 million, a three-hundred-fold increase in real terms. But it has one thousand times more components than the Spitfire … mind you, they're a bit faster than the Spitfire!

It is difficult to identify the exact cost of one unit of the HIMARS system that the US has supplied to Ukraine, but it is probably something like $8 million. Each missile costs about $100,000. It can easily be seen why the cost to the United States for supporting Ukraine is coming in at tens of billions of dollars. A Patriot missile system, of the type used to protect Kyiv, costs $1 billion. Each Patriot missile costs $4 million – expensive to down a $20,000 Russian drone! Each Patriot system needs a support staff of about ninety, who have to be trained, which takes at least a month.

Second, the military-industrial complex (explained in detail in *About War*) conducts major research throughout private industry. One would not expect any commercial organisation, especially if listed on a stock exchange, to be negative about a particular technology in which it was investing. They would seek the research budgets and hope for a commercial application somewhere down the line.

Third is to consider technological innovation versus application and development. In Paul Kennedy's *Engineers of Victory: The Problem Solvers Who Turned the Tide in the Second World War*, he defines in brilliant detail how Allied innovation turned the tide against the Nazi onslaught. For example, in the early stages of the Second World War, convoys crossing the North Atlantic were terribly vulnerable to German U-boats. Continuing development of aircraft in terms of range meant that by the end of the war air cover could be extended across the whole route. The point is that much of this was only partly due to new technology, and more to do with the innovative development of existing technology.

Fourth, all weapons should be seen as weapons *systems*. The expression and manifestation of almost all weapons is on the battlefield, however defined: land, sea, air or cyberspace. Behind each weapon there is a long period of discovery, manufacture, delivery and maintenance. The logistics must also be considered. For example, back in the 1960s, the Americans developed a machine gun, the M134 Minigun, which could fire between 2,000 and 6,000 rounds a minute. It was based on the Gatling-style rotated barrel assembly, with external power, usually an electric motor. It sounds good until you realise that any machine gun firing this many bullets per minute would require hundreds of boxes of ammunition on a regular basis, all of which had to be carried up to the front line, or found space for on the aircraft.

Then there is the logistics tail. All these weapons have to be manufactured, boxed and transported to the battlefield, maybe overseas. This has always been a military challenge and it's not new. According to the archery website *Bow International:*

Documentation of production, storage, and use of arrows is particularly rich for the time of the Hundred Years War (1337–1456) with France. For example, it is recorded that in the year 1360 alone, 500,000 arrows were delivered to the royal armouries in the Tower of London; the year before it had been another 850,000.

Not only is that quite a lot of straight wood, bodkins and feathers for fletching, but it also means a lot of skilled workers and manufacturing time. Not to mention the transportation on awful roads!

Also, the more technologically sophisticated any weapon is, the more operator training will be required. In the recent past, sophisticated control systems in aircraft cockpits have proved too complex for pilots, particularly during combat stress. The 1960s Starfighter was such a plane. During training, 116 German pilots were killed. The verdict being that it was 'overburdened' by technology. A pilot nowadays needs to be a flyer, a nerd even, with nerve and nous.

Fifth is the ongoing debate within strategic/military circles about the concept of 'mass'. Do we really need to have a much bigger army with more tanks and artillery etc.; do we really need more planes, ships and missiles to win in any likely conflict? It is really about how 'smart' the military can be and whether a competitive edge can be gained from having 'smarter' doctrines, better command and control systems, and more powerful weapons. Unfortunately, the answer is: *it all depends*. And it largely depends on what sort of opponent we are facing. Although some effort goes into identifying security concerns and likely opponents, we can never be sure about how powerful or large the military should be.

HOW TO ADDRESS THE STRATEGIC ASPECTS OF TECHNOLOG-
ICAL INNOVATION? WHAT CAN BE INFERRED FROM THE RUS-
SIAN-UKRAINIAN WAR?

This trilogy, *Making Sense of War*, focuses on war as a political act as opposed to *warfare*, the practice of managing the battlefield. To analyse every aspect of technology used on the Ukraine battlefield would be an enormous task, even if all the information were available.

There has always been some hyperbole in considering the technological capabilities of an enemy. In fact, a sensible approach would be that, until you see the technology working, it may be safer to treat it with some scepticism. During the Cold War, the US Department of Defense was lobbied by the armed forces (and by the military-industrial complex) to 'keep up' with the Soviet Union, suggesting that if Russian technology was not in fact ahead of the Americans, it was certainly catching up. The so-called 'missile gap' was created. After the collapse of the Soviet Union, it was discovered that the same sort of lobbying happened in the Kremlin. They had a military-industrial complex too.

Today, we find that Putin boasts about 'wonder weapons'. Hitler believed in his 'vengeance' weapons, though these failed to turn the tide of war. Putin's miracle armoury includes the T-14 Armata tank, a marvellous machine with an active protection system and which fires 125 mm shells which could, one day, accommodate a small nuclear device.. As part of Russia's rearmament programme, 2,000 were supposed to be available by 2020. But they've yet to arrive.

What is arriving, supposedly to counter the German-made Leopard 2 tanks and the American M1 Abrams, is the Russian 'Marker Robot'. Russian-made videos of this track-mounted machine show a very impressive capability of recognising the above tanks from existing images, automatically engaging and destroying them. They sound like a wonder weapon, but there does not seem to be a great deal of concern in Ukraine or its allies about its capabilities. Their appearance on the battlefield and their effectiveness will be closely monitored. One is reminded that in the latter stages of the Second World War, Hitler promised a 'wonder weapon' to batter the Western Allies into submission. Despite 6,725 V1s being launched and nearly 3,000 V2s, they did not shake Western resolve. It may be that the Russians are better at making videos than developing and deploying weaponry.

Not so much forgotten, but often taken as read, is that Russia is the *largest nuclear-armed state in the world*. Its ICBMs can hit cities anywhere across the United States and, even if Europe were not involved, many cities across Europe as well. During 2021, Russia announced five major nuclear-capable weapons programmes. The idea was to ensure their capability to penetrate US missile defence systems and also, frighteningly, to guarantee a second-strike capability (explained in *War in Context*).

Before considering this, we might just mention Russia's capabilities in hypersonic weapons, again explained in *War in Context*. These actually do work, though there has only been one used to hit a western city in

Ukraine. But Putin claims they will ultimately be capable of carrying a nuclear weapon. There are two types of hypersonic weapons, but their virtue is that they can fly under any defensive radar.

Here, all strategic considerations come to a head. Should we in the West, as suggested above, treat technological developments with some scepticism, or, in the case of a nuclear threat, with the utmost seriousness. Of course, the latter. And, unpopular though it might be with the tax-paying public, even if there is the smallest possibility of a nuclear attack, it should be taken very seriously indeed, and a contingency plan made as if it were certain.

In Ukraine, Russia's nuclear capability has had a considerable influence on the war thus far. It is why the Biden administration has steadfastly refused to contemplate a no-fly zone over Ukraine. He does not want NATO warplanes (which would include the USAF, as they would have the largest number) engaging with their Russian counterparts over Ukrainian airspace. It would also be an aggressive form of political signalling. Russia is anyway reluctant to send their planes over Ukraine, preferring to use guided missiles.

A preoccupation for commentators since the war started is that Putin might use a tactical nuclear weapon, as he has threatened, but (only?) on states other than Ukraine who are supplying help and munitions – presumably NATO. The impact of any nuclear device is as much political as material. This is covered elsewhere, but just to recall that the main difference between a tactical or battlefield nuclear weapon and a full-scale ICBM is only partly to do with the size of the bomb. The problem with any nuclear device is the political panic that a detonation would cause.

An important political aspect is that nuclear-armed states have failed to limit nuclear warhead stock holdings or to negotiate agreements about tactical nuclear weapons. NATO still holds stocks of these weapons, as does Russia.

Satellite surveillance and navigation is now pretty standard for a myriad of uses. Gone are the days when an expert ploughman was one who could plough a straight furrow. Now, the tractor is guided by satellite. Satellites are obviously used for communication, and the speed at which data can be moved is vital for locating enemy positions and movements. Before Russia's invasion of Ukraine on 24 February 2022, the build-up of military equipment on the border and in Belarus was obvious. What of course was not known were their intentions.

Drones are now standard equipment on the battlefield. There are literally dozens of different types of drones. Their use is detailed in *War in Context*, the second book in this trilogy. There, was covered moral considerations about the use of drones, focusing largely on armed drones, which can loiter over a supposed enemy location, often a terrorist stronghold, select the target and fire a missile to kill an individual or a group.

Politically, there is no international law about the use of armed drones in war: what is against the law is the deliberate targeting of civilians. Collateral damage – bystanders, innocent people being killed – is inevitable, so the use of armed drones is something of a grey area. Bringing elusive, concealed and remote operators to justice is the problem. This is compounded by the fact that the operator may be on the other side of the world, perhaps in a Portakabin in one of about a dozen US airbases.

WHAT CAN BE DONE TO COUNTER (COMPETITIVE) TECHNOLOGY?

We need to distinguish between real innovation and application and development. Remember that the purpose of military force is political, and new technologies have more than military implications. One needs to be suspicious of the sort of meaningless jargon we find in the US 2022 National Defense Strategy: *deep need ... disruptive technologies ... faster-building technologies ... complicating escalation dynamics ...* There is a whiff here of tail wagging dog. Is this evidence of the private sector pushing for battlefield weaponry that isn't needed?

Nevertheless, we have to be aware of the dangers of competitors' technology. A RUSI report entitled *Operation Z*, by Jack Watling and Nick Reynolds, shows some PCBs and transistors that have been recovered from Russian military equipment, either captured or only partially destroyed in an attack. Many of these components are manufactured outside Russia, and therefore cannot be easily replaced. Sanctions have prevented that. However, 'reverse engineering' (allowing for a printed circuit board) can eventually replicate components, although the lack of availability of computer chips, the basis for any PCB, may cause problems.

Arms manufacturers in the West will be monitoring the effectiveness of weapons in the conflict. Lessons learned will be incorporated into new weapons, but the US, for example, will often deny key software to foreign customers, even NATO countries.

We must be constantly aware of any potential enemy's technological capabilities. Espionage may reveal how well developed and effective they are. But quality is useless without quantity: the capacity to make sufficient arms *and* to transport them to the sharp end of battle. And to train skilled operatives in their use. The development and application of any technology is as important as the technology itself.

STRATEGIC CONSIDERATIONS FOR TECHNOLOGY

As signalled at the start of this section, science, technology, application and development *and* the concept of the weapons system are all vital to the conduct of warfare and, in consequence, to war itself. In sum, they provide a competitive edge over a military competitor, one that must be developed and reinforced. But we must not confuse a technological edge, however exemplary, with strategy itself. Strategy is, fundamentally, *everything about the future.* So, we can identify three qualifications:

First, almost all technological advances will eventually be either replicated or countered; technological development is vulnerable to theft, reverse engineering and espionage. Application, development and the concept of the weapons system less so, but this, of course, can be observed by a competitor on the battlefield.

Second, science and technology can have an enormous impact on warfare, but *technology alone cannot win wars.* War is a political act, first, last, always. The Taliban beat first the USSR and then the United States and NATO in Afghanistan, clad in pyjamas, often wearing flip-flops and sporting rifles the British had left behind in the 19th century.

Third, technology, however advanced, is *no substitute for strategy.* War is a political act and real strategy – long-term, competitive, contingent and multi-functional – its expression. By all means focus on technology and all its contributing aspects. By all means focus on development and application, the logistical tail and the concept of weapons systems, but NATO and its individual members must not neglect the essential aspects of war and warfare.

SUPPLY AND LOGISTICS

The subject of supply and logistics has given rise to any number of aphorisms: ... *an army marches on its stomach ... get there firstest with the mostest ... armchair generals talk strategy; real generals talk logistics ...*

None of these would come as a surprise to any experienced soldier, sailor or aviator. What this Ukraine war has demonstrated is that consumption rates in modern, high-intensity ground fighting is phenomenally high; they require not only strategic stockpiles far enough behind the front line to be safe (if that is possible at all), but also it means secure and rapid lines of communication between stockpiles and front lines.

After the breakout of Allied troops following the Normandy landings in 1944, the front line ran too far ahead of its supply. No suitable port near the battle lines was available. The High Command instituted the 'Red Ball Express', which was a mostly secure and rapid route through northern France. It was almost all by road: no crossroads and no stopping except for fuel and to change drivers. It was essential to allow armour to roll – but for every gallon of gas delivered it expended one in getting there. Munition expenditure today is extravagant. Any belligerent country has to have the industrial capacity to replace destroyed equipment, to supply spare parts – quite often as whole modules – and ammunition, fuel etc.

Russia has not performed well logistically. Shortly after the initial invasion, there were queues of its tanks and support vehicles some 40 km long and vulnerable to attack – which is what the Ukrainians did. Some Russian vehicles had run out of fuel. Their troops were also short of food, ammunition and maps.

It would be a great mistake to imagine that this will continue. In June 1941, the German army attacked Soviet Russia across a broad front in Operation Barbarossa. In the first few months, millions of Russians were killed or captured. However, eighteen months later, at the end of 1942, having retreated all the way (through Ukraine) to Stalingrad on the river Volga, the Red Army rallied and eventually prevailed (at terrible cost). Subsequently, they managed to launch attacks across fronts measuring several hundred kilometres wide – possible only with mastery over logistics.

By the end of 2022, the Russians were firing as many as 25,000 artillery shells per day (possibly even 60,000) and dozens of missiles, something beyond Ukrainian capacity. You cannot do that without competent logistics. However, Russian use of predominantly long-range missiles indicates they might be running out of artillery ordinance.

ARTILLERY DUELS

According to *The New York Times*, the war in eastern Ukraine is more or less an artillery duel, with both sides blasting away every day; the Russians firing up to 60,000 (other sources mention 25,000) artillery shells and rockets per day. The Russians obviously favour volume over accuracy. The Russian approach in the Donbas echoes past tactics in Grozny, Syria and Mariupol in southeastern Ukraine, also conspicuously Severodonetsk and Lysychansk. In the spring and early summer of 2022, Ukraine was forced to withdraw from these towns. These advances were Russia's biggest territorial gain since the initial invasion.

The logistical problem of transporting as much as 1,000 tonnes to the battlefield are significant. Couple that with small arms munition, food, clothing and medical evacuation, especially in winter, it means a complex and resource-hungry logistics system.

EUROPEAN SECURITY

Russia's actions have focused the EU's attention on joint security. The problem with Europe's joint security is, as one might expect, divergences of political opinion as well as integration of weapon systems. In the early stages of the conflict, President Macron of France was urging conciliation, the German Chancellor was reluctant to offer aid and the new prime minister in Italy, Giorgia Meloni, was initially hesitant about helping at all. Russian atrocities prompted action. President Zelensky of Ukraine has stated that, if they had received all the munitions asked for earlier, they could have chased the Russians out already.

Despite a desire for each country to support their own defence industry, divergences in the design and manufacture of military equipment slowly developed during the earlier part of the 21st century and resulted in PESCO, the European Union's Permanent Structured Cooperation. In 2018, twenty-five EU member states agreed to incorporate their militaries into an EU force. According to *Forbes* magazine, it was met with a certain amount of cynicism over its capacity to meet the EU's defence needs. It is not much better now: *Forbes* in 2018 suggested that the EU had six times as many weapon systems in service as the US, comprising seventeen different types of main battle tank. By contrast, the US relies on just one tank: the M1 Abrams. It is a similar story through the entire range of weapon systems, with European militaries using twenty different types of IFV and twenty-seven different howitzers. The US relies on just two versions of each. All in all, the US has 30 major weapon systems while Europe has 178.

Cutting down or reducing the variety of weapons systems would save costs, make maintenance and training less complicated, and the supply chain easier to manage. The situation in Ukraine also throws a light on how important manufacturing capacity is. This would certainly be easier if managed on a European basis. PESCO, though a worthy attempt, is not really fit for purpose.

As this trilogy has mentioned on several previous occasions, the first and fundamental duty of any state or any polity is to provide for its citizens' security. And the primary need is territorial and physical security. Any alliance, association, treaty, accord, club or tacit understanding with other states should prioritise this. The European Union was formed after the Second World War so that such a war could not happen again. It was a political union based on ever closer union. But the utility of such a union is thoroughly compromised if each and every citizen is not secure. This applies as much to states as it does to individuals.

Europe relies absolutely on NATO. Yes, NATO European members contribute greatly to NATO's capability, but NATO is American inspired and American led. NATO cannot take action without American approval.

So, NATO …

ADDENDUM

COVERT CABAL

This is an example of a privately financed and privately run group of people who, in this case, create military and defence analysis videos. From their website, they start with a quote by Bertrand Russell, (1872–1970):

'War does not determine who is right: war determines who is left.'

Covert Cabal's goal is to create *unbiased* military analysis, which, they claim, is rare these days. A lot of the military analysis seen in the media seems to be partisan, or wrong.

Covert Cabal seeks to provide analysis based solely on facts. Their intent is to create at least one video a week. It is certainly worth looking at the videos on YouTube, which cover such topics as: *How many tanks does Russia have left?* or *Is Russia running out of missiles?* All good fun!

Covert Cabal also started a project to map every military installation in the world. This has been largely successful and has since been built upon by a community of like-minded enthusiasts.

8 DIAGNOSIS AND PROGNOSIS

As I write, we cannot imagine when this war will end or what any ceasefire, treaty or any armed peace might look like. We might, however, be fairly confident that there will *not* be a clear victor nor indeed a clear loser, except the tens of thousands of dead and injured Ukrainian troops and civilians and the hundreds of thousands of dead and injured Russian troops, some of whom were getting on in years and barely trained. Spare a thought too for the families of Russian soldiers who have been killed in the conflict, but who have only been told that the soldier is MIA rather than dead.

If, as seems increasingly *un*likely, the Russian Federation's invasion is entirely successful, it will bring the Russian border right up to those of Poland, Slovakia, Hungary, Romania and the littorals of Bulgaria and Turkey, to what would then be a Russian Federation Black Sea. If Russia takes over Belarus, then its border would be right up to Poland, Lithuania and Latvia, all NATO members, and near the Suwałki Gap with more direct access to Kaliningrad, surely a security risk to NATO members and to Europe as a whole. Of course, we did not know about the invasion until shortly before it happened, but did NATO have a strategy for such an event? Strategy is as much about contingency plans as about what we'd like to do. So, what is missing is a coherent consensus on strategy.

Putin has now placed tactical nuclear missiles in Belarus. This does not amount to much of an additional threat to the West and, though the Baltics and Poland are rightly concerned about it, it may simply be intended to harness Belarus ever closer to Russia and to degrade whatever autonomy Lukashenko thinks he has left. In some ways, of course, Russia has *already* taken over Belarus, yet Lukashenko will not commit his troops to help Putin. For a while, in 2023, the hosting of Wagner units in Belarus raised questions about why they were there and what their mission might be. Was this Lukashenko's attempt to wrest back a sliver of autonomy from the Kremlin or to furnish himself with a loyal alternative to a possibly unreliable Belarusian military – or a bit of both? We cannot say, but there has indeed been renewed speculation about potential threats to the Suwałki Gap.

Yet we might still query:

What is now Ukraine's strategy?

What is American strategy for Ukraine?

What is Western Europe's strategy for Ukraine?

How does this reflect Russia's strategy (which is?) and how should the West react?

Committing all these to paper and considering their congruence or otherwise might show up some egregious divergences, and also wildly varying ideas about timeframe.

WHERE TO FROM HERE?

There is little point in recounting the current news, with the appalling violence and the gratuitous missile strikes, some on materially important targets, some out of vindictiveness. For example, the Ukrainian sinking in the Black Sea of the *Moskva* on 14 April 2022 (sorry, *Pravda*; you told us it was an on-board fire) was followed by more strikes against civilian targets. Neither can words describe the atrocious behaviour of the Russian troops torturing and murdering Ukrainian civilians. With some armies, such behaviour is usually attributed to ill-disciplined troops, who also loot goods and artefacts from the defeated civilians. There is some consensus about the Russians in Ukraine in that this is a deliberate policy of using terror tactics on the Ukrainian population. It is gratifying that, as I write, war crimes tribunals are trying Russian soldiers in Kyiv.

At the end of 2022, Russia targeted infrastructure and power plants and distribution networks in particular, depriving Ukrainians of winter heating and water. As I write, this continues, and they are continuing to target civilian accommodation, the last strike having killed forty-one people in a block of flats in Dnipro. It might seem otiose to mention, but the strikes are in contravention of international law.

Professional commentators are reluctant to suggest how the war might proceed from here. The BBC has a coherent and cogent guide, largely parallel to my own thoughts, and I recognise their contribution below:

Short War I involves Russia escalating military operations with massive resources, solving leadership and logistical problems within their army, freeing up their force to act more effectively, managing this time to take Kyiv and achieve a change of government. This is thought to be unlikely.

In *Short War II,* Ukraine gets all the help, munitions and international support that they asked for and drives the Russians out of antebellum Ukrainian territory. More likely than the previous scenario, but still a long stretch.

Peristalsis: a *long war,* with Russian forces getting bogged down, hampered by low morale, poor logistics and inept leadership. This echoes Russia's long and brutal campaign that largely flattened Grozny, the capital of Chechnya.

It is possible that this war could develop into a *wider European war,* with other countries, such as Poland, getting involved or Putin, perhaps as a diversionary tactic, deploying troops into ex-Soviet, non-NATO republics like Moldova and Georgia or, of course, NATO members in the Baltic. Generally, this would invoke a NATO response and Putin would be reluctant to push his luck this far.

Many commentators are suggesting that this war will only progress if there is a diplomatic solution. Most wars end in negotiation, and we know there have been discussions between Moscow, Kyiv, Brussels and Washington. The BBC reports that 'the key question is whether the West can offer what diplomats refer to as an off ramp, a term for an exit off a major highway. Diplomats say it is important the Russian leader knows what it would take for Western sanctions to lift so a face-saving deal is at least possible'. There is a contrary view to this: that Russia, and by implication the population as a whole, should suffer, and be seen to suffer.

One solution, though it may not be as such, is that Putin is ousted. The scenario is as follows and cannot be put any better than by the BBC:

'Thousands of Russian soldiers die. The economic sanctions bite. Putin loses popular support ... there is the threat of popular revolution. Putin uses Russia's internal security forces to suppress that opposition ... this turns sour and enough members of Russia's military, political and economic elite turn against him. The West makes clear that if Putin goes and is replaced by a more moderate leader, then Russia will see the lifting of some sanctions and a restoration of normal diplomatic relations. There is a bloody (usual Russian practice!) palace coup and Putin is out ...'

THE MOST LIKELY SCENARIO ...
Spring offensives on either and both sides do not enable Russia to increase the penetration of Ukraine, or for Ukraine to push the Russians back to the antebellum borders. Russia is concerned about dwindling stocks of weaponry, and any great mobilisation and recruitment drive that Putin announces goes badly. Opposition to Putin grows as body bags return home. Sanctions begin to really bite. China intervenes, putting pressure on Moscow to compromise, warning that it will not buy Russian oil and gas unless it de-escalates.

In America, meanwhile, Biden is concerned about the Republican threat to his presidency and, in recognition of the presidential elections in 2024, and the Ukrainian war (which has already cost the Americans tens of billions of dollars), he gently suggests to Ukrainian President Zelenskyy that he might start thinking about a compromise and negotiating a deal with the Russians. Meanwhile, the Ukrainian authorities see the continuing destruction of their country and conclude that political compromise might be better than such devastating loss of life and property. So, diplomats engage, and a deal is done. Ukraine, say, accepts Russian sovereignty over Crimea and parts of the Donbas. In turn, Putin accepts Ukrainian independence and its right to deepen ties with Europe. The BBC concludes that:

These scenarios are not mutually exclusive … some of each could combine to produce different outcomes. But, however this conflict plays out, the world has changed. It will not return to the status quo ante. Russia's relationship with the outside world will be different. European attitudes to security will be transformed. And the liberal, international rules-based order might just have rediscovered what it was for in the first place.

THE TEDDY ROOSEVELT SOLUTION

Theodore Roosevelt (US president 1901–1909) was one of the outstanding US presidents. Perhaps it is in order to end with a somewhat modified version of his great contribution to political philosophy.

It is often said that what Putin and other Russian leaders admire is *power*. So, speak softly to Russia: guarantee their borders, only release their offshore funds for social improvement, infrastructure and to build a modern industrial society and eventually a democratic form of government with a free press and competing political parties.

Stop equivocating about the supply of heavy tanks, warplanes and longer-range missiles to Ukraine. Supply these in great quantity. Putin will get the message and, we hope, slink off to spend the rest of his wretched days in his dacha.

The original quote? 'Speak softly, but carry a big stick.'

In short, demonstrate raw power, diplomatic power, economic power but mostly *military* power, and wave it in his putrid face.

PUTIN: RECIDIVISM, PARANOIA OR MALEVOLENCE PERSONIFIED?

Western media defines Putin as the mastermind and inspiration for the attack on Ukraine, although he would not have been able to invoke it without the complicity of other senior politicians. Putin is portrayed as paranoid, lacking objective advice and fuelled by his recidivist worldview rather than informed opinion. Let his *actions* be witness to the international political environment in which he lives, and his mental state, and let us step back and consider a broader sweep of history.

Putin is a spy, first and last, and neither a soldier nor statesman. He has a few leadership skills, save threats. Yet, like Hitler, he can be subtle and something of a charmer. Such a talent for masking his humours, nature and intentions have worked well in the past with the younger Bush, Blair, Macron, Schroder, Steinmeier, etc. One would hope, however, that the mask is now fully down and irretrievable.

And Putin delivers not just threats of censure, but death threats, which are actually carried out. His career started in the Soviet KGB, and he was head of its Russian successor, the FSB, before becoming Prime Minister and then President. His predisposition is for the clandestine and the dishonest. He has fashioned a worldview to vindicate his policies that, to a western mind, are increasingly detached from reality. It is impossible to know how much of this he believes or to what extent he is persuaded by his own propaganda (see the panel on Maskirovka).

His assertions that the Ukrainians are destroying their own property or are seeking to acquire nuclear or biological weapons are simply sardonic or, in the demotic, bonkers.

Many adjectives are used to describe the leaders of delinquent states, such as autocrat, dictator or nationalist. But it is an essentially limited vocabulary. It would be more useful to describe Putin, despite his intelligence and low cunning, as simply incompetent in that role. He might well have recognised that the Soviet Union collapsed because it did not deliver the promised consumer paradise. Has he realised that working in the give and take of an anarchic and democratic world represents a different challenge? His reaction to dissent at home is to restrict the media and arrest protesters, coupled with a high level of propaganda that bears little relation to the truth.

It is possible, of course, that he *has* realised: he's not daft or stupid. But it's too late for that now. Would he, if he could turn the clock back to January 2022, do things differently? But the die was cast when the first Russian troops crossed the border into Ukraine. Like other dictators before him, he's now on the tiger's back. All he can do is postpone his own fall, and the only tool remaining for that now is to clamp and double down – much as the Third Reich could only double down even further on dissidents and defeatists once the war started going badly and the past mistakes and inevitable outcomes became all too evident.

This Third Reich analogy is increasingly apposite: the last six to twelve months has seen Russia set about vigorously promoting the cause of war and equating it with patriotism – going further than simply quashing opposition and dissent, but selling the war in schools and other institutions as well as shifting Russia towards a war economy – and with apparent popular support. The prospects for Putin's removal are no stronger than Hitler's would have been in, say 1943. He may mobilise on a grand scale – Goebbels 'Total War', where the only end for

Putin's regime would be the same as that required for the Third Reich – complete and unconditional surrender. It sounds attractive but in the nuclear age remains unconscionable.

But this is only the day-to-day stuff. More important in the modern world is that corporate strength comes not from territory nor population but from organisational skills and human resources. Yes, natural resources are important, but many states manage without access to the enormous resources available to Russia – think of Singapore. It is here that Putin has failed desperately: over the years, many skilled Russians have been driven to leave and sought careers in the West. When he announced a widespread mobilisation, there were queues of young men at the border trying to escape the country and the draft. Also, the simple demographics of births, deaths, aging, immigration and emigration are working against him. Russia may have lost as many as two million people over the past three years from various causes, over and above that what they might have expected. Life expectancy has declined, and the COVID-19 pandemic wiped out far more than the official Russian figure of 390,000. Add to this as many as 250,000 Russian soldiers killed or wounded in the invasion of Ukraine, and it may not be too much of an exaggeration to say that Russia is a failing state, and has entered into a doom loop. He has failed to build a modern, technology-based industrial state, using instead the revenues from oil and natural gas to prop up his regime.

Putin's Russia is stuck in a time warp, with little evidence that this is recognised and is being resolved. How the Russians, or the international community at large, copes with this is a major challenge for the rest of the 21st century. But, rather than triumphing over the failed Soviet state and the hoped-for freeing of Ukraine, the West, and particularly Europe, should identify future security threats emanating from a resentful and dangerous Russia. There is also the dual problem of Russian regions that may wish to secede from the Federation, and the already independent former Soviet republics, such as Kazakhstan, wishing to distance themselves from the Russia Federation itself. Belarus may follow eventually.

Given that Russia has a permanent seat on the United Nations Security Council (Soviet Russia was expelled from the League of Nations after the attack on Finland in 1939), given that Russia is the most nuclear armed country in the world and given the various machinations amongst European countries about their reaction to the Russian invasion, the future for Europe's security, and for Europe's periphery – NATO's 'arch of insecurity' – looks bleak for the whole of Europe. Spending on consumer goods looks good and wins elections, but it is a poor substitute for security in all its senses, the main and most important function of any state.

What future the United Nations, and particularly the Security Council, might have with its five permanent members, is something which only gets addressed in the most specialised journals. However, there is mounting pressure that large and powerful states such as India, Brazil and possibly Japan should really have a seat on the UNSC. Although the invocation to 'leave things as they are' is generally interpreted as being something suggested by 'stick in the muds', it may be that attempting to reform the United Nations would be the opening of a Pandora's box. Recall that the United Nations is not simply represented by the General Assembly and the Security Council but by a whole host of other bodies, such as the World Health Organization.

Part Two: the Nation-State

9 THE NATION, THE STATE AND THE NATION-STATE POST-EMPIRE

The main actor in international relations today is the nation-state, and although this term is in common usage, 'nation' and 'state' are divergent concepts. What are the implications for security, domestically or internationally?

To address this we need to look briefly at historic 'war actors' and consider the utility of the current nation-state model, and the designations used. First came empires ...

EMPIRE

The shift from a hunter-gatherer to a sedentary lifestyle with a fixed location, with arable and animal husbandry is generally thought to have been about 10,000 BC, but this did not happen everywhere to everyone at the same time. Since cities – more like large villages – needed to defend themselves against marauding bands and other cities, partly for security and resources and partly for glory, and expanded their influence over bigger and bigger areas until they could be called empires. The first Empire is thought to have been the Akkadian Empire in Mesopotamia, about 2334–2154 BC. Yes, empire has an ancient origin, though the exact nomenclature has changed over the years – Henry VIII would often assert that *'England is an Empire'*, a polity *entire in itself, not part of something else; fully autonomous and independent and owing no fealty or tribute to any foreign authority'*. An empire typically comprises several or many different territories, countries, polities and peoples.

There is no general model; no usual terminology. The British Empire comprised colonies, territories, possessions, trade outposts (some run by private companies) and several other forms. The centre of the Empire (in the British Empire: London) exerted *political* control over the constituent parts which may have continued with their own laws, customs and access to human and civil rights. Foreign policy is usually closely controlled from the centre.

There were various routes to Empire; some were expanded by treaty, some by conquest, some by mercantilism, and in some cases British colonialists, feeling that they were inherently superior to the natives, simply moved in and took control. Such empires were originally established to create markets, to extract resources at a low cost and to prevent other European countries gaining control of that territory with its associated benefits. Little thought was given to what were then called the 'natives'.

The French claimed to be civilising the colonies – *'la mission civilisatrice'*, but it's difficult to discern any success they might have had in that area and what success would have looked like anyway. Whatever, for most of human history, empire has been a usual form of governance. For Spain and Portugal, empire was also about saving souls – lives were of far less important. Also, of course, the gold.

The real imperial age for Britain was actually quite short, perhaps from when Queen Victoria was made Empress of India (1877) until the 1920s. The British seemed to wake up to the fact that they had one, that perhaps it was something to be proud of after all and expanded deliberately.

The imperial rush was driven by the emergence of newly unified countries in Europe: Germany, Italy and Belgium in particular. Though late to the party, they wanted their slice of the pie – no self-respecting European state could *not* have an overseas empire in the last two decades of the 19th century. It was really only then that the smash and grab began – especially in Africa and China.

The point about empire is that underlying the mercantilism, or the Imperial need for raw materials, was the use of or threat of military power. Putin does not seem to have got the memo with regard to Ukraine. One wonders if it ever occurred to him that instead of invading, he might have made it economically worthwhile for Ukraine to become a member of the new Russian Federation. Trade deals and technology transfer could have been used. It almost certainly never crossed his mind!

Take two historic though contradictory examples, the Assyrian Empire (perhaps 2000–600 BC) was little more than a vast protection racket, in which the Assyrians fleeced neighbouring populations and, if they didn't cough up, wiped them out. The Roman Empire, although not differing a lot from the Roman Republic in this regard, had a different offer. If you wanted to join the Roman system you had to pay tribute to Rome and supply troops for Roman armies. Rich Romans would turn up and use your city as a trade base, but generally the whole population was better off, and did at least get amphitheatres where you could see the games. Any participation by the local senate in foreign policy was forbidden.

On the other hand if you did not bend your knee to the Romans, they simply wiped you out. 'They made a desert and called it peace' (from lines attributed by Tacitus to the Caledonian warlord, Calgacus) is the appropriate aphorism.

The Ottoman Empire was perhaps the most lasting, from 1299 to 1921 and, at first sight, seems preferable to today's fractured Middle East. Syria, a modern nation-state, can hardly be called a success, and there can be no doubt that the Syrians were better off under the Ottomans. And despite some years of French rule, so were the people of Lebanon.

The British Empire, which was the largest and most populous empire ever, was arguably the most benign of the European empires. Though with a new generation, say over the past twenty or so years, it has had a particularly bad reputation. This was largely based on accusations of racism ('the lower races') and lack of human rights, conveniently ignoring the same in their own countries. This also ignores the fact that, when the British departed, they left behind the most successful and wealthy republics in history of mankind, the United States of America: okay, it involved violence, but most transitions did. The birth of the largest democracy ever in the world, India, involved much violence, but not against the British. There are also beacons of democracy and prosperity such as Canada, Australia and several African countries. Contrast this with Belgium's departure from the Congo, which only achieved independence in 1960.

The original idea of empire continued right up to the First World War when the Ottoman Empire, the German Empire and the Austro-Hungarian Empire, the Habsburgs, fell apart. It was an abrupt ending. These empires in central and Eastern Europe were like pressure cookers. Their defeat in 1918, and the retreat of Russia in 1917, effectively blew the lid off the pressure cooker. Nationalism in these territories had moved from being a romantic and cultural idea of the young bourgeoisie (1848) to an economic imperative. Grievances and territorial mix-ups over ethnic boundaries and the status of minorities inevitably surfaced, much as after the fall of Yugoslavia in the 1990s.

The Russian (czarist) empire suffered under the terms of the Brest-Litovsk settlement, but being such a large land area, continued as the USSR; their imperial ambitions only temporarily muted.

The worldwide British Empire, despite feeling itself inviolable, continued in some form for another fifty years, before its final political expiration. Nevertheless, what is still considered to be the glory and the benefits of the British Empire endures in many British minds.

We must express some surprise, intrigue even, at the rapidity and enthusiasm with which 'it was decided' (with apologies for the passive tense) that the age of empire was dead, and the future was nation-states. But the original idea of empire did not quite die. For the victors of the First World War, the concept of empire mutated. The US arguably remained an effective imperial power well beyond the end of that war and the next. It didn't need direct rule to achieve this. You didn't need the formal structures of empire to maintain your influence. There was a flutter in 2010 when Michael Ignatieff, a Canadian politician and academic, suggested the concept of 'Empire Lite' but it was pooh-poohed by likely subjects.

THE END OF EMPIRE

The concept of the nation-state is now the norm. In many ways, it has been a great success. After the end of the Second World War many more nation-states were formed, several intergovernmental bodies such as the United Nations, the African Union, ECOWAS (The Economic Community of West African States) and ASEAN (Association of Southeast Asian Nations) amongst them, as well as dozens of trade agreements. Recall that when we consider the United Nations, we comprehend a whole range of UN bodies. The full list is enormous: the IMF, UNESCO, the World Bank, the International Telecommunication Union, the International Atomic Energy Agency and the World Trade Organization. Even in our chosen subject here, the UN covers the International Organization for Migration, the Comprehensive Nuclear Test Ban Treaty and the Organisation for the Prohibition of Chemical Weapons.

But empire did not quite disappear. Empires were established both to create markets for the imperial powers and to extract resources at a low cost. To a large extent, this aspect continued, although it wasn't called imperial, and there was no need the formal structures of empire to achieve this.

Once the idea – or at least the old model – of empire was officially out of the way, they got a bad press, partly because they were seen to prevent the local populations managing themselves, which was largely true, and partly because they were often racist (again true), treating the 'natives' as inferior. But that's not quite the whole story.

Inspired by distant memories of the Westphalian settlement (see *War in Context*), endorsed by some of Woodrow Wilson's 14 points (see panel) and informed by a combination of greater literacy, a wider distribution of media and more travel, empires, at least in their original form, largely disappeared and the nation-state, long in the realisation, became the norm.

Whatever the success or otherwise of the nation-state, almost the whole world, except the Russians and maybe the Chinese – recall Tibet – now accept this as the normal way of governance for the world, rather than empire.

The main actor in international relations today is the nation-state, but several other terms, as in the subheading, are in common usage. At the risk of being pedantic, they need to be defined as they have a different legal status in international law, and different rights about the use of military force.

10 POLITIES, NATIONS, STATES, COUNTRIES AND THE NATION-STATE

A *polity* is a general term used to denote any group of people who can be identified as such and are capable of acting as a group. A polity therefore has political significance. The term could encompass the nation, the state and the nation-state, and also country. It is a useful term because the group might be seen as a precursor gaining political significance, both in themselves and to the wider world.

A *nation* then is a substantial group of people who consider themselves to be united by common bonds of language, history, culture and/or ethnicity. There may also be a religious element. Various stories are told of past heroic deeds. Many in Great Britain revel in the 'Dunkirk Spirit', conveniently forgetting that Dunkirk was both a disaster and a defeat. Historically, British Empire maps, resplendent in classrooms in the 1950s, had vast swathes of pink – colonies, overseas territories, possessions – all over them. As schoolchildren, we were impressed, as though this was the natural order of things. France's Marianne, leading the French people in revolution, is their personification of liberty, equality and fraternity.

Told in American schools, the story of the birth of the United States is one of heroism and resolve to achieve freedom from the colonial British master. Paul Revere's Midnight Ride and Washington crossing the Delaware River are both heroic deeds, but there is some myth involved. In fact the American War of Independence was a series of messy and disjointed battles, finally brought to head by British incompetence and French intervention.

For most of history, countries were ruled by monarchs – kings, pharaohs, czars, emperors, caliphs, etc. – who claimed dominion over their, and sometimes others', lands. Some monarchs claimed a 'divine right' to rule, the notion that hereditary royalty is a God-given sanction.

During the 18th century, the idea changed from the monarch having a God-given right to rule, to being accountable to the common man. Women were not considered. Witness Thomas Paine's *Rights of Man*. In his book, published in 1791, Paine proposed that government should be based on justice, as an expression of not only mankind's natural rights: life, liberty, free speech and freedom of conscience, but also civil rights: security and protection. It is astonishing and distressing that over 230 years after Thomas Paine, this does not apply in every corner of the globe.

There may also be external factors: nations may also be partially defined by external influences and experiences. The Irish nation was treated appallingly by the English and the resentment lasts to this day. The Irish diaspora, particularly in the United States, still has a strong feeling of community and belonging to their homeland. This is in contrast to the Scottish nation, who were not so much treated badly by the English, but carelessly. Yet there is a strong feeling of nationalism amongst the Scots, manifest in a desire amongst half the population to become completely independent of the United Kingdom, though some may see that as simply England. Without Scotland, there is no Britain or British. We simply go back to being English again. There is also a substantial Scottish diaspora.

Look at Germany, and however stomach-churning, 'ein Volk, ein Reich, ein Fuehrer' is pretty powerful stuff. Hitler used external influences – the then major powers denying Germany their place in the world – and historical circumstances – the Versailles treaty – which punished Germany unnecessarily harshly. Hitler's case is questionable, and it is disturbing to find echoes of Hitler's justification in what Putin says today. The argument about whether the Versailles treaty was too harsh, or too weak, continues today. It is disturbing to see every single 1930s appeasement argument being trotted out again by Putin's useful idiots – even men of intelligence such as Mearsheimer and Peter Hitchens. At least it keeps historians busy. None of this is particularly novel, but the concept of the nation, as a constituent part of the nation-state, must be recognised in any commentary.

What, then, is a *state*? In defining the state, we might have hoped that there was one clear definition. Alas, there is not, although there are many differing interpretations through history. Was the Roman Republic a *state*, or a militarised venture capital operation?

The Westphalian Settlement of 1648, which ended the Thirty Years' War, fully described in *About War*, defined and legitimised the concept of the state as a mostly contiguous territory over which sovereignty was exercised. It established fixed borders between states. Westphalia implies a separation of the domestic and international spheres and confers equal recognition of all states, large or small. We might also define *sovereignty* as being a fundamental concept in international law. Sovereignty confers the right and power of a governing body to govern itself without any interference from outside sources or bodies. It concerns territorial integrity, legal authority, independence, recognition and non-intervention. Sovereignty implies that other states have no right, or obligation to intervene in other states' affairs. This developed into the modem international system, enshrined in the United Nations Charter, which states that 'nothing ... shall authorise the United Nations to intervene in matters which are essentially within the domestic jurisdiction of any state'. It is tempting to say at this stage, that the incidence of interstate war diminished. Tragically not.

The term *country* is often used. It usually means nation-state, but, over the years, the use of the word has changed. In 2010 *The Economist* suggested that 'finding a clear definition of country soon runs into a thicket of exceptions and anomalies'. Nevertheless, the most frequently used term in international affairs is *nation-state*, largely synonymous with *country* when describing either in a political sense. And so we arrive at the key player: the nation-state.

ADDENDUM

WOODROW WILSON'S FOURTEEN POINTS...

…was a statement outlined to the US Congress in 1918 by the then President Woodrow Wilson (President 1913–1921). It was ambitious in its scope, leading some allied leaders to be sceptical about 'Wilsonian optimism'. The relevant clauses of the fourteen points are (author's emphasis):

V. A *free*, open-minded, and absolutely impartial adjustment of all colonial claims, based upon a strict observance of the principle that in determining all such questions of *sovereignty the interests of the populations concerned must have equal weight* with the equitable government whose title is to be determined.

X. The people of Austria-Hungary, whose place among the nations we wish to see safeguarded and assured, should be accorded the *freest opportunity to autonomous development.*[28]

XIII. An *independent Polish state* should be erected (original wording) which should include the territories inhabited by indisputably Polish populations, which should be assured a free and secure access to the sea, and whose political and economic independence and territorial integrity should be guaranteed by international covenant.

And finally, and most poignant:

XIV. A general *association of nations* must be formed under specific covenants for the purpose of affording *mutual guarantees of political independence and territorial integrity to great and small states alike.*

Clause 14 gave birth to the **League of Nations**, and although in general the United States wished to join, it did not get through Congress. The League fell apart – some blamed the League for the outbreak of the Second World War, although that was mainly due to Adolf Hitler. Most of the concepts were taken over by the United Nations, launched in 1945.

11 THE NATION-STATE

The expression 'nation-state' rolls off the tongue easily, but it's not a necessary conjunction. Few citizens reflect on the way that the state has taken over the nation; how legitimacy has been wrenched from what the people – the nation – might have thought of as their sovereign rights. Few notice how the state has intruded into every aspect of the nation's affairs and the daily life of its citizens or, in monarchies like the United Kingdom, subjects. Indeed, the very history of the nation – its heritage – may have been usurped, through propaganda, by the state, in order to legitimise itself. Those people who imagine they live in a democracy may wish to examine some of their received history in a revisionist light.

In some instances, there are several nations within the state, such as the United Kingdom, with Wales, Scotland, England and Northern Ireland, or the majority nation with minority ethnic groups, such as Israel with Israeli Arabs. The several nations within a state may compete and, unless held together by a strong and, most of all, *capable* state or quite often an autocratic leader, conflicts may be inevitable. Iraq's continuing conflict between Shia and Sunni may also be an example.

WHY IS ALL THIS IMPORTANT?

From the point of view of the propensity to initiate war, or to defend the nation-state against an aggressor, there are three aspects to be recognised: the interplay of nation and state in terms of their own self-image and their position in the world; and the inherent problems with the multi-nation-state, and the legal monopoly of violence for the state (after Max Weber).

INTERACTION BETWEEN NATION AND STATE

The nation and the state work together symbiotically to produce the nation-state, the main actor in modern international affairs. The nation seeks and requires statehood for its legitimate place in international affairs and the state requires the nation or nations to ensure unity and a sense of national pride, but may be more state pride. It is in the interests of the state to promote a feeling of this national/state pride to ensure coherence. Successive United Kingdom governments have not been a great success with regard to Scotland, Ireland and Wales.

There can also be external forces helping to forge a national identity, and thus strengthen the state. Obviously, this is happening in Ukraine, but West Pakistan's treatment of East Pakistan was so appalling, that it provides all the stories, myths and symbols required to produce Bangladesh in 1971 (see the Bangladesh genocide, described in *War in Context*). Many states wish to encourage the idea of the nation, realised in the nation-state, to ensure coherence and ultimately survival.

THE (MULTI) NATION-STATE

It's difficult to say how many nation-states are multi-nation-states and how many might be single-nation-states. This is as much a part of self-perception as differences in culture. In some instances the nation is congruent with the state, a good example being France. In some instances the nation is rather suspicious of the state, rather like Italy.

Many nation-states have multiple nations within them. In some instances, usually the most successful and wealthy nation-states, this is of no consequence. When the multi-nation-state is seen to be treating one particular nation more favourably than others, this can cause problems. Of course this is not a permanent fixture, and might change with historical circumstances – sometimes quite quickly, such as in Bangladesh, the former Soviet republics, South Sudan or North and South Cyprus.

Yet, in an age of globalism and travel, it is remarkable how powerful national feelings are. Perhaps this is a wish to be part of a group, perhaps a case of 'better the devil you know', perhaps a feeling of obligation to the state that brought you up. Whatever, it helps many people, for better or worse, to feel more secure in what might look like a threatening world.

A shorthand definition of nation, state and a nation-state might be that the nation is the subjective, emotional aspect, the state an objective codified element. They come together to form the modern nation-state.

THE LEGITIMATE MONOPOLY OF VIOLENCE

Max Weber defined the state as a 'human community that (successfully) claims the monopoly of the legitimate use of physical force within a given territory'. He also noted that 'under a feudal system, no lords, including the king, could claim a monopoly over the use of violence'. Under international law, the only polity recognised is the nation-state, or country. Under the Westphalian settlement, the state, with the legitimate use of physical force, can use the force to suppress any rebel or insurgent groups. The only counter to this is international opinion. This is why civil wars, which are quite often sponsored and supported by neighbouring countries, are so expensive in terms of blood and treasure. The nation can claim no such right.

THE NATION-STATE AND WAR

The *concept* of the nation-state has had some great successes: it has facilitated the organisation of post-empire polities into coherent and sovereign political entities that can govern themselves and more easily play a part in international affairs. The first and most important role of any nation-state is the security of its people. Looking more generally, let us examine how well nation-states, in whatever form, have coped with their own internal security challenges.

Since 1945, wars, in general, have not abated. During the Cold War, many wars were proxy wars between the United States and the USSR, but since the collapse of the Soviet Union, only a small proportion of wars have been between nation-states. Since 1990, the end of the Cold War, war *within* states has become the norm rather than foreign invasion. This is why the Russian invasion of Ukraine was such a shock.

Currently, most wars, somewhere between 80 per cent and 95 per cent, have been down to national breakdown rather than foreign invasion, although, as we noted in *War in Context*, most internal wars are supported in some way by other nation-states or international insurgent operations such as Al Qaeda or ISIS. Some authorities suggest that such war deaths since 1989 might amount to between six and nine million souls.

Why are there so many wars of national breakdown? The main actors: the nation and the state, each with its own resources, objectives and, ultimately, power. The tension between these may stimulate dissent which may ultimately descend into violence, in whatever form: rebellion, insurrection or ultimately civil war. Established nation-states are, great proponents of Max Weber's maxim about the legitimate monopoly of violence, and so demand that the *state must triumph* ...

After the French revolution, and particularly between 1793 and 1796, the Vendée, with its stronger support for both the church and the *ancien régime*, decided that they did not wish to be part of the *liberté, égalité, fraternité* of the new French state. In the subsequent war, some 200,000 people died: the *state had to win*. And it wasn't just royalists who were savagely put down by the new state. One infamous example was Lyon, besieged by the Jacobin government in 1794. When it fell, more than 1,600 of Lyon's citizens of both sexes and all ages were executed – some blown apart by cannon, others tied into carts in their dozens and then drawn into the river to be drowned.

In Israel, it seems that the Israeli state cannot tolerate a Palestinian state – the two-state solution – on its border, and the whole issue seems to be decided by violence. The British state could not contemplate a united Ireland because it would have been 'surrendering to terrorism' and although the 'troubles' did not descend into a full-scale Civil War, again, the British state considered that it *had to win*. Attempts at Catalonia's independence from the Spanish state did not descend into violence, but it certainly presented tricky legal issues for both the Catalonian leaders and the Spanish state itself. Thankfully, violence was minimal.

There are many more examples like this. Any list would be extensive and reveal a dynamic interaction between many factors which would feed on others, such as religious grievances stimulating economic deprivation. Think of the Catholic community in Northern Ireland before the 'troubles' (1967–1998) or the French state's treatment of its Muslim population.

It is a moot question as to whether the multi-nation-state can cope where there is limited economic development, with no history of different nations within the state working together, or without the coercion of autocratic or dictatorial leadership. We might question whether the sovereign nation-state is best model for achieving and maintaining an internal national peace.

One particular post-empire problem is that many of the word's nation-states were poorly defined by their former colonial masters. Current borders of former colonies often cut across religious, tribal and other cultural or ethnic groupings, making for unstable existences. A comparison was made by the Kenyan UN ambassador during the first UN debate on Putin's invasion in February 2022. He was one of the few African representatives to take a bold condemnatory stand against Putin and Russia and compared Ukraine's plight to the colonial legacy in Africa.

He suggested that internal borders in Africa had been 'badly drawn', and had inherited national boundaries imposed on them by departing colonial masters. They often made no sense, he claimed. The same might be said of the Sykes–Picot line, which was a 1916 secret treaty between the United Kingdom and France, with assent from the Russian Empire and the Kingdom of Italy, to define their mutually agreed spheres of influence and control in an eventual partition of the Ottoman Empire.

The Kenyan UN ambassador went on to say that if every African nation sought to address what it regarded as the wrongs of history in respect of their frontiers, mass carnage would surely follow, hence the principles of the UN charter as pertaining to a neighbouring country's sovereignty had to be respected, no matter how badly that historical border had been drawn. It was 'what they had' he argued. In fact, it was as early as 1964, at a conference in Cairo that the African Union agreed to respect the colonial borders, however formed, within the African continent.

12 CONCLUSIONS: PROSPECTS FOR THE NATION-STATE, ALLIANCES AND THE WORLD

Political memory tends to be short. Even today in the UK, older women might just recall when women did not even have the vote. It was only comparatively recently that adult women – even professional women – had to get their husband's approval to open a bank account.

Knowledge of the power of the state is scant: the British Emergency Powers Act gives the government enormous and, one might say, even 'unprecedented powers'. Yet it's been invoked a dozen times in the last hundred years, in each case during periods of industrial action – strikes.

At the same time, the United Kingdom government has shamelessly ignored the nations that make up the United Kingdom. Vast areas of Wales, Scotland and Northern Ireland have been deindustrialised, and the investment in London and the South East, compared with these regions is egregious.

But here we are talking about *war*, and the propensity of the nation-state, or the multi-nation-state in the case of the United Kingdom, to use violence – military force – to achieve political ends.

The objectives of this chapter have been twofold: first to affirm the definitions of *nation* and of *state*, and suggest that the term *nation-state* compounded two different but complementary concepts. The second objective was to highlight both the strengths and weaknesses of the nation-state and of the nation-state within the international system.

Strengths: It enables nations to realise legitimacy within the international community and to organise themselves as they wish, with their own laws and social values, unless of course they are led by an autocrat or dictator.

Weaknesses: Legitimacy, sovereignty and a Westphalian injunction about other states interfering in their own internal affairs may hide human and civil rights abuses and the use of corrupt laws to persecute their citizens. The multinational nation-state is a good model, but there is almost bound to be a dominant nation, with the attendant danger that other nations are treated less well or even neglected. Would half the population of Scotland wish to secede from the union – the United Kingdom – if investment there had been on a similar level to South East England? And, as an extreme example, would Ireland as a whole have sought independence for many years had the absent English landlords not abused the population. Even then, in the multinational nation-state, nations can get carried away, spurred by self-interested or power-hungry leaders, such as in Basque Spain or Catalonia. In a benign example, Quebec had a period of wishing to secede from Canada, a federal nation-state.

Internationally, the nation-state is so much the normal expectation of other nation-states that any other constitutional arrangement would not be realised or accepted. This has denied legitimacy for the Kurds for 100 years, the Palestinians for 70-odd years and the Jews for some 1,980 years before that, until 1948. And, in a mirror image of the sovereignty provision, this might allow smug, wealthy countries to ignore the plight of oppressed people.

The UN has condemned the actions of the supposedly legitimate government in Syria, but the international community should be ashamed of the horrors – including chemical weapons – inflicted upon the Syrian people. Although Turkey has housed millions of Syrian refugees, the rest of the world has stood by and done nothing. It was a poor excuse to say that we could not counter Russian involvement there. Indeed, Russian involvement might have been avoided. The aftermath of Iraq and Afghanistan made the West – the US in particular, reluctant to get involved – the Russians saw that and moved in to fill the vacuum.

The problem is that the overall record is not good. As we mentioned at the beginning of the chapter, between 80 per cent and 95 per cent of current wars are between different factions within the same nation-state. Insurrections, civil wars and insurgencies represent security concerns for all countries, not just the nation-state itself, but other contiguous nation-states in the region. Other world problems, such as drug cartels and environmental damage can only be tackled on a multinational basis.

All nation-states surrender some of their sovereignty with membership of international or supranational bodies, or trade deals, or defence arrangements. This is the most flagrant aspect missing from the advocates of Brexit in the United Kingdom. Currently, the concept of the Westphalian nation-state; sovereign, independent and jealous of its supposed rights, is simply not addressing the issue of war or other security threats, either intrastate or international.

To achieve anything like a lasting peace, the current model need not be thrown out, but it needs to change and adapt, particularly in terms of working with other nation-states, and have more concern for human and civil rights around the world.

Part Three: European Security

13 EUROPEAN SECURITY ARCHITECTURE

The Russian invasion demonstrated in stark clarity the globalisation of security concerns: Russia purchased drones from Iran, and munitions from North Korea. Turkey, on the other side of the Black Sea to Ukraine, and NATO's most unpredictable member, still maintained contacts with Vladimir Putin. The United States has contributed generously to the war, but some factions within the political establishment in the US see it as a distraction from what they see as their main enemy and security concern: China.

Given that Europe's security architecture is complex and multi-dimensional, and that NATO seems to consider itself as having a global role in terms of security, how did Europe *in general* cope with the Russian invasion of Ukraine 2022?

The Russian Federation's invasion of Ukraine was considered to be a great shock to all concerned, even though Ukraine itself and the CIA warned of it some weeks beforehand. But short-term warning of an attack has little

utility in terms of resisting it in the first place and then restoring the antebellum status. The CIA claims credit for this prediction, but any analysis of the situation on the ground should have been taken after Russia's annexation of Crimea, and certainly with Russian actions in Donbas.

Let's make this plain: from the West's point of view, the Russian annexation of Crimea was a political failure, both in terms of the event and the reaction to it. The Russian invasion of Ukraine was an egregious intelligence, political and diplomatic disaster, only partly redeemed by the support offered since then.

There were two second-order shocks which I introduced in the first section. First, Russia, whether czarist, Soviet or supposedly post-Soviet 'liberal/democratic, etc.' was still following its age-old agenda of seeing power as the acquisition and subjugation of territory. Vlast: see reference to Orlando Figes in Chapter 7.

Even acknowledging Russia's expansion since Ivan the Terrible and Peter the Great, consider Soviet actions since the start of the Second World War in 1939. This includes Finland, the Baltic, Ukraine, Poland, Korea, Hungary, Czechoslovakia and Afghanistan. In post-Soviet Russia, refer to Georgia, Chechnya, Syria, Armenia, Azerbaijan, Belarus and of course Crimea and Donbas. All involved horrendous casualties (less so in Crimea and Belarus), both for the inflicted country and for the Russian military.

Through such a prism, the Russian Federation's invasion of Ukraine should not be seen as anything outside the norm; we might even have anticipated Russia's actions.

The second shock was intelligence. Nobody, except the Ukrainians themselves, expected their military to put up such a competent resistance. This means that Western intelligence, American military and diplomatic intelligence, Five Eyes intelligence and NATO intelligence all failed to appreciate how much the Ukrainian army had learned in Donbas since Russian incursions there from 2014, or how well they would fight.

Neither did the intelligence community appreciate the weaknesses in the Russian Federation army, although the individual aspects that make up that weakness were suspected. Did nobody consider these together and come up with an objective assessment of exactly how well the Russian army had developed, or rather, not? Considering the phenomenal amount of money that is spent on intelligence, one might pause to think what the taxpayer is getting for their money.

However, OSINT has really come into its own: see reference to OSINT in Chapter 7.

The Russian attack focused Europe's attention on joint security, which is, as one might expect, subject to divergences of political opinion. In the early stages of the conflict, President Macron of France was urging conciliation; the German Chancellor was reluctant to offer aid – it might 'fuel the conflict/cause escalation' – and the new prime minister in Italy, Giorgia Meloni, was initially hesitant about helping at all. The United Kingdom, albeit with a limited supplies of their own, stepped up to the plate in very short order.

Russian atrocities at Bucha in the early stages of the war prompted action. At the time of writing, supplies of munitions have geared up considerably, but only after much agonising and disagreements about the supply of armour. At the time of writing, the offensives and counteroffensive from Ukraine is going ahead, some say with mixed results, but without what any general would call adequate air cover.

This chapter is concerned with the implication of Russia's invasion on European security: in a word, is it good enough to resist the Russian bear? Or, more pertinently, is it sufficient to *deter* the Russian bear from taking action against other countries, contiguous or otherwise?

As this trilogy has mentioned on several occasions, the first and fundamental duty of any state, or indeed any polity, is to provide for its citizens' security. And the primary need is territorial and physical security. Any alliance, association, treaty, accord, club, community or understanding concerning relationships with other states should prioritise this. The European Union was formed after the Second World War so that such a war could not happen again. It was a political union based on 'ever closer union'. But the utility of such a union, or Europe in general, is compromised if each and every country, NATO, EU or not, is not secure. This applies as much to states as it does to individuals.

To its shame, Europe has complacently hidden behind the American security guarantees and their nuclear umbrella for the 77 years since the Second World War, and has consistently referred (deferred?) to the Americans for security and, to some extent, diplomacy. It was a cheap option that President Trump resented. This may have suited the Americans well, extending their worldwide hegemony, but American, European and UK foreign policy, although each distinct in their own way, is broadly that of 'The West'. For interest, try googling 'UK foreign policy'. The results are illuminating, or rather, not ...

This is not necessarily a bad thing: at least it ensures coordination. But it seems that there is very little consideration of how Europe in general might achieve President Macron's 'strategic autonomy' within – or even without – an American framework. A European assumption seems to be we should, in general, wait for the cue from the Americans before taking action. The NATO standard of 2 per cent of GDP spend on defence illustrates this. Had the Americans not stepped up so generously with munitions to Ukraine, that country would now be occupied by the Russian Federation, but also the devastation of the death that this would cause would be appalling.

Europe, whether the EU or NATO members (there is considerable overlap), relies absolutely on NATO for their security, two-thirds resourced by the Americans. Yes, NATO European members contribute greatly to NATO's capability, but NATO is American inspired and American led. NATO cannot take action without American approval. In terms of equipment and capability, America – one country out of thirty-one – contributes disproportionally to NATO's capabilities.

COMPONENTS OF EUROPEAN SECURITY ARCHITECTURE

The term 'European security architecture' is a catchphrase for the design of the interstate institutions whose role is the collective security of the

European area. This is sometimes described as such, sometimes simply as 'Europe' and sometimes as the 'North Atlantic area'. This need not distract us here, but the concept needs a consensus in terms of the northernmost boundaries – do we include Svalbard and the Arctic; the eastern boundaries – obviously at the moment Ukraine – and the southern boundaries – do we include North Africa, in which case how far do we consider security into the Sahel and West African states?

See Appendix A for a fuller definition of What is 'Europe'? What is 'The West'.

There are several, or even say a plethora, of organisations concerned with security and defence in Europe. The question is how effective they are, individually and collectively, in fulfilling their role.

Appendix B has an outline of contributors to European security architecture International Bodies, such as the United Nations and the OSCE.

EUROPEAN SECURITY: THE THREATS

One might imagine that there are simply too many bodies concerned with European security: the European Union, NATO, the United Nations and other international organisations, for example OSCE, all with similar or at least parallel roles and objectives. See Appendix B for a fuller list.

But the answer lies not in the number or diversity of these bodies but how effective the whole system is in providing for and, in the event, taking action to protect Europe's security. Europe here, meaning the European archipelago itself, but also contiguous states from North Cape (or Svalbard?) to North Africa, and from Portugal to the Black Sea, to include the Mediterranean with Syria, Lebanon, Jordan, Israel, and Egypt. See Appendix A.

This might represent a minimum: problems in Georgia (throw in Abkhazia and South Ossetia for good measure), Armenia, Azerbaijan and Iraq might also compromise European security. Neil Ascherson suggests that if Putin loses the Ukrainian war, some of the statelets around the Black Sea, such as Artsakh (aka Nagorno-Karabakh), South Ossetia, Abkhazia, the two Donbas republics of Donetsk and Luhansk, and Transnistria, will 'explode in blood', causing an exodus of even more refugees.

What role does NATO consider it has here? Furthermore, does NATO have any contingency plans for some of the aspiring states in the Russian Federation, thinking they might strive for independence. Dagestan comes to mind, and they may feel that, although the Georgian breakaway was bloody, it might be worth the cost for independence. Turkey – a NATO member – borders the Black Sea as well.

The main point is that, with the current focus being so much on *military* support for Ukraine, the political aspects might have been, if not forgotten, then at least relegated to second place. One recalls General Eric Ludendorff's comment just before his spring offensive in 1918. When asked what the strategy was, and how this his offensive might contribute to a political settlement with the Western allies, his response was tragically simplistic: '... we will punch a hole into [their line]. For the rest we shall see ...'. Small wonder military historians will now dub him 'successful tactician, failed strategist'.

RUSSIA AND 'RUSSIA IN AFRICA' ARE NOT THE ONLY THREATS TO EUROPEAN SECURITY

The preoccupation with Russia as a security threat might divert attention away from other threats to European security. There are three obvious sources. First, internal conflict within countries. The Balkans might be troublesome, Belarus is keeping the lid on dissent, and the countries round the Black Sea are only starters. Second, international terrorism, which has not gone away, and may use the west preoccupation with Russia to cause trouble. According to the Global Terrorism Index for 2023, 'The deadliest terrorist groups in the world in 2022 were Islamic State (IS) and its affiliates, followed by al-Shabaab, Balochistan Liberation Army (BLA) and Jamaat Nusrat Al-Islam wal Muslimeen (JNIM).' There are many others.

Finally, international crime, much of it drug-related, remains a major problem worldwide, particularly when linked to weak states. And it is not just gangsters, there is also penetration of state institutions, corruption, and dangers to Governance. According to the Website Global Financial Integrity, the largest transnational crime is counterfeiting, amounting to maybe $1 trillion, with drug trafficking at about $500 million. Also, illegal logging ($100 billion), human trafficking (£150 billion), illegal mining ($30 billion), IUU (Illegal, Unreported and Unregulated) fishing ($25 billion), illegal wildlife trade (surprisingly amounting to somewhere between $5 billion and $23 billion), crude oil theft ($8 billion), small arms and a light weapons trafficking ($2.5 billion) and, horrendously, organ trafficking which might amount to £1 billion. (Most of these numbers are reported with broad spreads, so the numbers above are largely illustrative.)

EUROPEAN SECURITY ARCHITECTURE: FIT FOR PURPOSE?

A perfunctory response is that in the event – Crimea, Donbas, 24 February 2022 – Europe, however defined, failed to deter the Russian Federation and failed in terms of the immediate reaction. It seems there was a lack of intelligence and contingency planning. There is little doubt that had the Americans not stepped in, and stepped in quickly, that

Ukraine would be now occupied by the Russians, and many Ukrainians dead or injured, and much infrastructure ruined.

Most commentaries about the solution to these problems focus on a 'this needs sorting' model, mentioning percentage expenditure, air power, the US involvement in NATO, logistics, strategic autonomy and resilience, as well as many other topic headings.

But what is needed is a comprehensive *vision* for Europe's security, one that recognises the security threats on the eastern flank; with the possibility of incorporating Russia into the European security apparatus, but if not, providing enough suitable deterrence. Subordinate to any vision is strategy. Strategy does not work if you don't know where you're going or why. Indeed, an oft-heard expression is 'if you don't know where you're going, any road will take you there'.

George H W Bush – the 41st President of the United States (Dad) 1989 to 1993 – eschewed the notion of 'the vision thing'. But in this case we have to comprehend not just expelling the Russian Federation from Ukraine to suit Ukrainians, but also a manageable approach, and capability, for deterrence, as well as how Europe might have to live with the Russian bear on its eastern flank.

Even if the vision is not realised, strategists need to think in terms of direction. We need therefore to consider all the contributory factors to a vision of lasting peace in wider Europe, and, although as this might be difficult to think of, a better and lasting relationship with the Russian people.

Strategy is everything about the future: It's rather like climbing a mountain: you might not be able to see the peak, but you can be pretty confident that moving uphill might eventually get you there.

Europe, whether taken to mean a geographic area, members of the European Union or, for example, the European Political Community, must develop and agree on a comprehensive vision for Europe's security, and that must include political as well as military aspirations.

It must include dealing with Russia as a pariah, but with the aspiration that the country might be welcomed into the international community in due course. Notwithstanding the Russian population and their culpability for the war, 140 million people, even spread out across the whole of Asia, need to be considered.

NATO

NATO is a political-military alliance formed in 1949 at the dawn of the Cold War. It's original and primary purpose was collective defence. The main target was Russia, but in the early days, Russia was not generally mentioned, only an 'enemy' or sometimes an 'unknown enemy'. The British general Lord Ismay, NATO's first Secretary General, famously said the purpose of the Alliance was 'to keep the Soviet Union out, the Americans in, and the Germans down'.

Now, NATO comprises thirty-two member countries, and is a vital component of European security. Security generally includes many aspects, for example crime, migration, energy supplies and the environment. NATO, although sensitive to these aspects, is largely focused on defence and the need for military force.

It is intriguing to note that thirty-one, the number of member countries is parallel to the number of countries in the European Union, which is twenty-seven. Perhaps there is an intrinsic constraint of trying to reach any consensus with more than this number. The African Union has fifty-five states, and ASEAN only ten, though they are not quite the same sort of organisation.

Although the EU does not have a permanent military command structure along the lines of the NATO, since 1999, the EU has been responsible for implementing missions such as peacekeeping and the verification of various treaties. Many EU member states are also NATO members, and although the EU sees NATO as responsible for the territorial defence of Europe, there is no *official* stance on this. Indeed, the diplomatic attitudes to the EU – NATO relationship varies between member states and there is no absolute consensus.

In 2019, as NATO celebrated its 70th anniversary, YouGov carried out a survey across NATO's population. The results were that Europeans remained more enthusiastic about NATO than Americans, but that support for membership has fallen in several European countries over the previous two years. Britons, French and Germans were less approving of NATO, Nordic countries also less approving, but not quite so much. One would expect this to have changed after Russia's invasion of Ukraine, but public opinion may not then be willing to see taxes increase to meet the new security threats.

NATO, AS A POLITICAL-MILITARY ALLIANCE

As a political-military alliance, NATO has failed in Ukraine. The military side has worked well but this does not redeem NATO as a political player, concerned as it is with the security of its member countries. Sure, it is individual NATO countries, mainly and largely America, who have stepped up to supply munitions, logistical support and intelligence, but the contributing nations are worldwide: even Albania sent two military ambulances.

Even then non-NATO members and the whole of Europe, however pathetically, relies on NATO, that is the Americans, for its joint and collective security. One can hear the rejoinder already: NATO's political side is beholden to the thirty NATO members, or just the American lead. NATO's politics is bedevilled by the strain of achieving consensus among thirty different sovereign nations. But this is no excuse. Think of the thousands of senior military officers, the thousands of diplomats all over Europe: what are they doing, except commentating? Remember Henry Kissinger's question: 'If I want to speak to Europe, who do I call?'

NATO, or perhaps we should say its constituent members, seem to have ignored the notion that war, the coercive use of armed force, is a political act. It is largely irrelevant that NATO did not commit ground, air or naval resources to counter Russia. Russia sees the war as one nation pitted against NATO anyway, so what would be the difference?

NATO's failure is a failure of deterrence. Now deterrence is often – actually almost always – linked to the word *nuclear*, as in *nuclear deterrence*. Deterrence was a success during the Cold War in that the face-off between the West and Soviet Russia never became a 'hot' war. (Deterrence is covered in detail in *War in Context.*)

Deterrence is considered to have been a success in that there was no hot war between the West and Soviet Russia. But deterrence is as much about conventional arms and political will as it is about nuclear threats. For example, the *Taipei Times* in November 2020 carried an article entitled 'Following the Swiss Defence Model'. It was obviously concerned about deterring a Chinese attack on Taiwan. To quote the *TT*:

Switzerland's national defence strategy makes it like a porcupine with short and dense spikes — when it encounters an enemy, it curls its body into a ball, with the spikes facing outward to resist the enemy's invasion and make it impossible for the enemy to swallow it, unless it is willing to pay a heavy price.

This is a small modification on the previous strategy, which was the exact and unacceptable price on any aggressor in terms of their losses in equipment and troops. *Taipei Times* also mentioned that Swiss men were required to perform compulsory military service from the age of twenty. We should note that, in spite being a neutral state, Switzerland is also a NATO 'partner' country. We cannot predict whether China will be deterred from attacking Taiwan, but raising the price in this way will give China more pause for thought.

Whatever NATO's conventional arms deterrence model was and despite the fact that Ukraine was not a NATO member, it is quite clear that the Russian Federation, and Putin in particular, were not deterred from acquiring Crimea or attacking Ukraine. Apart from a few mild sanctions following the Russian Federation's actions in Chechnya, Georgia and Syria et al., Putin clearly thought he could get away with it.

14 NATO AND WIDER EUROPEAN SECURITY

NATO recognises its role in wider European security, outside NATO members. NATO documentation and plans even suggest a global role. It's the implementation that is the challenge. Note that here we cover *European* security rather than just the security of NATO members. It seems that is part of NATO's declared purpose.

On the NATO website, there is a handy list of '10 things you need to know about NATO'. Number 2 in that list states that NATO is in the business of *'managing crises around the world'*. It claims to *'promote stability in our neighbourhood and protect our people at home'*, and this *'can sometimes mean taking action further afield'*. They then list Bosnia, Kosovo and Afghanistan … preventing piracy off the Horn of Africa and helping address the refugee and migrant crisis in Europe. It would be ungenerous to dismiss these claims out of hand, but one might query their extravagance. NATO does not seem to recognise that if any European nation feels insecure, then no nation, nor Europe as a whole, is secure. Defence, like justice, is indivisible. But where is Europe? See Appendix A.

After the NATO summit in Warsaw in July 2016, two years after Russia's incursion into Ukraine (Donbas and Crimea) and having been alerted to a more assertive Russia, NATO's communiqué described an 'arc of insecurity and instability along NATO's periphery and beyond' and suggested that these, together with security concerns in the Middle East and North Africa, could have 'direct implications for the security of NATO' – meaning Europe as a whole. So far, so good. NATO also agreed to the deployment of 'enhanced forward presence battlegroups'. These were to be deployed in the Baltic states and Poland. I refer again to the

War in Context appendix, where no less than twenty security concerns are identified in Europe's back yard.

NATO, or perhaps we should say its constituent members, are good at worrying about security, but slightly less proficient at dealing with it. So, what was NATO's new purpose after the Warsaw summit? NATO had taken the lead at the International Security Assistance Force (ISAF) in Afghanistan in 2003. But why? Sure, this action was mandated by the United Nations, the objective being to 'enable the Afghan government to provide effective security across the country and develop new Afghan security forces'. But it's a stretch to imagine that security problems in Afghanistan affected the security of the North Atlantic area. When he was Prime Minister, Gordon Brown claimed that the streets of Bradford (why Bradford?) were safer because of the British armed forces operating in Afghanistan. This was met with some derision.

NATO's main function is as a defensive alliance. As such, and although it not made specific, it is intended to *deter* any likely aggressor – originally the Soviet Union but, since Putin came to power, the Russian Federation. It is intended to deter Russia from attacking – or compromising the security of Europe, however defined. It is this *deterrent* function that is important.

The concept of formal, planned deterrence was originally conceived as an answer to the nuclear threat from the Soviet Union. Deterrence theory commanded a vast academic literature, some of it encumbered with complex theoretical considerations. Deterrence is sometimes thought of as being about threats: the Oxford English Dictionary mentions *restrain by fear*. Google dictionary also suggests *doubt or fear of the consequences.*

Deterrence theory is covered in depth in *War in Context*, but we repeat here Professor Sir Lawrence Freedman's maxim that 'deterrence can be a technique, doctrine and a state of mind. In all cases it is about setting boundaries for actions and establishing risks associated with crossing these boundaries'. Freedman suggests that instead of threatening punishment, deterrence should be more about defining barriers. A vernacular take on that might be that good fences make good neighbours. Despite undertakings to the contrary, Putin did not see the border between Ukraine and Russia as being accepted and agreed. Freedman's *Nuclear Deterrence: A Ladybird Expert Book* is disarmingly simple in explaining this subject, but none the worse for that. It is thoroughly recommended.

But, of course, it's all theory. The difficulty with the theory of nuclear deterrence is that, as is covered in *War in Context*, it cannot be tested or verified. When considering conventional war, how then does deterrence theory cope?

NATO's current posture raises important questions in the context of the Russian-Ukrainian war, but let us first remind ourselves of NATO's reaction, and that of the West in general, to Russia's use of military power in the past. What was NATO's reaction when, for example, Georgia was invaded or Grozny (Chechnya) flattened; when Litvinenko was murdered; when the Skripals were poisoned (with one local collateral death) or when Russia appropriated Crimea; when Russia committed war crimes in Syria or sent mercenaries to Libya and the Sahel; or attempted to subvert America's elections? Condemnation, a few sanctions, but mostly short-lived or ineffective. 'Engagement' seemed to be the maxim, rather than any action.

Keir Giles works with the Russia and Eurasia programme at Chatham House. He knows something about Russia. In June, he suggested that there would be no early end to the conflict. Far from commenting on whether the Russia was deterred from the crimes above, he suggests that the reluctance to provide Ukraine with war-winning equipment in sufficient volume is an example of the US and others' *self-deterrence* (my emphasis) out of fear of provoking escalation. All this, Giles suggests, gives Putin the drawn-out war that he needs. Putin's obvious hope is that the US and the West will tire of supplying Ukraine, saying that there is little prospect of winning in the short term and then start to wind down support. This is a counterpoint to Ukraine's president Vladimir Zelenskyy saying on several occasions that if he had had the weapons in the quantity he required, he could have chased the Russians out already. But there is a bigger message here: the whole idea of deterrence is to deter an enemy from attacking you. It's not supposed to be self-deterrence!

Military support, to be effective, has to be measured, yes, but against the Russian Federation, with its considerable resources, it would have been more effective had it been supplied in greater quantity, and sooner. More specifically, and to widen the brief:

1) How does NATO's *deterrence* role function in the event of a *conventional* Russian attack on a NATO country?

2) The Russian invasion of Ukraine brought that war right up to the Polish border, a NATO member. This is surely a security problem. Does NATO recognise *non-contiguous* threats? On its western borders, Ukraine has four other countries: Romania, Hungary, Slovakia (all NATO members) and Moldova (not a NATO member, and the north-eastern sliver of Moldova has been carved off in a separatist entity called Transnistria, currently home to some 2,000 Russian troops).

3) In the context of the twenty non-contiguous threats identified in *War in Context*, what role does NATO consider it has? Does NATO have contingency plans to deal with these threats?

4) Neil Ascherson suggests that if Putin loses the Ukrainian war, some of the statelets around the Black Sea, such as Artsakh (aka Nagorno-Karabakh), South Ossetia, Abkhazia, the two Donbas republics of Donetsk and Luhansk and Transnistria will *explode in blood*, causing an exodus of even more refugees. What role does NATO consider it has here? Furthermore, does NATO have any contingency plans for some of the aspiring states in the Russian Federation, thinking they might strive for independence. Dagestan comes to mind, and they may feel that, although the Georgian breakaway was bloody, it might be worth the cost for independence. Turkey, a NATO member, borders the Black Sea as well. And we might also record that Georgia, Armenia, Iran, Iraq, and Syria all border that NATO state (Turkey).

5) These are not casual questions. Some of the countries or regions concerned are only 'one country away' from a NATO member. Europe and NATO need to recognise these security threats and generate contingency plans. Without such plans it will be too late in the event of a real security threat; there would be no time for the British political establishment to argue about succession or the French to be suggesting conciliation ('don't humiliate Mr Putin') or the Germans to be reticent about doing anything at all ('not buying Russian gas might affect our industry').

6) Do we have a long-term strategy to defeat Putin? Even if Putin is deposed or disappears or dies, how are we going to deal with this resentful, unsuccessful (almost a failed state) behemoth on Europe's eastern border? Was it wise for the West to wait upon Ukrainian military gains before supplying the kit they needed?

15 NATO'S ROLE IN UKRAINE

NATO's overall strategy for Ukraine is to support their territorial integrity, and security. This is facilitated through the Ukraine-NATO Annual National Programme (ANP) and the Ukraine NATO Annual Target Plan (ATP), which together outline reforms in defence and security sector reform, democratic governance, and the rule of law, something that Ukraine will have to tackle when this war is over as a way of getting rid of endemic corruption.

In fact Ukraine-NATO cooperation started not long after the Soviet Union fell apart. In 1991, the newly independent Ukraine joined the North Atlantic Cooperation Council and in 1994, Partnership for Peace. In 1997, the two parties signed the Charter on a Distinctive Partnership, which established the NATO-Ukraine Commission (NUC) to take cooperation forward. At the Warsaw NATO summit in July 2016, the cooperation between NATO and Ukraine was set out in the Comprehensive Assistance Package (CAP), focussing more on practical support.

Since the initial Russian invasion in February 2022, NATO and allies from all over the world have provided unprecedented levels of support to Ukraine.

It is something of a relief is that United States support has stayed the course. In April 2023, spokespersons for the US Department of Defense stated that (edited for ease of quotation):

'Russia cannot be allowed to invade and destroy its neighbour Ukraine … our goal is a free, prosperous and democratic Ukraine able to defend its sovereignty and deter further aggression the US has committed more than $36 billion in security assistance to Ukraine including artillery, air defence

and armour ... this substantial commitment of the US military assistance reflects American interests and values that are at stake ... our support for Ukraine self-defence is an investment in our own security and prosperity.'

NATO's strategy is parallel with diplomatic efforts by other international actors, such as the EU and individual NATO member states. Although there are differences of opinion about levels of support, the provision art of armour and air power, the U.S and European consensus, at the beginning of what is known as Ukraine's spring offensive, seems to be holding.

NATO has been a key player in military support to Ukraine. Military stocks, pre-planned logistical arrangements and intelligence have all been vital in helping Ukraine counter the Russian onslaught. Ukraine is not a member of NATO and NATO is not obliged to react. For NATO, three important points emerge from Russian actions:

First, the imprudence of not taking more seriously Russia's annexation of Crimea in 2014. A few sanctions were imposed, but evidently not enough to deter Putin from pressing on. Neither did his actions in the Donbas invoke any sanctions which seriously deterred him.

Second, the political message it sends to the Russian Federation that there is indeed a line on a map which divides a Russian Federation sphere of influence, and the other side being truly European. Even without the invasion in February, this idea needs to be repudiated.

Third, and probably the most important, is that should the Russian Federation occupy the whole of Ukraine, then their border would be contiguous to a NATO state, a grave security risk.

But security, defence and deterrence is not something that is solely concerned with contiguous states. The United States takes very seriously the security threat from China, which of course is the other side of the Pacific to metropolitan US, thousands of miles away. Russia's Black

Sea Fleet is based in Sevastopol in Crimea; rarely reported, this was *leased* from Ukraine, the lease running out in 2017. This can be quickly deployed to NATO states such as Romania, Bulgaria and Turkey.

Moldova, some 400 km across the sea from Sevastopol, is not currently a member of NATO, and it's notable that there are Russian troops stationed in the breakaway region of Transnistria, a small sliver of land in the north of Moldova, bordering Ukraine. Whereas of course there are none in the other three countries.

In *War in Context*, we ask the most fundamental question of all, one that is often ignored: can the United Kingdom defend itself? Can, indeed, any other NATO country defend itself except America? *No* is the answer, but we and other members operate with and within NATO, where Article 5 of the treaty commits *'each member state to consider an armed attack against one member state, in Europe or North America, to be an armed attack against them all'*. Article 5 has been invoked once: by the United States after the 11 September attacks in 2001 on the World Trade Centre and the Pentagon.

But, before the Russian invasion of Ukraine, would it have worked? In 2019, President Macron of France suggested that NATO was 'brain dead', perhaps a reaction to President Trump's ambivalence towards NATO. Popular support for NATO and the provision of Article 5 across Europe is mixed; only about half of the respective electorates felt they would want to support NATO in a military venture. To put it bluntly, would British parents be happy seeing their sons and daughters die defending Bulgaria?

Even then, many people misunderstand Article 5. The definition above is taken from the NATO charter, but it goes on to say: *'each Party (member state) will assist the Party or Parties so attacked by taking forthwith, individually and in concert with the other Parties, such action as it (the member state) deems necessary, including* (but not necessarily –

my emphasis) *the use of armed force, to restore and maintain the security of the North Atlantic area'*.

NATO's primary purpose is the collective security of its member states, it does not clearly define the 'North Atlantic area' in its founding document. Implicitly, this is, based on the supposed threat from the Soviet Union during the Cold War the member countries located mainly in Europe and North America. But, possibly to give itself some meaning and some role, especially after the demise of the Soviet system, NATO has expanded beyond this North Atlantic area, with deployments in the Balkans, Afghanistan, and Libya, thus addressing security concerns outside its original boundaries. These were offensive actions, whereas the NATO contribution to Ukraine has been for what has been described by the US president as defensive purposes.

NATO'S STRATEGY IN UKRAINE

What was NATO's *strategy* with regard to Russia in general and in particular, the Russian invasion of Ukraine? Strategy is *everything about the future*. There are many aspects to the analysis, the generation, and execution of strategy. This trilogy emphasises that strategy is first, last and always political. Like war in general, there is no general model for strategy. The key being to think *strategically* rather than following any specific template. Thinking strategically must mean thinking politically. It is worth reminding ourselves of some of the basics of strategy.

The first task of the strategic challenge is to appreciate exactly what strategy is and the difference between *objective* strategy – the search for a lasting political settlement, and *subjective* strategy – the category usually considered – which cojoins the word with functional specifics, such as military, or logistics, or, almost tautologically, political strategy.

An important caveat here: much writing about strategy imagines that there is a caucus of strategists lurking somewhere within government, think tanks or universities. There may well be people who are capable of advising on strategy, and others who can provide detailed analysis, but the responsibility for overall *objective* strategy rests with the most senior politicians, and this is especially so when considering the use of armed force.

The second task is to locate *where* it happens, a forum, or at least to be aware of the protocols involved. Lest this be a statement of the bleedin' obvious, note the comment in the Chilcot report (covered in detail in *About War*), that the various strategies – there were several – involved in the invasion of Iraq passed 'like ships in the night'. And this just concerned the United Kingdom alone. Things are much more complex when there are thirty players, even if there is one overall lead, being the United States.

The fundamental principle of strategy is that it concerns ends, ways and means …

Ends in terms of the political situation which you want to achieve. This may change over time depending on the success or otherwise of the operation.

Ways in terms of what coercive power you might use, and how it might be used. This is usually thought of us being military power, but there are various other manifestations of power such as sanctions, cyber-attacks and strategic communication.

Means is the measure of resource they are prepared to commit to achieving the ends. For minor problems on the other side of the world, any nation-state might not be too keen on providing resources. However, where the threat is existential (as in the Second World War) then of course many more means would be deployed. Also, a point often missed when considering strategy, is that that means will also include those which can be developed during the operation. See the comments about Paul Kennedy's description of the North Atlantic campaign.

We cover the general issue of logistics above, but there are signs now that even American manufacturing industry will be pushed to produce the necessary munitions to meet a major threat. If American manufacturing capacity, and that of the Europeans, cannot keep up with the war in Ukraine, how will they cope with a major war against the Chinese? They might respond that they have higher tech weapons than the Chinese, but, to put it bluntly, I wouldn't rely on it.

So what is the *end* result that the West/NATO/Europe wanted to achieve?

Is it ... simply to chase the Russians out of Ukraine and then leave an inevitably fragile armed peace behind?

Or ... is it, as Lloyd Austin, the current United States Secretary of Defense suggested in the early days of the conflict, to 'see Russia weakened' so that it cannot 'do the kinds of things that it has done in invading Ukraine'? There was also talk of 'containing' Russia: see panel on the Truman doctrine. Austin also said that the US wants 'to see them (the Russians) not have the capability to very quickly reproduce similar military capability'; but then, in an intriguing adjunct, that the US 'wants to see the international community more united, especially NATO ... and ... we've moved very rapidly to demonstrate that we're going to defend every inch of NATO.'

Or ... is it to punish Putin and by implication the Russian people by destroying as much of the Russian Federation's armed forces as possible? Similar to the above, but bloodier.

Or ... is it to take heed of Neal Ascherson's comments about the Black Sea 'exploding in blood', and to prepare accordingly?

Or ... is it to anticipate a potentially failed state brought about by sanctions, the immense cost of the war, the depletion of the population, particularly well-educated youth, the pariah status which Russia would have to face for perhaps a generation?

There might be a realisation by some of the Russian regions that the Russian military might was not quite what they thought it was, which might raise hopes of secession.

These ends are largely congruent, but not quite. All would require different strategies from NATO. And, however the Russians behaviour in Ukraine has been, we will still have to live with them after everything is resolved.

Finally, are these ends congruent with Ukraine's? **What now Ukraine's ultimate goal?** Publicly they have stated that they want to chase the Russians out of every part of antebellum Ukraine, including Crimea. Most commentators think this – Crimea – will not be possible. In any case, what is their strategy for doing this, and is it in slight contrast to American objectives, which are to ensure that Ukraine is not defeated and that NATO does not get drawn into a direct conflict with Russia. The latter with the intended risk of escalation, and maybe even nuclear escalation.

There is a small danger that lack of consensus about the overall goal, let alone strategy might make post-war recovery more challenging. For example, the Russian bear …

And … what thought has been given to how we live with the Russian population afterwards? We should not, actually could not, contemplate anything along the lines of the Morgenthau Plan, which was a punitive policy to weaken Germany at the end of the Second World War by removing its manufacturing capabilities, particularly those associated with arms. It was designed by US Secretary of the Treasury Henry Morgenthau in 1944. In the event, it wasn't quite rejected so much as faded away. The point is that we must have a clear plan for helping the Russian population shake off the vestiges of Putinism.

SECOND, WHAT *WAYS* WERE CONSIDERED?

NATO, or rather the US president, agreed that Ukraine should be supported with technology, weaponry and munitions so they could manage the war on their own ... or at least with their own troops. A sort of proxy war. The Pentagon is heavily involved with advice and logistical support. But an important part of any modern conflict is airpower, and originally President Biden would not allow NATO aircraft to engage Russian aircraft over Ukraine. Neither would he allow Poland to contribute airpower. This has now changed, later revoked.

FINALLY, WHAT *MEANS* WERE PLANNED?

This is where the whole strategic edifice collapses. Once the West/ NATO realised that not only were the Ukrainians willing to fight, but they were fighting well, they decided that they would provide them with munitions and other help, such as intelligence. What seems to have happened is that the better Ukraine's armed forces did, the more and better munitions they received.

THERE'S A MAJOR CAVEAT ...

The West must not be lulled by Russia's failures into a false sense of security. Russia remains a powerful country with a strong sense of itself. They see their leader, whether dictator or elected president, as the legitimate heir to the mighty czars of the past.

Orlando Figes is a British historian and writer, and is known for his works on Russian history. His *A People's Tragedy* is an intriguing study of the Russian Revolution. He points out that, in Russian culture, this is a 'form of despotism and enslavement of society that goes from the Mongols to Stalin'. The Bolshevik Bukharin described Stalin as 'Genghis Khan with the telephone'. He goes on to say that the very word for power in Russian (vlast) comes not from action, as in Western languages, but from the term for a fiefdom, a territory owned by its ruler.

Putin is thought by the West as a pariah now, although there is little recognition of this outside the Western and European allies. Perhaps President Emmanuel Macron, of France, has a point in suggesting that we should not humiliate Putin, but engage with him, unsavoury as this might be. 'To Jaw-Jaw is better than to War-War', as Churchill didn't quite say, which in fact was, 'Meeting jaw to jaw is better than war'.

Russia still celebrates the triumph over the Nazi hordes between 1943 and 1945 in the Great Patriotic War, though the cost in human life may be unknown to most. But squeamishness over the butcher's bill has never been a Russian sentiment.

The essential Western support is of course reliant on continuing support from the West, particularly the US, and by happy coincidence, Joe Biden's support. It was particularly heartening to see him embrace Volodymyr Zelenskyy on the latest visit to Washington just before Christmas 2022.

The Russian Federation also has more nuclear weapons than anyone else, nearly 7,000 at the latest count, compared with the United States who have slightly fewer.

PARSIMONY OR SURGE?

Yes, Ukraine has continued to liberate Russian occupied territories. This has encouraged Washington and Brussels to continue to support Ukraine, but on the other hand Russia is digging in and, as any military person will know, an assault against entrenched positions can be very expensive in terms of blood and equipment. Yet the West, despite the enormous quantity of munitions already supplied to Ukraine, continues to be parsimonious. Perhaps that's too harsh a judgement, but the supplies, in terms of heavy weapons such as tanks, are not sufficient for Ukraine to 'finish the job'. Winston Churchill's plea to the Americans before they entered the war in 1941, is a fitting tribute to Ukraine:

'We shall not fail or falter; we shall not weaken or tire. Neither the sudden shock of battle, nor the long-drawn trials of vigilance and exertion will wear us down. Give us the tools, and we will finish the job.'

It's a stark contrast to the Iraq War troop 'surge' of 2007, where President George W Bush increased the number of US military combat troops in Iraq in an attempt to counter an insurgency and provide security for the local government.

Almost anybody with an interest in international affairs or war in general will be familiar with the Normandy campaign in 1944 (coincidentally enough, I am drafting this section on 6 June 2023, seventy-nine years after the original landings). A massed army of Allies, eventually 1.5 million strong, landed against a hostile shore in northern France, supported by thousands of ships and many aircraft. It was the largest mass movement of troops ever, and it's unlikely that it will ever be repeated. The reason for such scale was that the German armies in northern France were hard and experienced troops, and this was thought to be an appropriate resource. Even then, it was an horrendous battle, with more casualties than on the Somme in 1916, with nearly one quarter of a million casualties.

But supposing the Allies had said to General Eisenhower, 'Look, Ike, we have difficulty in getting enough resources for your invasion, so why don't you just see how you get on with a few divisions. If you are successful, we'll supply more but if not, will withdraw, regroup and think again...'

Such a position would have been complete and utter disaster, and set the end of the Second World War back by years.

It's a long stretch to see this as a parallel with what has happened in Ukraine: they've only received more munitions when they've been doing really well. Zelenskyy has repeatedly asked for more and better equipment. Indeed, at various stages, he has suggested that if he had had all he asked for earlier in the campaign, he could have chased the Russians out already.

THE 2023 VILNIUS SUMMIT

Such was the seriousness of the situation in Ukraine, that another conference was held in July 2023 in Vilnius, the capital of Lithuania.

The summit was largely dominated by Ukraine's ambition to join NATO. Although there were some reservations from America and Germany to offer a clear timetable, the members accepted that one day Ukraine would become a NATO member. This was reflected in recent announcements from Lloyd Austin, the US secretary of state for defence. Although unsurprising, this was the most notable outcome of Vilnius: Ukraine would eventually become a NATO member, with a caveat that could not happen while part of its territory was occupied by Russia. This sounds ideal, but, as of summer 2023, the emerging view that it is unlikely that Ukraine will recover all its occupied territory, so this caveat one represents something of a conundrum.

Apart from Ukraine's future membership of NATO, another important item on the agenda was the new plans for NATO that had been developed by the Supreme Allied Commander Europe (SACEUR) General Chris Cavoli, a graduate of Princeton and Yale, a fluent Russian speaker and considered to be one of the leading officers of his generation. These plans manifest themselves in three regional plans, for the north, centre and southern European NATO areas. There are also plans for space, cyber-operations and special forces.

The idea is that there is now clear guidance for every armed force in European NATO and North America about what to do should there be conflict. For a layperson, the only surprise here is that these did not exist in the first place! Under these new plans, NATO will have some 300,000 troops ready to deploy to its eastern flank within 30 days.

In a last-minute deal, Turkish President Erdogan agreed to Sweden joining NATO, Finland having already been accepted as a member. In fact, Sweden and NATO have been close partners for years, undertaking joint exercises. Sweden, with its long littoral on the Baltic, some of which is opposite Kaliningrad, the Russian exclave, has some submarine resources.

All Scandinavian countries are now members of NATO. Norway and Denmark members since NATO's inception in 1949. So all Scandinavian defence planning can now be integrated within the NATO framework.

What is emerging is that although America will go the distance in supporting Ukraine, they will be looking to the Europeans to help handle facilitate Ukraine's rebuilding of its economy. Also, the unspoken thought is that, with the United States preoccupation with China as a strategic competitor, Europeans, either through the EU or as a group, should look to their own security. The United States as such will always be there, and we might anticipate a difficult time transitioning from a US-led NATO to a European-led NATO, the latter of which might present some challenging problems.

THE NATO BUDGET

In The Economist for 24 November 2022, they suggested that President Joe Biden's Inflation Reduction Act, which involved $400 bn of handouts for energy, manufacturing and transport and included make-in-America provisions '...resembles the industrial policies that China has pursued for decades'. So much for free market liberalism. It was Europe, 'The Economist lamented, that still holds to its quaint insistence on upholding World Trade Organisation rules on free trade'. The Economist concluded that Europe looked like a sucker, but also that this subsidy spat exacerbated tensions between America and Europe.

Donald Trump insisted that each NATO member should contribute more to NATO. Most members of NATO have failed to meet the goal of spending 2 per cent of GDP on defence, the exceptions being, in order, Poland, the US, Greece, Estonia, Lithuania, Finland, Romania, Hungary, Latvia, the United Kingdom and the Slovak Republic. France sneaks in with just 1.9% as of mid 2024.

Though Donald Trump will run for president in 2024, it's is becoming increasingly clear that he may get elected. Whatever, his sentiments might persist, and a new US president might insist on NATO spending rising across-the-board to 2 per cent or more. An even bleaker scenario might be revival of the US pivot to the Asia-Pacific region. This might result in the US diverting its attention there instead Europe. Europe could do worse than usefully prepare itself for such a pivot.

16 THE FUTURE FOR NATO AND EUROPE'S VISION: SEVEN DIMENSIONS

At the risk of self-contradiction, in some ways NATO has performed well in the Ukraine crisis. The military arrangements, command, logistics, intelligence and an 'enhanced forward presence' have all worked well. But to what effect? Well, obviously to drive the Russians out of Ukraine. But that is only one part of the story. What is the overall *political* objective, the *ends*.

President Macron of France is derided for suggesting that Putin, and by implication Russia as a whole, should not be ridiculed, but he is right. Few other European leaders are providing Macron's strategic leadership. Most of all, there has to be a clear strategy to deter Russia from trying such actions again. And that must cover conventional arms deterrence as well as nuclear deterrence. Lloyd Austin's wish to see Russia 'weakened' may be a step too far and we must recognise that any treaties or agreements with the current Russian administration might be impossible to enforce.

But none of that is an excuse: the need for security for each and every European country – and recall that there are fifty of them in all – is paramount as well as the security of Europe as a whole. European governments, their leaders and diplomats must work hard to come up with workable solutions, those that can provide peace and security for all, including the Russians themselves.

There is little sign of that so far, but we have every hope that this will be addressed and implemented forthwith.

Following American leadership, although it took some months to happen, Europe has stepped up well to the challenge of supplying

Ukraine with munitions for them to resist the Russian onslaught. At some point in the future, the Russian-Ukrainian war will end, though it's almost impossible at this stage to guess what the settlement might look like. The danger is that, once that war is over, Europeans in general will relax and feel that they can continue with current policies on individual and group security. This would be a major step error. Most informed commentators say that any concessions to Putin will be 'banked', and then they will 'come again', whether in Georgia, Moldova, Armenia or even the Baltics. Recall that Finland lost some 10 per cent of its area during the 1940 Winter War against the Russians. (Even after eighty years, they would probably like it back.)

Whether Europe is defined as individual nation-states within the EU or outside, within NATO or outside, or members of both or neither, there needs to be considerably more focus on the security needs, individually and *of the whole*. Security is vital for every one of the fifty countries in Europe from their own point of view, and thus the security of the whole. Somebody, somewhere, be they an international statesperson a national leader or a functional head must recognise this – many do – but also provide leadership and herd the nation-states within Europe towards an integrated security policy. We suggest seven dimensions for this:

First, strategic autonomy: not in competition with the Americans, but congruent with them. This must be the overarching principle of Europe's approach to security, underwritten by the ability to act alone if necessary. Perhaps this is of most importance, should the Americans be distracted elsewhere.

Strategic autonomy refers to a nation's ability to shape its foreign policy, defence interests, economic strategies, technological development, and social provisions independently, without undue influence from international organisations. It doesn't imply complete isolation, but rather the capacity to prioritise national interests while considering others. It is to the credit of the European Union as a whole that they have managed to influence policies such as those regarding national debt, industrial subsidies and employment practices without the member nations sacrificing too much of their sovereignty.

The strategic autonomy concept is evolving slowly but steadily in the EU, within a changing global landscape marked by Brexit, the Trump presidency, BRIC's aspirations for influence and China's rise. The EU did demonstrate strategic autonomy during the COVID-19 pandemic, aligning with WHO guidance while asserting its overall sovereignty.

Challenges persist, such as media freedom issues in some member states, where the EU's response has been limited. Balancing this with traditional alliances, like the one with the United States, is the major challenge, especially as the US refocuses on China. Finding a strategic and political role in harmony with American interests should be a future pursuit.

Second, Europe must recognise its global context, must acknowledge its prominent role in wealth, governance, domestic and international law, technological development, foreign aid, and as an exemplar of democratic prosperity. It should serve as a testament to how formerly war-torn regions can come together in peace and prosperity, despite internal wealth disparities driven by democratic processes.

The European Union itself, does sees itself as having a global role. This involves the Common Foreign and Security Policy, trade and economy, diplomatic engagement and being an active participant in international organisations such as the United Nations, and the World Trade Organization. The EU is also committed to addressing climate change and promoting environmental sustainability.

The focus must now be more on security: there is still some way to go in defining and pursuing Europe's interests.

Third, and within the context of its global role and strategic autonomy, security must be paramount. Under the constitution, the European Union cannot participate in military operations, but in the case of Ukraine this has been neatly managed by arranging finance for the purchase of munitions.

Thus the relationship with NATO is vitally important. Europe looks to, and relies on, NATO for its security, and although NATO is conceived as a political/military alliance, it is largely focused on the military aspects of any threat.

In the context of the at least twenty non-contiguous threats to European security identified in *War in Context*, what role does NATO consider it has? It will have contingency plans to deal with any 'arc of insecurity' or the 'twenty non-contiguous threats'. Yet these plans will be for military deployment rather than political engagement. What the EU can contribute is a comprehensive political approach to these problems and work with NATO to solve the overall problem. It is this area that needs some improvement.

These are not casual questions. Some of the threats are only 'one country away' from a NATO member. Europe and NATO together need to recognise these security threats and generate contingency political and military plans. Without such plans it will be too late in the event of a real security threat; there would be no time for the British political establishment to argue about secession (Brexit), or the French to be suggesting conciliation ('don't humiliate Mr Putin') or the Germans to be reticent about doing anything at all ('not buying Russian gas might affect our industry'). Thankfully, Germany has now been successful in weaning itself off Russian gas, and is an ideal exemplar to other countries.

Thus, Fourth, the EU and NATO must work well together. The vision here must be that relationships between the EU, Europe in general and NATO represent something which is more than the sum of their respective parts. After all, the two organisations share a majority of members, have common values, and face similar threats and challenges.

The 'sum of the parts' would manifest itself in a common approach not only to defence and security issues, but also deterrence and post-conflict resolution. By that standard, they have come a long way since their respective inceptions.

In January 2023, their respective presidents signed the third Joint Declaration on EU-NATO Cooperation, further strengthening and expanding their strategic partnership. It was the third such joint declaration, the previous two being in 2016 in 2018. The official stance is that cooperation between the EU and NATO is an established norm and takes place within the key guiding principles of openness and transparency and with respect for different the decision-making processes. It is clearly the intent and belief that a strong EU and a strong NATO are mutually reinforcing. There have also been some institutional initiatives to enhance the relationship between the two organisations. The Berlin Plus Agreement of 1999, the European Security and Défense Policy itself, the Permanent Joint Council and the NATO-Russia Council and Partnership for Peace were all initiatives in his direction.

Inevitably, with two such distinct organisations, there have been some challenges in their relationship. There have been various sources for this, such as institutional and national rivalries, and disagreements about the scope and purpose of NATO-EU cooperation. Some of the challenges are essentially second order problems, such as overlap and duplication, mixed memberships, different decision-making processes and competing initiatives, all capable by being resolved by firm and consistent management.

Some are more serious and can detract from the 'sum of the parts'. NATO has a more autonomous decision-making process. There might be differing priorities: NATO's focus is on collective defence and military cooperation, while the EU looks to a broader range of security challenges, including crisis management, conflict prevention and civilian missions. Although these differences could lead to disagreements about resource allocation, if security is seen in the round, the two aspects should be complementary, and part of an overall vision and consequent strategies.

For example, NATO might rightly see that their priority is defeating Russia, facilitating Ukraine's success in their war. Although the EU/Europe might will agree with this in full measure, their attention might also be on how Europe as a whole lives with a Russian bear post-conflict.

Yet the NATO-EU partnership is largely tactical rather than strategic. The challenge of how Europe's defence capabilities as a whole can be developed without compromising the integrity of NATO, may yet need to be resolved.

The concept that Europe does the diplomatic and political work might sound attractive, but the difficulties of achieving this must be recognised. Straightforward though this might seem, this must be resolved. A major threat to Europe's security, and NATO itself on the horizon is the spectre of a new Trump presidency. Although America it is unlikely to leave the alliance, it is expected that their focus will shift more to China and the Pacific.

The bottom line is that Europe as a whole, the EU and NATO have, in diplomatic and political terms, little time to resolve this conundrum, and there are very few signs that the various governments are taking this seriously enough.

In terms of the population, wealth and technological base that Europe has, the objective should be that Europe, and 'NATO in Europe' should be much, much more than the sum of the parts, and as much an economic, political and security alliance as the United States or China, or as other major countries around the world such as India, Brazil and others several perhaps less to diverted by internal problems.

Fifth, the focus must be on deterrence: In June 2023, Professor Sir

Lawrence Freedman, introduced in other parts of this trilogy, wrote an article entitled: 'Salami Slicing, Boiled Frogs, and Russian Red Lines'. The concept was that although deterrence was the threat of retaliation against any overt military actions by another party, it was more likely that a hegemonic enemy would start salami slicing, that is carving off a bit of someone else's territory in the hope that other countries wouldn't notice, or thought that that particular bit of territory was unimportant.

When Hitler remilitarised the Rhineland in 1936, although it was against the Versailles Treaty, it was thought to be manageable and maybe even reasonable. When he then demanded justice for the Sudeten Germans, again it was seen as perhaps not reasonable, but manageable. We all know how that ended: he then took over the whole of Czechoslovakia, Austria and then eventually, he tried to take over the whole of Russia. It did not end well for any party.

Freedman quotes a 1986 BBC episode from *Yes, Prime Minister*, entitled 'The Grand Design', in which the Prime Minister's interlocutor suggesting that the enemy (well, Soviet Russia) would use 'salami tactics, slice by slice, one small piece at a time'. So, he asks, 'Will you press the button if they invade West Berlin?' The Prime Minister's response is classic: 'It all depends.' On what, we are never told, but the point is made. In the context of Russia's actions against Ukraine, the concept is clearly demonstrated, although Crimea was quite a big slice.

The concept of deterrence relies on an adversary's understanding that aggressive actions will prompt an armed response. Unfortunately for deterrence theory, this has been almost completely taken over by the idea of nuclear deterrence, even to the extent that conventional aggressive actions would be met with a nuclear response. This seems to go against some of the other criteria for considering deterrence such as proportionality.

Classic deterrence theory is that it should conform to the 'Three

Cs' model: Capability, Credibility and Communication. That is, first of all the body doing the deterring should be capable of carrying it out, similar to the credibility criterion. The importance is that you can't fool an enemy by having insufficient resources to carry out the threat. Intelligence, and even OSINT will reveal if you are nothing more than a paper tiger. Of course, the reverse is also true. If the other side are claiming they've got all sorts of resources which they haven't got. In the case of the Russian Federation, they obviously had the resources, but they weren't quite up to scratch. The final criterion, communication, is very important. It came to nothing when Russia took over Crimea, and nothing when the Russian Federation troops interfered in Donbass. Nul points for deterrence communication! Recall though, Freedman's concept about deterrence really being about boundaries, and 'good fences make good neighbours'.

Finally, salami slicing and boiled frogs can work the other way round. In a neat reversal, one can see Ukraine and its allies operating salami slicing themselves. Whereas there was a case for throwing NATO wholesale into defending Ukraine and ejecting the Russians, in fact the contributions, certainly before the allied Ramstein conference in January 2023, were more or less salami slices, none of which reached a Russian red line in the way that wholesale commitment of NATO might have done.

This shift in dynamics reflects the challenges and complexities of modern conflict and deterrence strategies. Welcome to the complex world of political/military strategy!

Deterrence must also recognise the naval dimension, sometimes avoided. This is the 'near waters maritime strategy', and to complete the picture, in March 2023:

'... the European Commission and the High Representative adopted a Joint

Communication on an enhanced EU Maritime Security Strategy to ensure a peaceful use of the seas and safeguard the maritime domain against new threats. They have also adopted an updated Action Plan through which the Strategy will be implemented...'

Whereas NATO's Alliance Maritime Strategy (AMS) is twelve years old and must be updated to better align with the Strategic Concept agreed last year.

Sixth, and, in the current circumstance, there must be more defence cooperation. This has been demonstrated in stark terms by the inability of European manufacture capacity to compensate for the appalling attrition during the Russian-Ukrainian war, despite the war bringing together European countries in ways that have rarely been seen since the seven alliances against Napoleon, possibly since the collapse of the Roman Empire. It is also the biggest challenge to European's capability to fight a major land war. Even though almost all European countries, EU or not, are planning to spend more on defence, Jens Stoltenberg, the NATO Secretary General now says that the oft-unmet 2 per cent of GDP spend on defence represents a minimum not a target. But there is a major – one might say overwhelming – problem. According to the European Defence Agency, in November 2021, under the heading 'The sorry state of European defence Corporation':

'In terms of defence spending, the positive trend seems to be accelerating, in line with announcements from the majority of Participating Member States. It remains to be seen whether PMS will follow a coordinated approach which would ensure greater efficiency and interoperability of armed forces and avoid further fragmentation.'

In short, Europe is spending more on defence but cooperating less.

One tragic aspect of this is that, despite three decades of political initiatives designed to improve European defence cooperation, things are getting worse on this front. Indeed, in a report by the 'Friends of Europe' (a Brussels-based, not-for-profit think tank for European Union policy analysis and debate) in June 2023, they assert, not surprisingly, and in the context of seeking a stronger and more resilient Europe, there are major constraints:

'... the innate short-termism of politicians who care most about the next election ...'

But also, horrendously,

'... ingrained resistance in national defence establishments to cross-border arms cooperation, longstanding rivalries among some of the continent's leading defence companies reluctant to share technology with each other and a propensity to trust the US more than fellow Europeans ...'

The numbers make stark reading: in a Centre for Strategic and International Studies (An American think tank based in Washington, conducting policy studies and strategic analyses of political, economic and security issues throughout the world) report of March 2023, they quote EU data, that:

'... both the total amount of cooperative spending and the number of cooperative initiatives have decreased significantly over the last decade. As of 2020, cooperative equipment spending fell to 11 percent of total defence spending, far short of the European Union's target of 35 percent and the lowest figure since EDA records began in 2005. The same trend applies to cooperative research and development (R&D) spending, which was 6 percent of overall R&D investment in 2020, far below the EDA's 20 percent target and another record low …'

The CSIS goes on to say that, and with no apology for using the word 'horrendously':

'… efforts to date have seen little progress or promise to overcome fragmentation … no improved coherence of the EU defence landscape has yet been observed … it remains to be seen whether PMS will follow a coordinated approach which would ensure greater efficiency and interoperability of armed forces, and avoid further fragmentation …'

And finally,

'… this indicates European nations favour spending on national or off-the-shelf equipment from non-EU countries over cooperation – especially equipment made in the United States …'

'… the result … is incoherence and capability gaps. Europe's military forces are not designed to fit together … a 2017 assessment showed EU militaries have 178 different types of weapon systems – 148 more than the United States, despite having half the budget …'

Forbes, in 2018 suggested that the EU has six times as many weapon systems in service as the US, comprising seventeen different types of main battle tank. By contrast, the US relies on just one tank – the M1 Abrams. It is similar through the entire range of weapon systems, with European militaries using twenty different types of IFV and twenty-seven different howitzers. The US relies on just two versions of each. All in all, the US has 30 major weapon systems while Europe has 178.

There is also a problem with the supply of ammunition. During the gung-ho but relatively simple military actions involving bombing Libya in 2011 – supposedly for humanitarian reasons – ammunitions shortfalls and a continued reliance on the United States for strategic capabilities were revealed. One is bound to wonder how European leaders (the culprits were the British Prime Minister David Cameron, and the French President Emmanuel Macron) could even consider resisting the Russian Federation when they can't even carry out a simple bombing raid on a war-torn country with a little in the way of a defence.

So: the supply of munitions to Ukraine was obviously in the right direction, though the accusation that there were *too few, too late* might still apply. The problem seems to be at every stage of the process: specifying the needs, design, development, testing, manufacture and deployment.

For the UK, in a House of Commons Committee report of July 2023 entitled *It is broke – and it's time to fix it: The UK's defence procurement system* (subtitled, rather hopefully, that *'the government has two months to respond'),* the committee concludes that:

'... the Ministry of Defence must finally admit, once and for all, that there is a real problem across UK defence procurement: the current system is indeed broken and multiple, successive reviews have not yet fixed it. With a major war now under way in Ukraine, now is the time to act ...'

Recall that this is well over a year since the Ukraine war started. RUSI is not so brutal: although the report represents a 'missed opportunity', They suggest that:

'Despite what the Committee says, the DE&S (Defence Equipment and

Support) is not broken, delivering well on three quarters of its highest value projects. But it does need improvement including increasing awareness of the needs of its UK suppliers if Government aspirations for operational independence are to be met (note that the Armed Forces needs are not mentioned here). *Overall, there is need for recognition ... huge variety of goods and services ... the most demanding purchases which involve extensive development work and advanced manufacturing techniques are extremely difficult and have multiple risks. There is likely more need for expectation management ...'*

So one might wonder how much funding RUSI get from the MOD.

This is pathetic and reflects the tragic British pathology of a continual or even continuous lowering of expectations; a very British trait since the end of the Second World War. It manifests itself in talk of 'declinism' or 'managed decline'. It is a toxic philosophy.

Many organisations around the world manage complex R&D, product design and testing, launch, manufacturing, maintenance and distribution competently and over the long term. Whether they are state, quasi-state, institutions or private companies, and even if they are variously constrained by politics, resources, management and skills shortages or budgets, aeroplanes fly, ships sail and massive, complex IT systems, together with the World Wide Web, actually work.

If this is really a problem with the MOD, this specific management issue must be addressed. They must avoid the usual response of governments and other public bodies to create yet another body to address the issue. For example 'delivery units', or 'nudge units' or other what are basically auditing bodies.

With apologies to the reader, and some slight scepticism about a *Private Eye*, quote, they suggest that:

'A major shortage of skills and experience in the MOD and in the arms industry is now hampering many significant military equipment programs. Three MoD projects were moved to a red (late, over budget) classification by the Infrastructure and Projects Authority (IPA: see above comment) *in its annual roundup of major government programmes.'*

Private Eye goes on to say that both Spear Cap 3 and the Brimstone air-to-ground missile are:

'... red rated because of challenges in resourcing sufficiently suitable qualified and experienced people across the programme and delivery teams and within the industry ...'

Recall: *Strategy is everything about the future.*

It's no good developing brilliant weapons systems if you can't manufacture them ...

It's no good if you can supply them but the operators don't have the skills to use them ...

R&D to battle space success is a long journey, and any glitch in the way it will ruin the whole system ...

In most fields of human activity, some delays and glitches may be expected and coped with ...

In the business of war, it could mean defeat and a waste of blood and treasure.

Seventh, security, whether seen through a deterrence, or a defence perspective, is expensive: Stoltenberg's assertion, mentioned above, that the oft-unmet 2 per cent of GDP spend on defence represents a minimum not a target. In fact this has been a major bone of contention for many years. It has been one of the main debates within NATO: how member states contribute financially to the alliance. The US has for some time argued that many European NATO members are not meeting their agreed-upon defence spending targets, which is set at the aforementioned 2 per cent of their respective GDPs.

This is seen this as an unfair burden on American taxpayers, who provide a significant portion – something like 70 per cent – of NATO's budget. A counterargument is that the 2 per cent target is arbitrary and that security contributions should be measured in a more comprehensive way, including capabilities, readiness and contributions to NATO missions.

Some European NATO members contend that the 2 per cent GDP spending target doesn't capture the full picture of their defence contributions. They emphasise their capabilities, such as troops and equipment they provide to NATO missions, as well as their role in regional security. They argue that a narrow focus on budget numbers overlooks their tangible contributions to NATO's effectiveness. As an example, the United Kingdom has the CASD (continuous at-sea deterrent) as a contribution to NATO, and Finland, a new NATO member, has an enormous amount of artillery on its border with Russia.

Putting NATO and the 2 per cent question to one side for a moment, defence spending is one of the great conundrums of modern times.

There *appeared* to be few concerns in terms of security within Europe between the fourteen years between collapse of the Soviet Union (1989 to 1991) and Putin's occupation of Crimea. There was an accompanying 'peace dividend' and great – rather too much as it turned out – rejoicing, with a reduction in the number of troops (sailors, aviators) and thereby budget.

Successful deterrence, whether nuclear or not, would mean that the Armed Forces would never need to engage in a full-on war but … it's very expensive. Even 2 per cent might not be enough. The greatest imaginable caveat is that, if war was inevitable, one can't magic up an effective army, navy or air force overnight. You need to spend the money now, and consistently into the future. Apart from the technology, which would have to keep up with, and go beyond, the enemy's; apart from the considerable manufacturing capability that would be required, training and developing personnel might take even longer.

As we are experiencing now, there will always be seemingly irresistible demands on the public purse. As any experienced politician would say, 'There's no votes in defence.'

'What price security?' is, as we say, one of the great conundrums of modern times. Given the issues of provisioning, manufacturing capability and management, there is no numerical answer. What we can say is that with the security threats we can see now, 2 per cent is nowhere near enough. Poland, contiguous of course with Ukraine and Belarus, has already announced that it will be spending 4 per cent on its defence capabilities from now on.

Finally, the one of the biggest dangers to European security, especially with other calls such as housing, social provision, R&D and, perhaps most of all, the green economy, is governments' parsimony in terms of resources.

Governments in general, and particularly in the UK, need to get over their reluctance to increase taxes. This represents a major challenge to the whole idea of security.

There is also compassion fatigue. With regards to Ukraine, people in many European may feel that that they have 'done enough' to save Ukraine, and support may ebb away. It remains a major political challenge to persuade the European population that Russia is not going away, and will, for the foreseeable future, represent a very 'clear and present' security threat. A similar sentiment applies to security and defence as a whole. There are many more threats to Europe's security than just Russia.

As part of this, organisation and governance must not be neglected: In terms of vision, this aspect is largely ignored. At first sight, it looks as if there are too many separate bodies all with overlapping roles and powers to make any progress. It's almost impossible to make any judgement on that. But, looking at who is part of what, and the complex decision-making procedures for the EU, and with particular reference to making decisions about security and defence, this represents both a very long-term (strategic) and very short-term (tactical) problem.

In short, and rather obviously, long-term strategic visions might be difficult to achieve because of short-term political considerations. On the other political organisations, particularly if they are working in alliance with other political organisations will find it very difficult to make tactical decisions in terms of defence and security.

Yet Europe is still beset by major and minor spats between various countries, divergence from democratic norms by others, and obsession with consumer goods and some long memories of previous conflicts. Let's not beat around the bush: Europe as individual countries, and as a whole, needs to resolve these issues as part of a journey to a more secure, peaceful and lasting settlement. Otherwise, the future will look bleak.

There may be something of a gap between aspiration and *actualité*, and the EU has made great, although slow, progress over the past few years, but there must be consistent focus on organisation and governance, and a willingness to modify this in the light of new challenges.

These seven coordinates may be seen through a geographic lens, an institutional lens such as the EU or the OSCE. But the security and the search for a lasting peace is every country's responsibility – to its citizens and to its near and far European neighbours. It was as recently as 1979 that Soviet Russia ran a top-secret military simulation exercise by the Warsaw Pact that depicted the Soviet Bloc's advance to the Rhine, for which purpose the Warsaw troops would have had to cross several

European countries, some of them two or three countries away from the then-existing Soviet border. The terrifying thing about this was the title of the exercise: *Seven Days to the River Rhine.*

Not even enough time to mobilise European troops, of course there would've been some warning of it, and certainly not enough time to gear up production for the incredible amount of munitions countering this would need.

EUROPE, NATO AND SECURITY: CONCLUSIONS

Europe, if we accept the 'cradle of civilisation' story for a moment, cannot defend itself against even a modest military threat. Its sons and daughters, 'huddled masses yearning to breathe free', crossed the Atlantic and forged a new nation – a Republic – which can defend against most external threats. Now, the Europeans with a similar aggregate GDP, have to rely on them for help. No wonder the Americans call European wars 'civil wars'. It borders on the pitiful.

In the aftermath of the Crimea, Donbas, and the Russian invasion of Ukraine in 2022, Europe found itself facing profound security challenges and vulnerabilities. It became evident that Europe's response was marked by a lack of preparedness, intelligence, and contingency planning. The rapid American intervention and the mobilisation of NATO prevented what could have been a dire occupation of Ukraine and massive human suffering.

Most discussions on addressing these issues revolve around tactical solutions, emphasising factors like military spending, air power, US involvement in NATO, logistics, strategic autonomy and resilience.

However, the real requirement lies in shaping a comprehensive *vision* for Europe's security. Such a vision must acknowledge the genuine threats on the eastern flank, consider the possibility of integrating Russia into European security structures, and, if that's not feasible, ensure robust deterrence capabilities.

A European comprehensive vision for security should encompass seven key dimensions: strategic autonomy, global awareness, prioritising security, seamless EU-NATO cooperation, deterrence as a primary function, much increased defence collaboration, and recognising the financial investments necessary for security. Organisation and governance should not be overlooked.

Strategy, of course, is crucial, and although ultimate ends may not be achieved, a well-defined vision provides overall direction. It's akin to climbing a mountain; you may not see the summit, but moving upward is the way to reach it. Europe, whether geographically, within the European Union, or the broader European Community, must unite behind a vision encompassing both political and military dimensions. This vision should address not only Russia's pariah status but also hold open the hope of welcoming Russia into the international community someday.

Relationships with NATO must be improved in every dimension. In the end, Europe as a whole must chart a path forward that ensures lasting peace and security and cultivates improved relations with the Russian people after the war, and even amid the complexities of geopolitics and security.

Consensus is the key, even the *sine qua non* of this venture. The alternatives: poor relations relationships with Russia, spats amongst European countries and a withdrawal of American support for NATO – however gradual – are the awful alternatives.

ADDENDUM

CONTAINING THE SOVIET UNION: THE TRUMAN DOCTRINE

The Truman Doctrine (announced in March 1947) promised support for 'democracies against authoritarian threats', a consequence of wishing to contain Soviet geopolitical expansion during the Cold War.

Over the next twenty years, deterrence theory, or more particularly nuclear deterrence theory, was developed on the basis of MAD (Mutual Assured Destruction), and that in turn was based on second strike capability. This is explained in detail in *About War* and *War in Context*.

The point is that it doesn't look as if American/Western/NATO thinking has moved very much beyond this. Although this may be an entirely appropriate response to the Russian bear, we still wish to 'contain' the threat and to deter Russia, although that does not seem to have worked very well with this war. The West should never make the mistake of assuming rationality in opponents. It made no sense for Putin to invade Ukraine. But that did not stop him.

Whatever the present outcome, Russia, a nuclear power, remains the largest country by land area in the world, and with considerable natural resources. Russia is bitter about their loss of empire and status. James Nixey, the Russian expert at Chatham House, argues that we must learn to live without Russia. That they have no interest in consensus and respect no agreement. If we no longer sit at tables with them, like the G8, and accept that we should not, we must adopt a consistent policy of *defensive quarantine*.

Part Four: The Future for Nuclear Weapons

17 NUCLEAR WEAPONS: PROVENANCE, (NON)-USE AND FUTURE USE

War is a paradox. Intelligent, cultured men and women with home lives and family send young men and women to kill each other, or send appallingly destructive missiles, bombs and shells to kill others, sometimes for no other reason than their own political future and a misguided idea of 'honour'. As Simon Tisdall puts brilliantly it in *The Guardian* for 14 October 2023, just after the Hamas attack on Israel:

'Old men start wars. Young men and women fight them. It's a phenomenon that has broadly held true throughout history. Now, once again, in today's violence-wracked Middle East, the aggressive blundering of angry old men rains curses on the young, twisting minds, blighting lives, imperilling futures … such men, in thrall to worn-out ideologies and prejudices, hold leadership positions by reason of longevity and guile, not wisdom or sense. They rule by fear and division, abuse the tenets of their faith and poison the minds of children. The young pay the price …'

Much the same could be said of Putin's invasion of Ukraine: Russian casualties now amount to about 300,000 Russian troops with somewhere between 50,000 and 190,000 permanently disabled or dead.

This much we know, but war is also a conundrum: what is to be done about it? What *can* we do about it? And that conundrum is even more critical when it comes to nuclear weapons. Can we undo the nuclear world?

This chapter looks specifically at the future of nuclear weapons, before considering the larger question: the future of war, particularly after Ukraine, in the next chapter. We also attempt to answer some of the questions that arise from studying the first nuclear age.

THE WORLD DISCOVERS NUCLEAR WEAPONS

At the dawn of the 20th century, the world was controlled by eight main empires: the British, Russian, French, German, Austro-Hungarian, Ottoman, Japanese and American. Almost all were established or expanded by a combination of diplomatic and trade manoeuvring, but the main factor was military power. The most extensive was the British Empire, controlling some 23 per cent of the world's population and 24 per cent of the total area.

By the end of the 20th century, all but two (American and Russian) had collapsed. A caveat would be that the Americans would never admit to being an imperial power and Russia had lost and then regained some of its western provinces.

America, a republic, had remained so; Russia had experienced seventy-four years of a corrupt and oppressive form of socialism – communism. (Marx would have been horrified.)

As is well known, there were dozens of wars during the 20th century but two obviously stand out. The causes of the First World War have been debated since the end of that conflict, but the consensus is emerging that the Germans were largely to blame, and in particularly Kaiser Wilhelm II ('Kaiser Bill').

The causes of the Second World War were clearer: Hitler claimed that the settlement imposed on Germany at the end of the First World War, including the Treaty of Versailles and Woodrow Wilson's 14 points, were too harsh. This was largely to shift blame away from the German military leadership, which he knew would be essential to achieve his megalomaniac plans. Another cause, of course, was his perceived need for living space – *Lebensraum*. All this set him on his path to war, by which he needed to 'prove' the superiority of the German race.

The Second World War was the most extensive and expensive in terms of blood and the most damaging war in the history of mankind, with some estimates of between 50 and 70 million dead.

It was essentially an imperial war: Hitler wanted Germany to have an empire by neutralising France and extending Germany into Russia. It should be noted here that although the British, French and to a certain extent German, pre-First World War Empires were essentially global, Hitler's concept was for a contiguous empire.

But the age of empires was over and at the end of that conflict, only two, American and Russian, had survived or were on their last legs. The British Empire staggered on for twenty-odd years, longer in the minds of some right-wing politicians. France found it difficult to abandon its North African Empire, even though the largest country, Algeria, had been officially a *départment* of France. At the dawn of the 21st century, France was still trying to come to terms with this 'loss'.

The Russian Empire, under the oppressive Soviet system, lasted until 1991, and for a brief turbulent period looked as if it might become a 'liberal' free-market democracy. Alas, Vladimir Putin had different ideas and although some of the Russian population enjoyed and still enjoy the pleasures of consumer goods, many have not seen their living conditions improve. Putin's dictatorial regime is arguably worse than the Soviet system.

All this is relevant to our consideration of the future of nuclear weapons. Currently, there are now just nine nuclear armed states in the world. The United States, the United Kingdom, France, China, and the Russian Federation are members of the United Nations Security Council. The others are India, Pakistan, North Korea and Israel, who do not admit to having nuclear weapons.

Although some 85 per cent of current wars around the world are civil wars, rebellions or insurrections, major state-on-state conflict may just involve United States/Russia, United States/China, North Korea and the rest of the world, India/Pakistan or Israel/Iran. The United States and Great Britain operate within NATO, but France remains outside NATO in terms of nuclear weapons deployment.

The final section of Part Four looks at the future for nuclear weapons; the final chapter covers the future for war – as a political act – from the point of view of both nuclear and conventional weapons.

THE START OF THE NUCLEAR WORLD

The test detonation of the first atomic bomb at Alamogordo, New Mexico, was on 16 July 1945, codenamed 'Trinity'. This date is often quoted as the start of the nuclear age, although some commentators nominate the date of first offensive use of the atom bomb, dropped on Hiroshima on 11 August 1945. Whenever, the nuclear age since 1945 divides conveniently into three phases:

The *first* period was from the Hiroshima bomb – or Alamogordo – to the end of the stand-off between the United States and Soviet Russia at the end of the 1980s and the collapse of the Soviet Union.

The *second* period was that brief, thirty-one-year period between the demise of the Soviet Union and Russian President Vladimir Putin breaking the 'nuclear taboo' (see below) on the occasion of his invasion of Ukraine in February 2022. Recall that his original threat on this occasion to was not to use a nuclear weapon in Ukraine, but to use it against any country or alliance who might support Ukraine. His particular antipathy is of course NATO as a whole, closely followed by the United States and the United Kingdom.

We are now in the *third* nuclear age, characterised by anxieties, fears even, about the Russian Federation's seeming willingness to use a nuclear device to achieve their goals, about proliferation of nuclear weapons in general and about nuclear material being acquired by either terrorist groups or one side in a civil war. The last two maybe coincident.

THE FIRST NUCLEAR AGE

In considering the nuclear age, we might equally say that it all started at the turn of the century. In 1905, the most famous postal clerk in history, Albert Einstein, established the equivalence of mass and energy. Perhaps the most well-known equation ever is $E = mc^2$. Since c, the speed of light, is a very large number, c^2 is massive. Thus, the conversion of even a small amount of nuclear material into energy, as in a nuclear bomb, releases a vast amount of energy. Modern thermonuclear bombs only convert a small part of their mass into released energy.

In 1919, Ernest Rutherford, a New Zealand physicist, became Director of the Cavendish Laboratory at the University of Cambridge. There, the neutron was discovered by James Chadwick, an English physicist, in 1932. He was awarded the 1935 Nobel Prize in Physics for this discovery. Also in 1932, the first controlled experiment to split the nucleus was performed by John Cockcroft and Ernest Walton, working under Chadwick's direction.

In 1934, Enrico Fermi, an American nationalised Italian, *nearly* discovered nuclear fission while bombarding uranium with neutrons. The sample was wrapped in aluminium foil, preventing him from detecting the splitting of the atom.

In 1938, German physicists Otto Hahn and Fritz Strassmann had discovered nuclear fission, but it was not until 1942, as part of the Manhattan Project, that the first controlled nuclear fission reaction was demonstrated in a basement in Chicago, using apparatus designed by Chadwick. This is shown in the film *Oppenheimer*.

Against the background of this atomic research, Albert Einstein wrote to President Roosevelt in 1939, that: 'this new phenomenon would also lead to the construction of bombs, and it is conceivable – though much less certain – that extremely powerful bombs of a new type may thus be constructed.' Einstein went on to say that 'a single bomb of this nature might well (for example) destroy a whole port and some of the surrounding territory'.

This was the start of the whole nuclear story. In response to this, and the outbreak of war, FDR established the advisory committee on uranium led by Lyman Briggs (an American engineer, physicist and administrator).

Chadwick went on to write the final draft of the MAUD Report in 1941, which went some way to inspire the US government to begin serious atom bomb research efforts. Chadwick was the head of the British team that worked on the Manhattan Project and was knighted for his contribution.

All this, of course, was before the United States entered the war on 8 December 1941, with the declaration of war against Japan. Then, on 11 December 1941, Germany declared war on the United States, possibly one of the biggest mistakes of the 20th century.

The United States saw Hiroshima as a way of bringing the Second World War in the east to a conclusion. It was the first offensive use of the atomic bomb. They then dropped a second atom bomb on the city of Nagasaki on 9 August 1945. The Hiroshima bomb, 'Little Boy', was an enriched uranium gun-type fission weapon with a yield of between 13 and 15 kilotons (15,000 tons of TNT). 'Fat Man', the Nagasaki bomb, was a plutonium implosion-type nuclear weapon, with a yield of about 21 kilotons (21,000 tons of TNT). After some constitutional agonies surrounding his status, Emperor Hirohito announced the unconditional surrender on 15 August 1945.

POLITICAL IMPLICATIONS

This book emphasises that war, a political act, is separate from *warfare*: the practice of armed conflict on the battlefield. As such, programmes such as The Changing Character of War at Oxford University tend to focus largely on warfare, whilst admitting that war itself as the political act has an enduring meaning.

Warfare has changed dramatically since the end of the Second World War and the advent of the nuclear age, primarily in two ways. First, the machinery of warfare is much changed, with, for example, satellite surveillance, electronic sensors, more powerful and directed munitions, and also faster and more potent aircraft and drones. The full list would be extensive. Second, there has been a radical development of doctrine, which is how warfare is conducted in particular circumstances. This is particularly the case with NATO forces, who now operate together in a different and improved way.

But – and it's a very large but – we cannot talk about the way that nuclear warfare has changed, because there has not been any war based on nuclear weapons.

Would that we could say the same about the approach to the political side of war. The main antagonists, the United States and Russia, are still at odds, and although nuclear stockpiles decreased dramatically on both sides at the end of the Soviet period, they are still enough to ruin the world completely, and those stocks are now being built up again.

These three phases of the nuclear age and the differences between them, cannot be contemplated without understanding their provenance. That is, going back to original decisions, both by the Americans and Soviet Russia in the early stages of the post-war period and the Cold War.

The Americans' attitude to nuclear weapons, their use and proliferation were governed, and to a large extent are still governed, by their attitude toward Soviet Russia in the period immediately after the Second World War and the start of the Cold War. This was despite the enormous amount of help that the Americans had given the Russians in fighting the Germans on the Eastern front (the Western front to the Russians). All in all, and at current prices, the Americans contributed something like $110 billion of aid to the Russians. It could even be said that the Second World War was won with American resources and Russian lives.

In retrospect, the Cold War seems puzzling to the layperson: here were two world powers who had managed to counter one of the biggest threats to civilisation the world had seen to date. Both had managed an unbelievable gearing up of their industrial resources, and with their relative geographic sizes and populations, it might be thought that they could have conceived of living in peace.

It was not to be. After listening to one of Stalin's speeches, George Kennan, a US diplomat in Moscow, sent, in February 1946, the now famous 'Long Telegram'. In it, Kennan emphasised that the Soviet Union did not see the possibility for long-term peaceful coexistence with the capitalist world.

A year later, Kennan published an article in the prestigious journal *Foreign Affairs* as 'X', clarifying his original analysis.

The attitudes and strategies suggested by these two documents formed the basis of America's approach to the Soviet Union for the rest of the Cold War. It found its articulation in Truman's policy of 'containment'. There were three elements to this:

1 Henceforth, the United States would provide political, economic, and military assistance to any nation under the threat of communism. In the immediate aftermath of the Second World War, both France and Italy were in danger of communist takeovers.

For Harry Truman, however, the initial focus was on providing aid to Greece and Turkey to prevent communist takeovers in those countries.

2 The Marshall Plan (1948) was named after George Catlett Marshall, the then US Secretary of State. Marshall, one of the great unsung heroes of the Second World War (his biography is called, rather modestly, *Organiser of Victory*). He did not concern himself too much with the details of it and the moot point was whether it was his initiative or Truman's. The Marshall Plan was also known as the European Recovery Plan, and provided economic aid to Western European countries to help them rebuild their economies. The United States aimed to prevent economic instability that could potentially lead to the spread of communism. Strange to relate in retrospect, Stalin was also offered participation in the master plan but refused, thinking it would draw some of his independent republics into the Western sphere of influence.

3 NATO was formed in 1949, and the United States played a key role in its establishment, as did Clement Attlee, the UK prime minister at the time. The alliance was seen as collectively deterring aggression by the Soviet Union.

There were also provisions about containment in Asia. The United States provided support to anti-communist forces during the Chinese Civil War (to 1949) and later the Korean War (1950–1953) to prevent the spread of communism on the Korean Peninsula, followed by the Vietnam War; each claimed nearly 50,000 American servicemen's lives.

Truman believed that the spread of communism posed a threat to democracy and international stability, and this policy of containment was the foundation of US foreign policy during the Cold War. Rather obviously, then, America's attitude to nuclear weapons was based on the mutual antipathy between the United States and Soviet Russia. This antipathy lasts to this day, three quarters of a century after they cooperated in defeating Nazi Germany during the Second World War.

Project Solarium is covered in detail in *War in Context*; the main output being National Security Council memorandum 162/2 which called for the containment of Soviet Russia and firmness. This largely confirmed Truman's doctrine. There was also an emphasis on deterrence and a suggested balancing of diplomacy and force. Thereafter, the United States would explore opportunities for diplomatic engagement, particularly in areas where they could pursue negotiations with the Soviets with a view to reducing weapons stocks.

Although diplomatic contact continued, no US president then met any Soviet leader until after Stalin's death. President Eisenhower met Khrushchev and Bulganin in Switzerland in 1955. The summit was intended to reduce Cold War tensions and discuss trade policy, the nuclear arms race and, reference the current Ukrainian war, German reunification and a Western refusal to withdraw West Germany from NATO.

During this time, and up to and including the Cuban Missile Crisis, there were some military leaders oriented towards what they saw as 'victory', who advocated a pre-emptive strike on Soviet Russia's nuclear resources. In the transcripts of one committee meeting about Cuba, one General suggested this. Kennedy is recorded as making the rather cool response of, 'Thank you, General'. Pre-emptive strikes are perhaps the most tricky military moves to pull off successfully. See panel.

There is thus a clear vector between:

Americans' antipathy to anything that looks like socialism, particularly communism: this runs deep, despite social support for food, housing and a disability benefit; despite defence welfare where enormous federal defence spending supports workers who might otherwise be unemployed; despite considerable federal spending on supporting industry and workers. There are assertions such as 'better dead than red' or 'better to die on your feet then to live on your knees'. Much of this is of course performative, as it is with most anti-statist commentators, who would be the first to complain if the state, local or federal, were to withdraw their support on any front.

The House Unamerican Activities Committee (HUAC) and domestic anti-communism: HUAC's role was to investigate and expose communist activities and organisations in the United States. During its early years it targeted individuals and groups it believed had ties to communism. During the post-Second World War era and the Cold War, HUAC shifted its focus to exposing communist infiltration in the entertainment industry, leading to the blacklisting of many individuals in Hollywood. Retrospectively, it is not thought to have been contributed very much to American freedom and democracy.

HUAC's anti-communist investigations are often associated with 'McCarthyism', after US Senator, Joseph McCarthy. In reality, they had no direct involvement with HUAC, which was a House of Representatives committee. For reference, McCarthy was the chairman of the Government Operations Committee and its Permanent Subcommittee on Investigations of the US Senate.

Truman's Policy of Containment: popular at the time, and with an enduring legacy.

For all the efforts of HUAC, the policy of containment, counter-espionage and nuclear secrecy, it was inevitable that the Soviet Union would, in the words of the time 'acquire the bomb'. The first Soviet atomic bomb was tested in August 1949, and they achieve nuclear parity with the United States by the early 1960s.

After a brief flirtation with 'massive retaliation', and Soviet nuclear parity, **deterrence** became the main theme of foreign policy with regard to Russia.

THE START OF NUCLEAR NEGOTIATIONS

Following the successful US test of an atomic bomb, the Trinity test, at Alamogordo, New Mexico, in July 1945, the Potsdam Conference, 17th July–2nd August 1945, followed, and brought together the leaders of the United States (Truman), the Soviet Union (Stalin) and the United Kingdom (Churchill) to discuss the post-Second World War order and the administration of post-war Germany. This was *before* the first use of an atomic bomb in war in August 1945 at Hiroshima.

During a private meeting, Truman informed Stalin of this test, although Stalin had already heard about it from his own sources. This announcement of the Trinity nuclear test was an important moment. It was the first time that the Soviet leadership was officially informed about the existence and successful testing of atomic weapons. It is reasonable to assume that this influenced Stalin's approach to the negotiations. The jibe that Stalin and Churchill had 'pored over a map and divided up Europe' – sometimes with a blunt pencil – was, and remains a constant grievance of eastern European countries and some parts of the Middle East. In Churchill's defence, there was no way that the British Armed Forces could have taken on the Russians and it's doubtful whether the Americans would have helped; they thought they had done enough, and they would have vetoed that idea.

Atomic weapons had far-reaching implications for the post-war order and the balance of power between United States and the Soviet

Union. It was the start of a nuclear arms race.

The United Nations was set up in 1945. In 1946, the UN established the United Nations Atomic Energy Commission (AEC), making recommendations on how to prevent the use of atomic energy for destructive purposes. Although the AEC made a significant contribution, it did not achieve its original objectives.

In the same year, the US presented the Baruch Plan to the UN for international control of atomic energy and the elimination of nuclear weapons, but this was vetoed by the Soviet Union. However, in the same year, the first substantive US–Soviet talks took place in Washington. The talks were largely about post-war issues but also the future of atomic weapons. These early talks did not lead to any important agreements.

Negotiations over nuclear treaties continued more or less continuously throughout the Cold War, such as the Strategic Arms Limitation Talks (SALT) in the 1970s and the Intermediate-Range Nuclear Forces (INF) Treaty in the 1980s. (See the appendix of *War in Context* for a more comprehensive list of nuclear treaties.)

The whole process collapsed under presidents Trump and Putin. For example, the new Strategic Arms Reduction Treaty (START II), the successor to the original START I treaty, was signed in April 2010 by President Barack Obama and President Dmitry Medvedev of Russia. It entered into force in February 2011.

This was to expire in February 2021 unless both parties agreed to extend it for 'up to' five years. Discussions about extending the treaty were held during the Trump administration, and President Putin expressed interest in extending it. However, Trump dismissed this on the basis that it was a 'bad' treaty – largely because it had been negotiated by President Obama. Fortunately, there was a change of US president, and shortly after taking office, President Biden agreed with President Putin to extend the new START treaty for five years, and this was announced at the end of January 2021.

President Trump's repudiation of the 'Joint Comprehensive Plan of Action', known as the 'Iran deal', in May 2018 had many consequences for international relations, particularly on relations with between the US and President Putin of the Russian Federation. Trump's Iran decision potentially positioned Russia as a mediator and partner to Iran, enhancing Russia's influence in the Middle East. The withdrawal from the JCPOA was part of a broader trend under the Trump administration to distance the US from international agreements.

Arms control discussions were badly affected: this uncertainty would have been a concern for Russia, which values strategic arms limitations with the US as a means of maintaining its 'great power' status.

The point here is not so much whether there is any treaty in place, but whether there is a good relationship between the negotiating parties. Whatever that relationship is between presidents, the teams of diplomats and officials typically get to know each other and are able to discern and understand the other party's postures and plans. This is no longer the case, making the world a more dangerous place.

THE SECOND PHASE OF THE NUCLEAR AGE

This was that brief, thirty-one-year period between the demise of the Soviet Union and Russian President Vladimir Putin breaking the 'nuclear taboo' (see below) on the occasion of his invasion of Ukraine in February 2022. In retrospect, we might consider the second phase of the nuclear age to have started at the Gorbachev/Reagan summit and ended with Vladimir Putin's accession to president in 2012, just twenty years after the inauguration of the Russian Federation, or even in 1999 when Putin became Prime Minister, just eight years later. This was a time of great optimism and positive contact between the two great powers.

The Gorbachev/Reagan summit, the Reykjavík meeting, had been held on 11–12 October 1986, between the Soviet leader Mikhail Gorbachev and US President Ronald Reagan. It was an important meeting during the concluding years of the Cold War. No formal agreements were reached, but there were some tangible developments. (Some wag suggested that one of the constraints to the meeting was that neither side had thought to bring a photocopier – for the want of a nail, the battle was lost – but in this case, it was not significant.)

The two leaders discussed nuclear arms reduction and various categories of nuclear forces and significant progress was made in the negotiations on The Strategic Arms Reduction Treaty (START). Gorbachev proposed that both sides eliminate all their intermediate-range nuclear missiles in Europe, and this provided a foundation for the later Intermediate-Range Nuclear Forces Treaty (INF Treaty), signed in 1987. The Treaty faced many challenges, such as alleged Russian non-compliance and both sides suspending the treaty. Tragically, it ultimately collapsed and is now moribund.

Reagan refused to drop his SDI, the Strategy Defence Initiative or 'Star Wars' as it was called at the time. The Star Wars programme subsequently faced technical challenges and political controversy and eventually mutated into a general missile defence system.

Reykjavík did not result in a comprehensive arms control agreement – perhaps that was too much to expect – but it was a momentous moment in US–Soviet relations. It may or may not have eventually led to the end of the Cold War. Perhaps the most significant progress outcome from the meeting was that the relationship between the two leaders improved, something that cannot be said under the presidency of recent Russian leaders.

There were also momentous changes in the geopolitical landscape. East and West Germany were soon reunited, and agreement was reached with the Russian leadership that the new Germany should be a member of NATO. This is one of Putin's major gripes, as he sees NATO, which he loathes, creeping up to Russia's borders.

In all, thirteen supposedly independent Soviet republics became sovereign states, and were recognised internationally as such (see Appendix E).

There were Soviet nuclear weapons located in Ukraine, and the new independent Ukrainian state was persuaded to give these up and they were repatriated to the Russian Federation in return for security guarantees. In retrospect this may have been a bad idea! Other important changes included the proliferation of nuclear capability: India had developed a nuclear bomb in 1974, Pakistan became a nuclear power in 1998, North Korea in 2006. New deterrence strategies were required as the world shifted from a bipolar world to a multipolar world.

Nuclear terrorism became more of a latent threat. The concern about rogue non-state actors acquiring, assembling and delivering nuclear weapons became a major global security challenge. While it is difficult for a non-state actor to assemble a bomb, there is still a danger of a terrorist group dispersing radioactive material over a wide area and causing a panic among the civilian population.

Despite this, it was a time of great hope for reconciliation and peace between east and west.

The second phase of the nuclear age saw a range of aspirations and diplomatic initiatives aimed at reconciliation and better relations between Russia and Western countries, particularly the United States and its NATO allies.

The most notable was previously mentioned (START 1), signed in 1991, which came into force on 4 December 1994. This bilateral treaty between the United States and the Soviet Union was the first significant reduction in the number of strategic nuclear weapons in both the US and the Soviet stockpiles. The treaty barred its signatories from deploying more than 6,000 nuclear warheads and a total of 1,600 ICBMs and bombers.

There followed non-nuclear problems almost immediately: there were territory disputes involving Russia and Azerbaijan, Moldova, Georgia, Lithuania, Estonia, Belarus, Ukraine, Kazakhstan and Armenia. All were ex-Soviet republics. In no case did the dispute improve peaceful relations. Poland was a 'socialist ally' in the Warsaw Pact, and Syria completely separate.

Nevertheless, in 1994, Russia joined the Partnership for Peace programme and, in May 1997, the NATO–Russia Founding Act (NRFA) was signed at the NATO Summit in France, enabling the creation of the NATO–Russia Permanent Joint Council (NRPJC), replaced by the NATO–Russia Council (NRC). The West, led by the United States, had its own agenda:

NATO expanded eastward into former Warsaw Pact countries and eventually the Baltic states. This raised concerns in Russia, who saw NATO enlargement as a security threat. There were also other western involvements in Kosovo and the 'colour revolutions' in former Soviet states, e.g. Ukraine and Georgia, seen – or at least portrayed – by Moscow as Western interference.

In 2014, the Russian Federation appropriated Crimea, claiming that it had always been Russian – part of Novorossiya. Relations between East and West deteriorated to a point where it was sometimes described as at its worst since the Cold War. Overall, the dynamics led to deteriorating trust and a return to a more confrontational stance.

ADDENDUM

PRE-EMPTIVE STRIKES

A pre-emptive strike is military action taken by one party in an actual or potential conflict in anticipation of an imminent or immanent threat or attack by an adversary. The classic example is the Japanese attack on the American naval base at Pearl Harbor on 7th December 1941. Other examples might be Drake's attack on Cadiz in 1587 – the year before the Armada – or the Argentinian attack on the Falkland Islands in April 1982, to pre-emp the culmination of many years of negotiation, which the Argentinians felt would only confirm the status quo which was that the islands belonged to Great Britain. Another example would be Israel launching a pre-emptive strike against Egypt, Syria, and Jordan in the belief that they were jointly planning an attack on the Israeli homeland. This was the 1967 Six-Day War. A contrary example is where the Western allies failed to counter Hitler's remilitarisation of the Rhineland in 1936. Might that have dissuaded Hitler from launching his attack on France in 1940, or even his attack on Russia in 1941?

The main aim of any pre-emptive strike is to deter an adversary from launching their own attack or to drastically reduce the adversary's capabilities. This could prevent them from obstructing the attacker's future plans. The key features are surprise, a belief that the other party has malign intent, and that the attack will in itself reduce the adversary's capabilities to a significant degree.

Tactically, the Pearl Harbor attack was, for the most part, reasonably competent, although much of the US Pacific Fleet was at sea at the time. The tactical objectives were poor. Although the US suffered several ships sunk, aircraft lost and over 2,000 casualties, it did not achieve the original Japanese objectives.

Strategically, and prior to that attack, the US could not prevent Japan expanding over much of Southeast Asia. This misnamed 'Co-Prosperity Sphere', which went as far as Midway Island, was an absolute disaster for Japan. It encouraged Hitler to declare war on the United States and woke the country out of its post-Great Depression torpor.

Under international law, pre-emptive self-defence is generally considered legal if certain criteria are met, such as an imminent threat and the proportionality of the response. And here is the rub: a modest pre-emptive strike may just annoy the targeted adversary, as demonstrated by Pearl Harbor and Margaret Thatcher's reaction to the Falklands, or suggest to the targeted adversary that the attacker represents an existential threat.

Generally, pre-emptive strikes risk untoward (to the attacker) escalation. Escalation control and risk mitigation are both tricky. Japan and Argentina got it wrong. Israel, by winning the Six-Day War, got it right, but at a terrible cost in blood – over 5,000 casualties – and treasure – 400 tanks and 46 aircraft.

18 THE THIRD AND CURRENT PHASE OF THE NUCLEAR AGE: ENDURING THEMES

Putin, with his scarcely veiled threat to use nuclear weapons against any country that might interfere with his invasion of Ukraine in February 2022, effectively ended the second phase of the nuclear age, and we are now in the *third* phase. It is tempting to say *lost* in the third phase. His threats stimulated other concerns about nuclear proliferation – other states and non-state groups acquiring nuclear weapons, or, the sum of all fears, a terrorist nuclear attack. Although this may seem rather far-fetched, his actions in Syria and in Iran might all point on this direction.

We must face the world as it currently is, not as we wish it to be. As we cope with this new, third phase, it is crucial to acknowledge certain persistent themes that have re-emerged since the more stable second nuclear age. Essentially, unlike the recent past, we continue to exist in a perilous nuclear environment. To truly understand this world, we must fully grasp a variety of factors. Some of these have existed in various forms since the beginning of the nuclear age, while others are responses to new developments like hypersonic delivery vehicles. It is important to stay alert to how these factors evolve, guided by political and technological intelligence. Some of these themes may verge on the familiar, but they are still potent influences on our nuclear posture. It may be banal, but the old saying that 'familiarity breeds contempt' is never more true of nuclear considerations.

FROM VICTORY TO NON-USE:

This is a rather obvious point but worth repeating: military leaders are oriented towards 'victory', or at least achieving the political goal – if such be clear enough. But recall Churchill's famous speech in 1940:

'We shall go on to the end, we shall fight in France, we shall fight on the seas and oceans, we shall fight with growing confidence and growing strength in the air, we shall defend our island, whatever the cost may be...'

The keywords here are *whatever the cost may be.* Churchill's speeches of course contain a fair amount of rhetoric but this *whatever the cost* contrasts dramatically with the overwhelming difference between conventional and nuclear war. As was agreed at the Gorbachev/Reagan summit, 'a nuclear war cannot be won and therefore must never be fought.'

This confirmed the belief that the using nuclear weapons in a conflict between the United States and the Soviet Union, would result in catastrophic consequences for both countries and for the world as a whole. It referenced MAD – Mutually Assured Destruction – and also the whole idea of the pre-emptive strike and second-strike capability.

It was a significant sentiment, and was an important factor in driving arms control negotiations and efforts to reduce the size and capabilities of nuclear arsenals during the Cold War. And although the ending of the Cold War was greeted enthusiastically by most observers, it also meant that Gorbachev was out of business within a few years of his meeting with Ronald Reagan.

ICBMS

ICBMs are the big daddy of nuclear delivery methods. (Recall the 'triad' system outlined in *War in Context.*) They are long-range missiles that can travel thousands of miles and deliver nuclear warheads to distant targets. Modern ICBMs typically carry multiple independently targetable re-entry vehicles (MIRVs), each of which carries a separate nuclear warhead, allowing a single missile to hit multiple targets.

So if an ICBM was carrying three nuclear warheads, each with an explosive yield of (say) 500 kilotons (33 Hiroshimas), this would give the overall weapon a maximum yield of 1.5 megatons, or about a hundred times the destructive effect of the bomb that fell on Hiroshima.

The key to appreciating Intercontinental Ballistic Missiles is the *ballistic* part. Ballistic comes from Greek *ballein* 'to throw'. ICBMs are powered only during relatively a brief period – most of the flight is unpowered. This means that although they can land within a few hundred metres of their intended target – their exact accuracy is classified – they cannot hit with pinpoint accuracy.

This lack of accuracy means that an ICBM, even with its enormous destructive capability, is of limited use for a pre-emptive strike. In such an attempted strike, one would need to know exactly where the enemy's underground silos were located and would need to arrange for all missiles to arrive at the same time in enemy territory. In any case, this has become a moot point because even large ballistic missiles can now be launched from a mobile platform transported on specially designed trucks. Another problem is that the cunning enemy may have disguised their ICBM truck platforms as, say, watch towers in the middle of a forest.

The provenance of deterrence theory, which in turn is based on second strike capability, means that whatever devastation an enemy might have caused on the home territory, even if it was the result of an attempted pre-emptive strike, or as part of escalation, there would still remain enough missiles and enough delivery systems (reference the triad system) to retaliate and devastate the attacking country.

ESCALATION

Sometimes known as 'escalation ladder', is a process whereby a small initial spat between two polities becomes more and more intense in terms of the use of military force. Here, polities could be different nation-states, a breakaway region of an existing nation-state or a supposedly independent republic such as we find in Belarus. Although no longer under the Soviet system, any deviation from political guidance from the Russian Federation would result in treatment similar to that meted out on Hungary and Czechoslovakia during the Soviet period.

Escalation may involve functional moves, such as using different aspects of military force, such as air power or cyber force. Or it may mean quantitative – more intense bombardment, for example – which changes the way in which a conflict is conducted. The conflict could expand geographically, involve third parties or indeed cause one side to expand its original objectives from simply neutralising the other polity's aggressive stance to eliminating them all together.

The concept of escalation has given rise to a discrete body of writing from academics and think tanks, but most is considered under the broader issues of strategy.

The most influential book was Herman Kahn's *On Escalation: Metaphors and Scenarios*, published in 1965 during the height of the Cold War which considers escalation in the context of nuclear war. He examines various levels of escalation in a hypothetical war, referencing historical examples, game theory and strategic thinking.

Kahn introduced the idea of an 'escalation ladder' to describe the step-by-step progression of actions that could lead to more intense levels or a wider level of conflict, including the use of nuclear weapons.

Although he started with a more modest ladder, he subsequently came up with a forty-four-step escalation ladder, starting with the first, *Ostensible crisis* going up to number forty-four, *Insensate war*, which presumably marked the end of civilisation and possibly the globe.

Kahn's escalation faced several critiques over the years: that his forty-four steps may be oversimplistic, and he ignores the psychological aspects which may be down to Thucydides' *fear, honour and interest*. My own criticism is that his steps focus too much on the military aspects of any particular crisis rather than the political aspects. In addition, he does not examine the military-political interface in sufficient detail.

Nevertheless, Kahn's book is considered a classic in the field of strategic studies and is useful in starting discussions about nuclear deterrence and international security.

But there's the rub: in focusing almost exclusively on nuclear war, Khan has maybe given too little attention to conventional war. As the Russian–Ukrainian war has demonstrated, escalation can happen functionally, quantitatively and geographically, all at once.

So to some extent the concept of escalation looks like an extension of the Security Dilemma, where one polity, in attempting to maintain its security, is seen by the other side as a hostile act.

And although a useful reference point, it's difficult to see how Khan's forty-four steps can be of any help if Vladimir Putin decides to use a nuclear weapon in the Ukraine or against any of the allies contributing munitions.

THE NUCLEAR TABOO

The nuclear taboo is an understanding amongst nuclear-armed states that they will not use or threaten to use nuclear weapons except in the most extreme circumstances. It is linked to the 'no first use' provision in that world opinion would condemn any state initiating a nuclear conflict. There would be the risk of severe diplomatic, political and reputational consequences. It is essentially a set of expectations and behavioural norms that determine any nuclear armed state posture.

The nuclear taboo evolved over the first phase of the nuclear age. Whist there was some justification for the use of atomic bombs in Hiroshima and Nagasaki to end the Second World War, recognition of the terrible cost to the Japanese increased understanding of the results of nuclear warfare and contributed to the emergence of the taboo.

There was some discussion within the American military leadership about using an atomic device in the Korean War (1950–1953), the first major war after the Second World War. Indeed President Eisenhower thought that a semi-secret intention to use an atomic weapon would deter the Chinese from restarting the war. At that stage the Chinese did not have such weapons.

Some commentators argue that Eisenhower wanted to ensure the credibility of nuclear deterrence. Eisenhower's flexible nuclear strategy included the option of 'massive retaliation', which meant using nuclear weapons in retaliation, even in the event of a conventional attack. It may be that Eisenhower wanted to eliminate the idea of the nuclear taboo to preserve its deterrent effect.

The use of nuclear weapons was also discussed during the Vietnam War, but closer analysis showed that it would take hundreds of smaller tactical nuclear weapons to make any political difference at all. It was recognised that there was no point in using a major, strategic weapon against North Vietnam, as it would not contribute to a satisfactory political outcome for either the north or the south, or, of course, the US.

The nuclear taboo is not simply based on humanitarian concerns and moral repugnancy. Although, in an anarchic international system, the nuclear taboo is not legally binding, there are strategic implications.

All this changed when Vladimir Putin threatened any state supporting Ukraine after the Russian invasion with nuclear reprisal. It is often assumed here that the weapons used would be tactical, and used in the Ukraine to aid the Russian offensive. In fact, though, the threat was to supporting countries. It is difficult to see how a tactical nuclear weapon aimed against the United Kingdom, France or Germany, could have the desired political effect on those countries. In essence, it would be an attack on NATO, for which NATO would have to respond. This means there would be a grave risk of a strategic attack on Russia from NATO.

Nevertheless, the idea behind the nuclear taboo is still current. There are still ethical, moral and humanitarian considerations about the use of nuclear weapons. This is apart from the fear of retaliation, the catastrophic consequences and the difficulties of managing escalation.

The nuclear taboo is not simply about moral angst, but also strategic considerations. It is profoundly based on societal norms, public opinion and international institutions.

Since we live in an anarchic international system, some scholars have suggested that the whole idea behind the nuclear taboo was and remains a chimera. They imply that in the event of a real, hot, nuclear war, such ideas would be out of the window. In such circumstances, even the faint memory of the nuclear taboo, may help in constraining escalation.

The nuclear taboo and 'no first use' are not legally binding frameworks, simply a set of norms and expectations. It may not have been deterministic, but it has contributed to decisions about the use of nuclear weapons and to world peace.

The nuclear taboo emphasises the enormous responsibility that the possession of nuclear weapons entails. Indeed, one of the themes that are now mentioned in relation to nuclear weapons is the importance of stewardship. This is defined as the responsible management, maintenance, and oversight of a state's nuclear weapons and infrastructure. It covers a range of activities associated with the safe, secure and effective control of nuclear weapons and their delivery systems.

'NO FIRST USE ...'

A 'no first use' policy means that a country guarantees not to launch a nuclear attack unless it has first been attacked or is facing an imminent and overwhelming threat. The understanding of this policy has changed over the years. Originally, it meant 'no first use' unless the country had first been attacked with nuclear weapons. This provision seems to have diminished lately, and now some states threaten to use nuclear weapons against a non-nuclear but overwhelming attack.

Pakistan has considered and then rejected the idea of no first use.

China has always had a no first use policy, but this may be currently under review.

North Korea has no first use policy, though it is thought that they would use a nuclear weapon against a non-nuclear state if the regime of the Kim family were threatened.

Israel does not admit to having nuclear weapons so logically cannot have a no first use policy. However, they did launch a surprise attack in 1980, which destroyed an unfinished Iraqi nuclear reactor, to prevent Saddam Hussein developing his own nuclear bomb.

Which leaves NATO members **The United States, France** and the **UK**, none of whom have a no first use policy.

The United States has traditionally left open the option of first use of nuclear weapons in certain circumstances, such as in response to a significant threat to national security. Historically, the no first use policy has been vigorously debated in the United States – Obama was against it – and some American politicians have claimed that there is a *de facto* no first use policy anyway.

Russia had a no first use policy during the Cold War, but its current policy is more ambiguous. Russia's stance now is that it would consider the use of nuclear weapons in response to even a conventional attack that threatens the existence or survival of the Russian state.

France maintains a policy of deliberate ambiguity about no first use. The French position is that it would only use nuclear weapons in response to a major aggression against its vital interests, the specific conditions and circumstances are not publicly disclosed and remain classified for security reasons.

The United Kingdom, like the French, maintain a policy of deliberate ambiguity about no first use. The nuclear posture involves some flexibility, and the UK government has not ruled out the first use of nuclear weapons in some scenarios, rooting against non-nuclear armed states.

To some extent, no first use is more about diplomatic signalling that it is about strict constitutional or military rules.

It is inconceivable that a nuclear armed state suffering an existential threat or an incursion into its territory that could not countered with conventional force would not at least consider a nuclear response notwithstanding the nature of the threat.

An illustrative example is **India**, where they guarantee 'no first use', but with the proviso that if things were serious enough, they would be the first to initiate a nuclear response. They've obviously read Napoleon where he says, 'It's best to get your retaliation in first.'

No first use has contributed to improved international relations and decisions related to nuclear weapons. It has confirmed that countries with a 'no first use' policy see their weapons as a deterrent rather than offensive. This may be useful in a crisis, such as the Cuban Missile Crisis in 1962.

'LAUNCH ON WARNING'

This is a policy whereby a country would launch a nuclear attack on another in response to indications or warning of an imminent nuclear attack by an adversary. That is to say, without being attacked with nuclear weapons first.

It would mean that a 'launch on warning' country would launch a retaliatory attack before the incoming enemy missiles reach their targets. As such, it would represent a retaliation against the attacking country, or possibly the launch of anti-ICBM missiles in an attempt to destroy the incoming attack.

Nuclear armed countries rely on distant Early Warning Systems (EWS systems) including radar, satellites surveillance and other sensors to detect and track incoming missiles.

It is obvious that this is a high-risk strategy: errors and or misinterpretation of data could lead to accidental nuclear war. (See the list of nuclear risks in *War in Context.*) Despite what might be considerable effort put in to prevent escalation, 'launch on warning' could escalate a conflict too rapidly for adequate political control.

It might be thought that a 'launch on warning' would contribute to deterrence, but this ignores the risks involved. Overall, a 'launch on warning' policy, in the event, would involve complex considerations regarding the perceived threat: technological aspects (is the data secure?) in what would obviously be an overwhelming desire to avoid accidental nuclear conflict.

DELIVERY SYSTEMS: THE TRIAD

Rather obviously, nuclear bombs have no utility if they cannot be delivered to the targets at an appropriate time.

War in Context covers the conventional triad of delivery systems with ICBM, Submarine Launched Ballistic Missiles (SLBMs) and strategic bombers. Each of these delivery methods has its own advantages: ICBMs, located secretly within a country, can provide a rapid response capability; it's difficult to locate enemy submarines and aircraft may be able to get through when every other delivery system has failed, and can be recalled in the event of a mistake or emergency.

But each has also disadvantages: once launched, an ICBM cannot be recalled and, in any case, as we note above, the accuracy is not sufficient to take out an opponent's own ICBM launch silos. There is also another twist: should an aggressor launch an ICBM with a non-nuclear warhead, it's impossible to tell this from the target country's radar systems. They might then be encouraged to respond with a nuclear weapon.

SLBMs, which most nuclear armed countries have as part of their arsenal are perhaps the most reliable nuclear delivery system. The ballistic missiles they carry are launched from beneath the ocean surface, the submarine itself being difficult to detect. They provide a survivable second-strike capability.

The problems are that whereas they can *receive* messages by trailing an aerial while still submerged, they cannot partake in a dialogue with their own Fleet HQ or with their own government. Should they send a message, they'd instantly be located by the enemy and vulnerable to attack.

Furthermore, in the event that the captain of the nuclear-armed submarine had reason to believe that a nuclear exchange had taken place, and that he had received no instructions from fleet HQ, it is left to his own discretion as to whether to launch one or all of his missiles. Although there is a strict protocol with various levels of security, and, one imagines, designated targets, there could be no political involvement and the strike could aggravate whatever negotiations were going on.

Another problem here is that several countries are developing autonomous surface and subsea drones which can roam the oceans and locate nuclear-armed submarines. Should such a drone render a nuclear-armed submarine incapable, or even sink it, this would mean a number of unexploded nuclear warheads at perhaps an unrecoverable depth of the ocean.

In the 1930s, there was the suggestion that 'the bomber will always get through'. This is no longer the case. During times of heightened tension, the enemy might mistake a bomber armed with conventional weapons as one carrying nuclear weapons and respond with a nuclear launch.

HYPERSONIC CRUISE MISSILES

These are covered in detail in *War in Context*. For reference, there are two main types of hypersonic missiles, both of which will, eventually, be able to carry nuclear weapons. There is the HCM, the Hypersonic Cruise Missile, and also the HGV, the Hypersonic Boost Glide Vehicle. The HCM is powered by a scramjet, which is a supersonic development of the ramjet. The scramjet relies on the missile getting to a very high speed before it will actually work, something like Mach 4. This means they have to be launched with a rocket, such as an ICBM. Putin has boasted that the Russian Federation is working on a hypersonic cruise missile that can carry a nuclear weapon. This may be hyperbole, but it also may be too much to ignore.

Some authorities suggest that there is no defence against the hypersonic missile as they are 'fast, effective, precise and unstoppable' (*New York Times,* June 2021). Ballistic missiles (ICBMs) travel at hypersonic speeds, over Mach 20, but these are not dirigible in their final stages. What makes hypersonic cruise missiles so worrisome is that they can, whilst in-flight, evade anti-missile defences and only commit themselves to a target at the last stage. This might mean that the second-strike capability is impossible.

IN SUMMARY

We need to recognise the complex and evolving nature of nuclear strategy and thereby doctrine and stressing the critical distinction between conventional and nuclear warfare. We highlight the enduring relevance of deterrence theory, based on well-known and accepted doctrines such as 'second strike capability', ICBMs accuracy, the management of escalation, and new technological advancements like hypersonic missiles. Taken together, these factors illustrate the ongoing challenges in maintaining strategic stability and preventing nuclear war. The evolving nature of these policies and strategies reflects the need for continuous vigilance and adaptation in the face of changing geopolitical realities and technological advancements.

Harking back to our original definition of war, it's useful to recall that war is about, or should be about, achieving a *better* relationship between polities. Since much of nuclear strategy is about *avoiding* nuclear war, and is preoccupied, one might even say obsessed, with the doctrine and protocols, this may obscure the ultimate goal: a lasting and stable peace.

19) THE FUTURE FOR NUCLEAR WEAPONS

In trying to anticipate the future for war, it becomes apparent that the concept of nuclear war is distinct from the consideration of war in general. The language is specialised, the commentators are authorities in that particular field, and the world into which a nuclear exchange leads is terrifying in its unique and novel aspects. The politics are the same, but the effect of mistakes or misfortunes are amplified considerably. However, here is a small and dangerous overlap; witness Putin's threats – seen as nuclear – when he invaded Ukraine.

The final chapter of this book, *War after Ukraine* presents a conclusion of the whole *Making Sense of War* trilogy in terms of the future for war, of international relations, of achieving a lasting peace with justice and of the various aspects that may affect the path to war. This chapter looks at the future of nuclear weapons specifically from the perspective of their use in war.

As outlined above, one small nuclear weapon would have a limited effect on the battlefield, and several would have to be used to turn the tide of an attack or an assault. So, even if the nuclear device used was small, and although the effects might be containable, they would still cause alarm about escalation to the use of larger and more destructive weapons such as ICBMs. It is at this point that the world would stare into the abyss.

In *War in Context,* we examined the difficulties of predicting war. Whilst we recognise that most forecasts are almost bound to be wrong, it is the degree to which they are wrong that is surprising. It is not so long ago that Japan was seen as a likely peer competitor to the United States and there were a number of novels about that subject.

We distinguished between forecasting and prediction. Forecasts are based to a large extent on extrapolation, collecting, analysing and understanding past data. One can immediately see there are many value judgements. When and from where is the data collected? Are correlations weighted? If so, how? Is each piece of data given equal weighting or are they weighted exponentially? Is it a moving average? What about outliers? On that subject, and although there are well understood statistical methods for identifying outliers, these may indeed be the most important ones. Statistically, the Second World War was an outlier!

Predictions, we suggest, are a more general concept, based to some extent on forecasts but tempered with the idea of the probability of various other independent variables. These inputs are again bound to be influenced by human agency, which may be predisposed to wishful thinking. Prediction can also be persuasion about how we should cope with the future. Predictions can legitimise the preferred future of powerful commercial interests, or those of allies and organisations, or simply to bolster a country's self-image: 'we are a nuclear power and therefore a world power'.

There is also the problem of self-fulfilling prophecies. Seeing a nation-state as a competitor does not mean that the competition will necessarily escalate into military conflict or that any conventional war would 'go nuclear'. Yet it is remarkable how quickly Russia turned from being a responsible and welcome guest in international affairs to a military competitor. Of course, almost all of that was due to Putin's fear of democracy, the rule of accepted law and Russia's historic and chronic insecurity. Yet we could imagine a world – indeed we *did* imagine a world – where Russia would become a peaceful, liberal state and a responsible member of the international community. Somehow, we missed Chechnya and Georgia from our considerations.

Let us just say that, without allocating any blame at all to the West, more consideration could have been given to what Russia was all about. There may even be echoes of the Cold War.

How does this relate to the use of nuclear weapons? The problem here is obvious: apart from Hiroshima and Nagasaki, no nuclear weapon has ever been used in a hot war. In 1945, the use of nuclear weapons appeared to be a logical extension of previous wars. Munitions became more and more powerful during the Second World War and nuclear weapons were just one more step forward. This is no longer viable: greater yields, more precise targeting and faster delivery, taken together, mean that the concept and practice of a nuclear war lives in its own world.

Recognising that looking into the future is always an inexact business, we may suspend the usual caveats about 'forecasts always being wrong' and 'unknown unknowns' and consider some of the historic influences and decision points. No factor will be deterministic, but they could be illuminating.

There are several sources that might inform our thinking: First, we might revisit the legacy of the nuclear-related decisions made in the early stages and through to the end of the Cold War. Second, there are many novels about future war, almost all with Russia, some less credible than others. The BBC's fictionalised *BBC Special Report of NATO-Russia Conflict* in April 2018 is stimulating, but may be over egged and over dramatised. There was little political dialogue between NATO and Russia, Russian resources seemed to be inexhaustible, and the whole episode seemed to happen in double-quick time. It may be worth watching for the CGI pictures of an underwater nuclear explosion and also the civil defence expert claiming that, in the event of a large-scale nuclear war, the British government's advice was more or less nonsense.

Fortunately, there other accounts written by well-informed professionals and designed to be as realistic as possible. Two stand out:

John Hackett's Cold War era novel, *The Third World War* and a post-Cold War BBC programme *World War Three: Inside The War Room*.

Third, we consider Professor Sir Lawrence Freedman's final chapter in *The Evolution of Nuclear Strategy: Can there be a Nuclear Strategy?*

Fourth, and whilst accepting the marginal utility of counter-factual history, we could also examine another approach to the Russo-Ukraine war: no Budapest agreement, no relinquishing the Soviet nuclear assets positioned on Ukraine soil, a successful assault by Russian Federation forces.

THE LEGACY OF COLD WAR DECISIONS

Following Eisenhower's Project Solarium in 1953, an enormous amount of intellectual effort went into determining US strategy for this new nuclear age. Much of that strategy was impacted by the language that was used. 'Containment' of the Soviet Union was redefined and extended to protect and expand what was known during the Cold War as the 'free world'. John Foster Dulles, US Secretary of State at the time, may have over-interpreted one of the conclusions and advanced the notion of 'massive retaliation'.

It is difficult to assess to what extent the Soviet Union's objectives and strategies were taken into account. There was a fundamental belief that the Soviet leadership pursued the expansion of communism globally and intended to exploit any signs of Western weakness. One team imagined that the Soviets would retreat if confronted directly, another assumed that the Soviets would be willing to respect others' spheres of influence.

The outputs were not all about confrontation: whilst Solarium focused mainly on countering what were imagined to be – and probably were – Soviet ambitions, it did recognise the potential for diplomatic engagement. One of the teams looked at a strategy of coexistence with the USSR, even if this strategy wasn't the principal one adopted. There seems to have been little consideration that Khrushchev may have had different ideas to Stalin, although many hopes were subsequently dashed by Khrushchev's decision to invade Hungary in 1956.

It may seem otiose to relate language used some seventy years ago, but the title of Enthoven and Smith's 1971 book *How much is enough? Shaping the Defense Program, 1961–1969* asks a question that is still current: *what*, and *how much* is required to deter the Soviet Union, and now, it seems, The Russian Federation? Enthoven and Smith asserted that:

'... such nuclear superiority as the United States maintains is of little significance since we do not know how to use it to achieve our national security objectives. In other words, against the United States, superior US nuclear forces are extremely difficult to convert into real political power. The blunt unavoidable factors of the Soviet Union could effectively destroy the United States even after absorbing the full weight of a first US strike and vice versa ...'

The 1962 Cuban Missile Crisis is often cited as when the world came close to a nuclear war, although neither side wished that, and this is probably overstated. What is sometimes missed is that it was *conventional* US military power in the Caribbean that deterred Russia from pursuing their missile bases in Cuba. Again, how much (nuclear resources) is enough?

Defence planners and policymakers might claim that deterrence has been successful on the nuclear front, in that we have not had a major nuclear war during the Cold War or during the third phase of the nuclear age. But –and it's a very big but – whatever the West was doing in terms of conventional arms, it did not deter Putin from invading Ukraine.

There is another clue in pronouncements accompanying the 2023 UK *Global Britain in a Competitive Age: The Integrated Review of Security, Defence, Development and Foreign Policy* paper, which said:

'In 2010 the Government stated an intent to reduce our overall nuclear warhead stockpile ceiling from not more than 225 to not more than 180 by the mid-2020s. However, in recognition of the evolving security environment, including the developing range of technological and doctrinal threats, this is no longer possible, and the UK will move to an overall nuclear weapon stockpile of no more than 260 warheads.'

No rationale is offered, and this particular statement got very little press coverage or think tank commentary. It is difficult to imagine what *no longer possible* means. Let's ask the question again: how much is enough? We can add another: *How much nuclear deterrence do we need compared with how much conventional deterrence?*

This massive retaliation policy must have encouraged the Soviet Union to think along similar lines, and the 1970s saw a much wider interest from diplomats and officials about the nuclear question. At the same time, it was realised that perhaps one didn't have to be an expert at nuclear matters to ask essentially strategic questions. Nuclear matters are complex and replete with technical terms such as *yield* and *throw weight*; diplomatic accords like the Lisbon Protocol and the Mendoza Agreement; and performance factors such as *range, circular error probable*, etc. These may tend to inhibit thinking about nuclear weapons altogether, on the basis that they are too awful to contemplate or that they operate outside normal strategic rules and concepts. Nuclear matters are essentially strategic and thereby political.

Much of this thinking can be associated with Robert McNamara, who served as US Secretary of Defense from 1961 to 1968 under Presidents Jack Kennedy (JFK) and then Lyndon Johnson (LBJ). McNamara resigned in 1968 because of disagreements with Johnson about Vietnam. By this time, and under Kennedy's influence, McNamara was moving away from Eisenhower's policy of massive retaliation in favour of 'flexible response' that relied on increased US capacity to conduct limited, non-nuclear warfare. McNamara found sanctuary as the president of the World Bank, a position he held from 1968 to 1981.

For the rest of the Cold War, the twenty years from 1970 to 1990, and with the exception of the early 1980s (see Able Archer, described in *War in Context*) there was not so much an improvement in relationships between the US and Soviet Union but a certain stability evolved. It was not until 1986, when Ronald Reagan met Mikhail Gorbachev in Reykjavík that it was clear that the Cold War might be coming to an end. The two leaders had met at their summit in Geneva in 1985 and they jointly agreed that *a nuclear war cannot be won and must never be fought.*

The Cold War had many roots and causes, suspicions and misunderstandings. Despite much effort in intelligence gathering and interpretation, it was ever difficult to discern exactly what the Kremlin was thinking and what leaders' motivations were.

Were the Soviets really hegemonic villains, dedicated to the expansion of communism, or did they face similar political problems to those in the West. For example, it may have been thought that the military-industrial complex, where private capitalist firms developed technology and persuaded military leaders that they 'must have it' was a more or less Western thing. In fact, it was discovered that a very similar syndrome operated within the Soviet Union, with military leaders demanding more and better arms from their politicians. But for all that, we might mention instances where language itself may have played a part.

Massive Retaliation: for which the response might be for exactly what infringement? Could either side be sure?

Mutual Assured Destruction: before or after you have not adopted a 'no first use' policy? Have you?

Deterrence: what exactly are you seeking to deter – nuclear attack or *any* attack?

SOME CREDIBLE BUT FICTIONAL ACCOUNTS

The Third World War: The Untold Story by General Sir John Hackett, was published in 1982. 'Shan' Hackett was an Australian-born British soldier, author and, from 1968 to 1975 Principal of King's College, London, the author's alma mater.

He had considerable knowledge and experience of military matters. He had served in North Africa and fought in Operation Market Garden, better known as the battle for Arnhem. His controversial 1968 letter to *The Times* was critical of the British government's apparent lack of concern over the strength of NATO forces in Europe. He had signed it as a NATO officer, not as a British commander.

In writing The Third World War: The Untold Story Hackett consulted many military and political experts and one review of the book said that it 'represented a very high order of strategic thinking and was even a signal to the Soviets by way of warning'. Re-reading a synopsis now is terrifying, with many echoes of Putin's attack on Ukraine.

The narrative imagines that the Politburo (the Soviet Union's highest policy-making authority within the Communist Party), recognising that the Soviet economy is stagnating and that the Soviet Armed Forces may not be able to keep up technologically with the US and Western Europe, decide that their best interests are served by expanding influence through an invasion of Western Europe. This demonstrates a contrasting, alien strategic culture: how on earth did gaining hegemony over more of Western Europe help their economy?

They decide not to use nuclear weapons in the first instance but a conventional invasion, holding nuclear weapons as a backup should the invasion not go well. The Politburo is also conscious that they need to prove that the Soviet Union is still a potent world power.

The storyline is reasonably straightforward. In July 1985, the United States Marine Corps (USMC) intervenes against a Soviet incursion into Yugoslavia, as then was. In response, the Warsaw Pact mobilises on 4th August 1985, the 71st anniversary of the start of the First World War. They attack from East Germany (then under Soviet rule) towards the Rhine, and also attack Norway and Turkey.

However, there is stiff resistance from NATO, and even Ireland – it's historically neutral – sides with NATO. (Ireland is still to this day – 2024 – not a member of NATO, cherishing, as they imagine, their neutral status.) As a matter of interest, now that Sinn Fein are in government in the Irish Republic, the reunification of Ireland is being actively discussed. One wonders whether that might encourage Ireland to put quite a lot of the past behind them, and apply to join NATO.

The lack of Russian progress then faces significant internal destabilisation of the Russian Armed Forces. There are mutinies, desertions, and internal dissent.

In Hackett's scenario, there are other worldwide conflicts, for example in Cuba, Vietnam and Egypt – and Japan seizes the Kuril Islands.

To compensate for the lack of progress, the Soviet Union launches a strategic missile – that is an ICBM – against Birmingham and the whole of Birmingham is destroyed. In response, the US Navy and the Royal Navy launch a nuclear attack on Minsk in Belarus – then under Soviet control – and Minsk is devastated.

Political dissidents organise prison breaks across the country, internal Russian troops side with the citizenry and a coup d'état is launched – ironically by Ukrainian nationalists, who overthrow the Politburo and the Soviet Union collapses.

In the interests of full disclosure, there is an alternative ending. In this, NATO has acquiesced to the anti-nuclear lobby and scaled down nuclear forces and nuclear sharing capabilities in favour of conventional forces aside from France's Strategic Oceanic Force and the US's Strategic Air Command. In contrast, the Soviet Union maintain their nuclear forces, leaving the West at a major disadvantage.

In this scenario, the Warsaw Pact invasion overruns NATO forces in West Germany and the Low Countries. France withdraws from the conflict after the Soviet Union assures that it will escape occupation and attack. Unwilling to risk global nuclear war, American forces withdraw from Europe and the remnants of NATO sue for peace.

The United Kingdom is forced to accept Soviet Union control of British political, military and economic institutions, and national control is handed to a joint British–Soviet commission. Britain's EU membership is terminated. Much of the British military escapes Soviet control by putting themselves under American, Canadian or Australian commands.

World War Three: Inside the War Room is another BBC fictionalised documentary first broadcast in 2016. A committee of senior former British military and diplomatic figures comes together to role play a war game concerning a hypothetical 'hot war' in Eastern Europe, including an unimaginable nuclear confrontation. Considerable preparation went into the making of the programme by BBC researchers, and the professionals chosen to be 'Inside the War Room' were picked for their knowledge and experience. They included: Tony Brenton, British Ambassador to Russia from 2004 to 2008; Christopher Meyer, Ambassador to the United States from 1997 to 2003; Pauline Neville-Jones, Chairman of the Joint Intelligence Committee (JIC) from 1993 to 1994 (she also served on the National Security Council) and Richard Shirreff, a retired British Army officer and from 2011 to 2014, Deputy Supreme Allied Commander Europe.

Alan West represented the Royal Navy, having been First Sea Lord and Chief of the Naval Staff from 2002 to 2006. Also present were Baroness Falkner, Liberal Democrat Foreign Affairs Spokesman; Lord Arbuthnot, Chair of Defence Select Committee, 2005–2014; Dr Ian Kearns, Specialist Advisor, National Security Strategy, 2010; Dona Muirhead, Director of Communication, Ministry of Defence, 1997–2000; and Ian Bond, Ambassador to Latvia, 2005–2007. This ensured that the discussions were as realistic as possible. The BBC advertised the programme as follows:

'Following the crisis in Ukraine (the appropriation of Crimea; this was before the invasion in February 2022) *and Russia's involvement in Syria, the world is closer to superpower confrontation than at any time since the end of the Cold War. Now, a War Room of senior former British military and diplomatic figures comes together to war-game a hypothetical 'hot war' in eastern Europe, including the unthinkable – nuclear confrontation.'*

The challenge for any viewer watching this programme is not to evaluate the verisimilitude of the scenario or the wisdom or otherwise of the reaction from participants, but to consider aspects of the evolving situation and the dilemmas presented, some of which persist, others need to be resolved.

WORLD WAR THREE: INSIDE THE WAR ROOM: FANTASY OR INDICATIVE?

First, the programme is as realistic as it could possibly be. When Margaret Thatcher decided to retake the Falkland Islands, she consulted Harold McMillan, an ex-prime minister who has lived through, and contributed to the Second World War. He was the UK government's representative to the Allies in the Mediterranean. He recommended setting up a 'War Cabinet' and the War Room was a realistic example of this.

The characters all had extensive experience and knowledge of the security situation and, although thoroughly briefed, were honest and open about their reactions. Latgale was a good choice: it is the easternmost and poorer region of Latvia that might present the danger of revolt and, as we say, thinking that the 'grass is greener' within the Russian Federation. Many Latgalians are ethnically Russian, though speak a dialect of Latvian.

There was a realistic discussion about NATO's Article 5, which does not say, as it is sometimes thought, that other NATO members have to come to the aid of an attacked country in military terms, but simply to offer support.

The team recognise Putin's objective, being the fragmentation of NATO, which is entirely realistic.

Finally, the nuclear weapon above the Baltic – not over a population centre – was credible, as was the US President's retribution.

The final scene, where it is decided not to use a nuclear weapon on Russia is again completely realistic, though only a fool would imagine that this was official government policy.

Just before the programme, in February 2016, *Prospect* Magazine published an article by the journalist Annabelle Chapman. The headline was 'The BBC's *Inside the War Room* should never have been made', with a subheading: 'It is not just a television programme'. She cites that a 'fake documentary scene is set in Latvia', but suggests in the next paragraph that the programme reflects genuine concerns about Moscow's ambitions in the Baltic region since Russia annexed Crimea in March 2014.

She goes on to say that the War Room scenes are compelling but also recognises that it is unclear how NATO members would or could respond to a Russian attack on one of the Baltic states. She does pick up that the Russian media were incensed with the programme, referencing one of its last decisions: that Britain would not reply to Russia's nuclear strike.

Overall, the programme did not get very high ratings, yet it was important to communicate to the general public problems that the United Kingdom in particular, NATO in general and also the world has to contemplate when facing Russia. It is amazing that any journalist would wish to censor such a programme: journalists are usually the first to complain about censorship or sensitivities.

20 CAN THERE BE A NUCLEAR STRATEGY?

In the concluding chapter of his classic reference volume, *The Evolution of Nuclear Strategy*, updated and completely revised in 2019, Professor Sir Lawrence Freedman, together with Jeffrey Michaels, asked the above question. Here, as well as a commentary, we take a critical look at some of the concepts and provide some reflection on the overall conclusions. Classic strategic theory contends that strategy is the link between politics and military action, but there more factors to include.

It is obvious how awful the use of a nuclear weapon – strategic or tactical – would be. From the practical point of view, the death and destruction would be appalling. There would be horrendous radiation which might take years to abate. Even if the world survived such an attack, the political consequences would be considerable. The international community would be cautious in dealing with any 'first user' whose economy might suffer. Such actions could signal to less responsible nations that it was acceptable to use a nuclear weapon. North Korea might think that they could invade the south for example. There also might be a scramble from non-nuclear states to acquire nuclear weapons and proliferation might get out of hand.

Any deliberation about nuclear weapons requires considerable technical knowledge and experience. A newly appointed defence chief or president, or one presented with a nuclear problem, calling for an expert on nuclear weapons would be provided with someone who can 'talk nuclear'. It is too easy to get carried away with technical details of throw weights, targeting and delivery methods, and avoid the strategic/ political aspects of the use of nuclear weapons.

In fact, in not too gross a simplification, all a political leader needs know about nuclear weapons is that they have to be transported to the enemy country, usually via a missile, but sometimes using aircraft, which might be a challenge. They make a very big bang, and the effects might last for a very long time. Oh, and the enemy might retaliate with something similar but even more powerful on your own country. And there's also the not so small matter of a country's international reputation to consider.

Putin's war in Ukraine upset the apple cart. Until then, the mutual, tacit agreement between nuclear armed states was one of deterrence. Many commentators called this a strategy based on Mutual Assured Destruction, or MAD, and second-strike capability. Prior to Putin's war, deterrence had reached an almost theological level, with its own advocates, language and expectations. The problem was, and remains, that, in the case of Putin and Ukraine, it did not work. Neither did the 'nuclear taboo'.

What is unclear is whether Putin was not deterred because the nuclear deterrent is worthless, or because everybody has forgotten about conventional deterrence.

The theory of deterrence is that such effects can be achieved by fear of punishment – countermeasures – or by denial, representing to the putative enemy that the consequences of his action would be considerable in terms of human, financial and reputational costs. Academics warm to their trade by suggesting the 'three Cs' of deterrence theory.

First, the deterring party must have the *capability* to impose the costs that have been threatened. You can't send an ordinary submarine out into the ocean with a sign pasted on the side saying, *Caution: nuclear weapons on board.* Apart from the naysayers in the press, this would surely leak, or spiders would discover that it was a sham.

Second, the deterrer's posture must be credible to the potential deterree.

Finally, of course, the deterrent has to be communicated to and understood by the other party. Like all forms of strategy, deterrence is a form of negotiation, of understanding, and by the acceptance that a tolerable status quo is both required and accessible.

Deterrence is implicitly before the act, in the hope that the enemy is deterred – obviously. Deterrence does not need to end there. It seems little thought has been given to deterrence after the act. In the case of Ukraine, a post-invasion deterrent action might have been to build runways in eastern Ukraine that could take NATO jets, and set up anti-aircraft facilities with radar, missiles, etc. Mr Putin would undoubtedly have seen this as a hostile action, but Ukraine could have claimed that it was thoroughly defensive.

Hew Strachan is a prominent military historian and scholar of strategic studies, and has written extensively on war and strategy. One of his famous observations relates to the lack of clarity and the profusion of definitions in in strategic thinking. In his work *The Direction of War: Contemporary Strategy in Historical Perspective* (2013), Strachan suggested that the word *strategy* has become hackneyed in both military and civilian contexts. He remarked on the proliferation of terms like 'business strategy', and 'media strategy' which dilute the term's original meaning.

Strachan sees *strategy* in the classical way linking between *ends, ways and means,* archetypically Clausewitzian. Most of all, Strachan was talking about a bridge – a favourite word of Colin Gray's – between military *means* and *political objectives.* Commentators often get confused between ways and mean. *Ways* are to do with operations on the ground, whereas *means* refers to what resources would be involved. Just so you know!

Most of all, Strachan emphasised the need for clarity in definitions, particularly when discussing matters of war and peace. Without clear definitions, it becomes difficult to have a realistic discourse, to make decisions or create coherent policies.

And here is the nub of the problem: in the same way that nuclear war has its own language and disciples, the military 'ways and means' aspects of strategy have their own language too, with talk of victory and maybe even peace.

As an illustration, consider a 2020 article in *Foreign Affairs* by Jake Sullivan and Daniel Benaim. Sullivan is now a US National Security Advisor. The article is titled 'America's Opportunity in the Middle East: Diplomacy Could Succeed Where Military Force Has Failed' (who knew?). It only reinforces that old saw: 'If all you've got is a hammer, everything looks like a nail.'

In a word, Hew Strachan's definition of strategy is outdated. In international relations, in dealings with other states, we must consider every aspect of that relationship by way of strategy. In the last few years, the BBC foreign-language budget has been cut, foreign aid has been cut and British embassies around the world have been told that they need to focus on promoting British trade rather than peaceful relationships. The British Council is a shadow of its former self, in terms of promoting British culture. Suppose the United Kingdom as a whole had put effort into improving these actions instead of acting as a money laundromat for the Russians who stole Russian assets with Putin's blessing.

It would be absurd to suggest that had all these aspects, including intelligence and diplomacy, been better resourced and more focused, Putin would not have invaded Ukraine. But, say that the BBC still broadcast to Russia in Russian – they ceased broadcasts in 2011; their programmes are now only available over the internet, easily countered by the Russian authorities. Say foreign aid was more focused and generous. Say that British culture was promoted widely, together with English language schools and the whole range of other actions.

Might that have meant that some countries, sometimes referred to as 'the global south' would have been more willing to condemn Russia's actions and maybe even modify their trading relationships?

One major barrier to creative thinking about strategy is that, in general, strategists (whoever they may be …) tend not to differentiate between objective and subjective strategy. Objective strategy is trying to define the whole future of international relations as well as we are able and to identify how we might make the best of it.

Strategy is everything about the future.

The most frequent use of the word strategy is implicitly *subjective* strategy. Hence, we get broadcasters talking about a strategy for climbing a mountain or winning a game. People talking about strategy will also quote Mike Tyson who said that whatever plan you have goes out of the window when somebody hits you in the mouth. It's all very confusing. A parallel *objective* strategy for climbing mountains might be that you want to be the best mountaineer around.

A parallel *objective* strategy for winning a game would be that you want to win the series and establish yourself as a leading sportsman or woman.

And surely, if Mike Tyson pops on his boxing shorts and boxing gloves, and steps into the ring with a near competitor he might just expect that he might get hit in the mouth. Because whatever else strategy is, it is also contingent. To quote Freedman:

'*However important nuclear weapons were to national strategy* (that is objective strategy) *they could never be the whole story. Viewing nuclear weapons in isolation, or assuming that they provided a satisfactory vantage point to discuss strategy in full, distorted strategic studies.*'

He goes on to say:

'What is often forgotten in strategic studies, preoccupied with military capabilities, is that the balance of terror rests upon a particular arrangement of political relations as much as on the quality and quantity of the respective nuclear arsenals. Movements in these political relations could prove far more disturbing to nuclear stability than any movement of purely military factors. The major task for the future must be to address the problems of nuclear arsenals in a world of political change'

COUNTERFACTUAL HISTORY

This is of limited use unless it takes you back to the uncertainties of the time. If considered objectively, such a practice might reveal unwarranted assumptions, smart moves or what in retrospect were enormous mistakes. So it might be worth first looking at a scenario where there was no Budapest Agreement concerning Ukraine. This 1994 memorandum provided security assurances by its signatories relating to the accession of Ukraine and also Belarus and Kazakhstan to the Treaty on the Non-Proliferation of Nuclear Weapons (NPT). Importantly, the memoranda were signed by three nuclear powers: the Russian Federation, the United Kingdom and the United States.

What it meant in practice was that Ukraine gave up its nuclear weapons, and they were removed back to what had become the Russian Federation.

Would possession of nuclear weapons have helped Ukraine when the Russian Federation invaded in February 2022? What could they have done with a nuclear weapon to resist an attack? They could use one or several on their own territory, with the consequential damage and irradiation. They could have possibly used one or more against a location in Russia, for example the assembly areas at Rostov on don, but any incursion into Russian space would have meant, in all likelihood, the complete obliteration of the entire country; what good would that have been for Putin? But Ukraine's possession of nuclear weapons would have raised the risks of a Russian invasion (to the Russians) into a completely unknown realm.

And, reference comments above about the political angles, Putin's breaking of this agreement shows that he is never to be trusted and even when he has gone, there will be a lot of suspicion about any assurances that Russia offers in the future.

Another counterfactual argument might be to consider what would have happened if there had been a successful assault by Russian Federation forces, as expected by Putin and his gang. Russian forces would then be on the border with Poland, Slovakia, Hungary and Romania, all NATO members. A puppet government would have been set up in Kiev and Russian forces would be facing a desperate insurgency from Ukrainian partisans.

Judging by their actions in the spring of 2022, we might expect those insurgencies to be put down with the utmost brutality. The world would have been aghast, but their actions after Georgia and Chechnya, meant nothing would have done except some token tightening of sanctions. Oh, and Russia would have been condemned by NATO and by the EU in the 'strongest possible terms'.

Overall, Europe and the world would have become a much more dangerous place.

UKRAINE MUST WIN

Russia must be defeated and must be seen to be defeated. Even though Russia's resources are currently stretched, they will continue to encroach into Georgia, Moldova and Azerbaijan/Armenia (Artsakh and Nagorno-Karabakh).

And although Ukraine has had some success in countering Russian's exclusion zone in the Black Sea, that might be denied. Bear in mind that the coasts of Bulgaria, Romania and Turkey, all NATO members, are all on the Black Sea, and in Bulgaria and Romania's case the only sea access they have.

21 CONCLUSIONS: NUCLEAR WEAPONS HAVE NO FUTURE

War in Context, the second book in this trilogy *Making Sense of War*, starts by asserting that 'There never was Elysium, never any Garden of Eden and that The idea of a perfect land, a paradise where 'life is easiest; where there is no snow nor heavy storm' is a myth'.

There never was a time when war, in whatever form, was absent from the world, and durable and stable peace reigned. Even great steps forward in technology like steel weapons, gunpowder, indirect fire, aircraft, missiles and a whole range of technologies, which might have been expected to give one side overwhelming power, were always countered and managed.

So it's a strange conundrum that the latest technology in the history of war, that of nuclear weapons, takes us into a whole new world. No previous technology has been so powerful, so relatively easy to acquire and, if used, so devastating. Nuclear weapons cannot be countered and managed, other than by inflicting a reciprocal devastation on the enemy. It's a curious paradox: nuclear weapons may simply be too powerful to use.

Philip Larkin's poem *MCMXIV* (1964) is a war poem that focuses on the changes that came over England after the end of First World War. It talks of the men who have just signed up to fight in the war against Imperial Germany. They have no idea what is about to happen to them. The poem ends with the unforgettable lines:

Never such innocence
Never before or since
Never such innocence again.

The same could be said about nuclear weapons, and Larkin could easily have been talking about nuclear weapons: born in 1922, he died in 1985 in the closing stages of the Cold War.

At the start of the nuclear age, the United States imagined nuclear weapons to be an extension of conventional weapons: 'massive retaliation' was the key concept. The UK, whose foreign policy was, and still is an anaemic parallel to that of the US, followed suit. At a point where the Soviet Union reached nuclear parity with the US, it dawned on policymakers that any attempt to use nuclear weapons against them would result in a devastating response. Analysts and policymakers entered into a period of fevered conjecture, assumptions and extrapolations. It might be somewhat unfair, but we might also observe that the whole *policy* of dealing with the Soviet Union did not have the same focus on the *politics* of international relations as might have been appropriate. It is interesting that policy and politics is the same word in German. Policy comes before strategy!

It seems that there was little trust in either direction. From the Western point of view, there was little appreciation that the Soviet Union, whatever its core ideology, might suffer from the same constraints as the West; budget and the Military-Industrial Complex. Neither did either party seem to heed FDR's maxim that the best way to engender trust in another party is to trust them. Admittedly, this is perhaps a little more than could be expected of the Soviet Union, but there has to be some element of trust on either side. Ronald Reagan learned the expression 'trust, but verify' from Suzanne Massie, a scholar of Russian history, with respect to treaties with Russia. Strangely enough, the expression is an old rhyming Russian proverb: доверяй, но проверяй.

Might it all go back to 1946, when George Kennan sent his now famous 'Long Telegram'? After listening to a speech by Stalin, Kennan judged that the Soviet Union did not see the possibility for long-term peaceful coexistence with the capitalist world. Retrospectively, any observer might say the same about the free-market capitalism world. Did they see any possibility for long-term peaceful existence with the Soviet world? Indeed, if Russia wanted to be a great hegemon, such as they had been in the past, could the United States in the West in general actually deny that these were their objectives too? And whilst European states in general are not in thrall to the United States, memories of the Marshall Plan, which set Europe on the road to recovery, must last.

Stalin casts a long shadow, but he died in 1953 and Georgy Malenkov took over as leader of the Soviet Union, with the odious but powerful Lavrentiy Beria. Beria was bumped off in June of that year and eventually Khrushchev took over. Notwithstanding the Cuban missile crisis, could there have been a better understanding between the West and Khrushchev's Russia, and before the long, sterile years of Leonid Brezhnev? Overall, the objective must be peace.

Such were the preoccupations on both sides for the duration of the Cold War. But whatever policies were adumbrated, there was nothing like a true strategy, being one that recognises that there are regimes around the world that are not the same as your own, but that you still need to maintain peaceful relationships with them. Overall, that objective must be peace, and peace with justice for all.

To return to the implicit question: do nuclear weapons have a future? The usual model for discussion is a nuclear war between two major nuclear states, such as the United States and (now) the Russian Federation or China. If escalation could not be contained – and that would be challenging enough – the war would result in a total annihilation of both states, but also alienation from the rest of the international community. Having learned the lessons of nuclear war, they might 'arm up' or, more likely, boost efforts to ban nuclear weapons altogether.

It's salutary that, as early as 1967, Latin and South American agreed the Treaty of Tlatelolco, which established a nuclear-weapon-free zone in Latin America and the Caribbean. This treaty was a significant step in the effort to prevent nuclear proliferation around the world. Looking at various scenarios:

Large nuclear state versus small non-nuclear state would result in devastation of the smaller state but also opprobrium from the international community: would any state trust the larger state ever again?

Small nuclear state versus large nuclear state (such as North Korea attacking the United States) would result in the devastation of North Korea with many regional consequences.

We might conclude that it is unlikely that a strategic nuclear weapon would ever be used.

A more likely scenario is that smaller, tactical nuclear weapons are used in an established battlefield or against a port or assembly area, such as the US Atlantic Fleet HQ, now renamed United States Fleet Forces Command in Norfolk, Virginia or the Royal Navy's base in Portsmouth UK.

Many weapons would have to be used to really change the balance. The point is that *tactical* battlefield nuclear weapons carry the same *political* risks as the use of strategic weapons, with opprobrium and isolation within the international community, as well, of course, as the risk of retaliation. So we might posit that nuclear weapons, strategic, tactical, and the various ways of delivery will continue to be part of some countries' arsenal, largely through momentum – or, as Freedman suggests, lethargy.

It's rather like the changing a country's constitution. Relatively straightforward to set up *ab initio*; there's lots of help around, but any attempt to change an existing constitution would have many vested interests, such as right-wing, left-wing, liberal, religious, etc. vying for their own favourite changes. It would be almost impossible, although some countries have managed: France is now on its *fifth* republic.

There is *no objective nuclear strategy* that satisfies any political objective. That is, using nuclear weapons to achieve a durable and lasting peace. In fact, nuclear weapons would do exactly the opposite.

Deterrence is not a strategy, but a subjective part of it.

The price of security and peace is constant vigilance, continuing negotiation and a recognition that strategy is about every aspect of international relations, not just military.

General competition theory stresses that a competitor be strong in every aspect of its operation, but very strong in one particular aspect. That aspect could be diplomacy and search for lasting peace, worldwide. Recall that the ratio between the amount of money spent on war and the amount of money spent on peace worldwide is roughly a thousand to one.

There could also be a recognition of what strategy really is...

...everything about the future

All in all, nuclear weapons have no future, and the current increases in nuclear stockpiles is contrary to any policy that embraces peace.

Nuclear weapons also refute the old adage that *if you want peace, prepare for war.*

A more humane aphorism might be that *if you want peace, prepare for and promulgate peace*, not forgetting justice, universal and indivisible.

Part Five: War after Ukraine

22 WHAT HAVE WE LEARNED FROM THE WAR IN UKRAINE?

We (and *us*) in this context refers to the United States, NATO, the EU and Western Europe plus the 'Western-aligned' nations of the Asia-Pacific and elsewhere on the globe. We might add Japan, Australia and New Zealand, South Korea, Botswana, Nigeria, Kenya and Morocco. Perhaps even Israel.

ABOUT WAR (THE TITLE OF THE FIRST BOOK IN THIS TRILOGY) ...

o Despite an enormous amount of literature, analyses, conferences, books, meetings, concepts and statements of intent, some heralding a more peaceful future, *war*, the use of organised purposeful violence in international relations is still with us.

o And because war is still with us, we have no choice: we must take war considerably more seriously.

o The West's deterrence strategy, focused almost exclusively on *nuclear* deterrence, did not work in terms of conventional deterrence where it was assumed that would work by association.

o In terms of general conventional deterrence, it is clear that troop deployments are better than threats of economic sanctions.

o It is also clear that, even with a conventional war, air power is essential.

o Although staying ahead in technology has always been seen as vital in the waging of war, it is now overwhelmingly important, and the difference between victory and defeat.

In an interview with *The Economist* in November 2023, Ukraine's former military commander, General Valery Zaluzhny, admitted that the war against Russia was at a stalemate. (This was denied quickly afterwards by President Zelenskyy.) Nevertheless, the well-respected Zaluzhny suggests that all the technical solutions he needs already exist. He urges innovation and application in drones, electronic warfare, anti-artillery capabilities and demining equipment, as well as in the use of robotics. Of course, Joe Biden, is careful that America is not dragged into confrontation with Russia, but there is scope for more, and better support.

o Although modern war theory and tactics favour manoeuvre, the Russian – Ukraine war, where one side digs in, is more akin to the trenches on the Western Front in the First World War.

ABOUT RUSSIA

o Russia's word is not to be trusted, and always beware Maskirovka.
o Russia still honours the 'Great Patriotic War' against Germany (1941 to 1945) and its appalling casualties. This may make citizens more tolerant of casualties.
o The Russian public did not condone this war against Ukraine but does not want to be seen as losing.
o Historically, Russia sees territory, particularly contiguous territory, as part of its hegemonic plan: e.g. Chechnya, Georgia, Armenia, etc.
o Russia sees war as a constant struggle, and relations with other countries as a zero-sum game: whatever the other side wins, Russia loses.
o Ever since Peter the Great, Russia has put great faith in artillery. Recall that most injury and deaths in battle come from artillery and bombs rather than bullets.
o War is waged in many more dimensions than the practice in

the West. Prior to invading Ukraine, Russian 'special services' had recruited a significant agent network in Ukraine, and that remained viable post invasion, providing a steady stream of human intelligence to Russian forces. At the time of writing, Russia is putting much effort into suborning Bulgaria, a NATO member.

o The Russian armed forces are good at learning. It seems to have escaped the West's notice that during Operation Barbarossa in June 1941, the Soviet Army was completely trounced, whole armies destroyed or taken into captivity. However, only eighteen months later, they fought and won the battle of Stalingrad. From that moment on, and although there were some horrifying battles (many fought in Ukraine) the Germans were on the back foot. Soviet staff work was good, and they managed to deploy on a front some 200 km wide

o As the Russian invasion of Ukraine has shown, the Russian playbook is one of corruption, suborning key members of the target country's civil service, misinformation and brutality, all with hegemonic intent.

ABOUT LIVING WITH RUSSIA

o Overall, the West has to find a way of living with a nuclear armed, insecure and bruised Russia. It is unlikely that Russian Federation will abandon its hegemonic plans, whatever the outcome of this war. But Russia may be facing a difficult future. Over the next few years – and we cannot imagine how many – Russia will suffer from financial sanctions and demographic changes. The population will grow older and require more support. Also, industry and the civil service will suffer the loss of younger, tech-savvy people.

o Already some of the ex-Soviet republics – Kazakhstan and Belarus come to mind – are slowly distancing themselves from the Russian Federation. So far this seems not to have affected the various oblasts within the Russian Federation itself, but – see above – a survey carried out in 2023 amongst Western Russia experts revealed that half of them imagined the Russian Federation falling apart in the next few years. Let us hope that this is not met with smug satisfaction and schadenfreude in the United States.

o By a tragic irony, the United States have their own problems, with doctrinal splits and the fear of another Trump presidency. There is even talk about some states seceding from the Union. (It didn't go well last time.)

o The danger for the West is that a turbulent and disintegrating Russian Federation might well affect contiguous countries, all the way from the Far East to Europe. In that event, the Russian Federation might find even more common cause with China, Iran and North Korea.

o In the fullness of time there will be many more books, PhDs and conferences on this war. Probably a few films as well, no doubt completely ignoring European contribution to the war and starring some Hollywood actor displaying epic heroism and winning the war all on his own. More serious discourses will link international relations with diplomacy, with munitions, with tactics and doctrines on the front line. The consensus will be that the war was more of a surprise than a shock. As we explored in Part One of this book, Russia's hegemonic ambitions are not curbed by being the largest country by land area in the world, or any of the defeats that they have suffered militarily (Brest-Litovsk), diplomatically or after the collapse of the Soviet system.

o What we have learned from the Russian Ukrainian war is well documented in the chapter on that subject. To look wider, and having recognised these lessons, here we focus on the incidence and likelihood of war in general and as a social enterprise. The key question is, in the light of that war, whether war continues to be a way of resolving international disputes?

o It will come as something of a disappointment to observe that the Russian-Ukrainian war will not have – or certainly should not have – an enormous impact on any the future incidence or progress of war in general. Moat of what we are 'discovering', we knew, or certainly should have known, beforehand.

o That is to say that the politics of war have always been paramount, as has the requirement to have adequate munitions. This has been repeated time and time again, and one of the major lessons of war is that wars seldom turn out as expected. The main, and overwhelming lesson is that war may break out anywhere, and at any time.

o The overwhelming presence of the Russian threat has eclipsed some of the other security threats around the 'arc of insecurity' on Europe's north, east and southern borders. It has also inhibited thinking about any long-term strategy for dealing with the Russian threat.

ABOUT NUCLEAR THREATS

o Nuclear weapons still cast a long shadow over international politics. They have not been used in war since 1945, but they have not gone away.

o Putin's nuclear threats have not stopped outside aid and the supply of munitions, but they have caused some restraint in the extent, nature and pace of that support. Western military assistance, while vital, has been piecemeal, careful and cautious due to fears of escalation.

o Arms control is an important tool in a world of nuclear armed states. The New START Treaty has shown its value. This framework has still provided assurances to each side about the other's nuclear capabilities at a time of intense distrust. Thankfully, there is also the continuing communication on routine peacetime nuclear activities such as missile tests. A constant concern is that a missile test might be mistaken for a full-scale nuclear launch.

ABOUT US (AS DEFINED EARLIER)

o Strategic ambiguity (see the US attitude to Taiwan's defence) is no longer viable. Clear plans will deter likely competitors more than 'ambiguity' or 'latency'.

o The NATO alliance is a uniquely valuable institution, and it should receive all the political and financial resources it requires. Also, NATO must have a role in resisting the suborning of weaker countries' governments, such as may now be happening in Bulgaria.

o Our intelligence, both from the of military and diplomatic point of view, was either very poor or, given the many intelligence agencies involved, uncoordinated. The intelligence may have been good but was not heeded or acted upon.

o We ignored Russia's cyber-actions in Estonia, bombs and artillery and devastation in Chechnya and Russian troops in Georgia, influencing American elections and poisoning the Skripals.

o There was far too much smugness in the West after the collapse of the Soviet system. To illustrate, some American commentators said that Russia needed to 'eat their greens'. It may be a fair comment, but probably not the best one to wave in Russia's face when they faced a very difficult time in their history. Schadenfreude is not a part of usual diplomatic interlocution and certainly not a good basis for diplomatic relations. Remember what Churchill said: 'In War, Resolution; In Defeat, Defiance; In Victory, Magnanimity; and in Peace, Good Will'.

o For all the planning, new HQ buildings, concepts, war gaming, doctrine, etc. NATO was unprepared for the scenario where Russia attacked Ukraine. It would only be fair to mention that, under the new, current Supreme Allied Commander Europe (SACEUR), General Christopher G Cavoli, much of this has been resolved.

o Stocks of weapons, munitions, artillery barrels, missiles, tanks and the whole paraphernalia of war in NATO stocks were considerable, but woefully inadequate.

o Also, there was nothing like enough manufacturing capacity to feed Ukraine's need for artillery shells and other vital equipment.

o The West may have a strategy to counter this war, but any long-term strategy – how to live with Russians in the future – is missing.

o We do not seem to have developed a reliable way of dealing with, or even communicating with Russia. In a 2008 meeting between David Miliband and Sergei Lavrov, Russian Foreign Minister, Miliband was left tongue-tied after Lavrov demanded to know 'Who the f**k are you to lecture me?' when told of the EU's frustration with the Kremlin. The Russians are different, not inferior.

o We have to find a way of dealing with the Russians according to their sensibilities, not ours. Many years ago now, in 1960, Khrushchev pounded his shoe on his delegate-desk in protest at a speech during a Plenary Meeting of the United Nations General Assembly. It was considered very undiplomatic!

o Desperately needed is a plan for the end of the Russian-Ukrainian war. It's a difficult, almost impossible call. In the Hamas versus Israel war, it seems that nobody has a clue what a settlement might look like. For every idea as to what post-war Ukraine might look like, there is a compelling argument as to why it would be untenable.

ABOUT THE REST OF THE WORLD

o There seems to have been an assumption that after Russia's unprovoked and brutal invasion of Ukraine, that the rest of the world would fall into line and condemn it. In fact, there were a substantial number of abstentions in the UN votes, with many countries saying the war was only a European problem.

o Russian foreign policy in Africa has been effective in courting the various leaders – some of them dictators or autocrats – with aid and military assistance. The problem for the west is that Russia, now being established in Africa, will be very difficult to displace.

o And countries, such as Iran, are supplying substantial amounts to the Russians. The Chinese, although diplomatically supporting, are not thought to be supplying munitions, though they are buying Russian oil.

o Although there is much commentary about China wishing to launch a new world order, their Russian/Ukrainian peace plan which they published in February 2023 is reasonable. It is intriguing to note that it does not appear to have been discussed seriously amongst Western allies, or in Ukraine itself.

23 WHAT WE HAVE LEARNED, OR NOT, ABOUT WAR IN GENERAL

War after Ukraine is the third and final book in the trilogy *Making Sense of War*. The first book, *About War*, promised to define what war means, how it is directed and what role it might have in the future. It concluded that war is a paradox: modern, supposedly sophisticated states using controlled violence against similarly endowed polities; men, and increasingly women, being asked to fight, to kill and to destroy and then return to a peaceful civilian life; political leaders preaching peace yet, inevitably, preparing for war with considerably more effort and investment in the latter than the former.

The concept behind this trilogy is to encourage the reader to see war as a political act and in those terms to comprehend the provenance, progress and conclusion of any war. Any nation-state's approach to war must be multifunctional, integrating overall strategy with politicians and foreign policy experts, civil servants, university professors and, most of all, senior military officers. See comments in *War in Context* about Libya in 2011.

About War emphasised that the primary duty of a modern state is the security of its citizens. It touched on the causes of war and strategy, generally poorly done, as the link between politics and the use of armed force.

The second book, *War in Context*, examined how the emergence of the state both legitimised war and controlled it. It covered the problem of classifying wars and thus, perhaps, predicting them. It touched on a number of other topics such as nuclear deterrence, drones and pacifism. During the drafting of the second book, the world changed with Putin's invasion of Ukraine on 24 February 2022. This volume then included a brief summary of the situation in Ukraine at the time of writing, midway through 2022.

War after Ukraine recognises the major changes that have taken place during the many months of this invasion, by focusing on and analysing five main topics: Russia's use of military power for hegemonic reasons, whether czarist, Soviet or under Putin; the concept of the nation-state; the specific security of Europe and the role of NATO and, because Putin mentioned nuclear weapons when he announced his invasion, an analysis of the provenance of nuclear weapons going back to decisions made at the start of the nuclear age. The book covers the prospects for nuclear weapons.

War after Ukraine uses concepts defined in *About War* and *War in Context* as a framework to hazard a commentary on the prospects *for* war, not just in Ukraine. Again, we emphasise that it's the prospects *for* war as a way of resolving problems of international relations rather than the prospect *of* war, which, in the literature, usually means warfare.

WAR WILL ALWAYS BE WITH US

As explained in the first two volumes of the trilogy, war's beginning can be traced to when people could first walk upright. Being upright meant that things could be carried, and weapons manufactured and used. Social organisation also developed and, inevitably, pride and association with the group, and a concomitant disdain of the 'other'. Larger groups – nations and states – meant more people to fight and also the legitimisation of war for maintaining and developing the nation/group/state. Political philosophy developed considerably over the years from state to empire to hegemony. Various renaissances through the ages, the enlightenment, the industrial revolution, have all served war rather than restrained it.

The message must be that whatever the international structure, whatever international and domestic law might say and whatever the level of prevailing political philosophy, war will always be with us. War can certainly be controlled and managed, but, and it's a bleak thought, war will always break out somewhere probably somewhere where it's least expected.

THE CAUSES OF WAR ARE DIVERSE AND EVER-CHANGING

There is no single model of war; all wars are different. The causes of wars are subject to an everlasting debate and although history might teach some useful concepts here, there are no definitive answers.

However, peace had to be invented. the late Michael Howard, the doyen of war writing in the United Kingdom and the first professor of a War Studies at King's College London War Studies department wrote *The Invention of Peace* in 2001. It is an intriguing thesis. He asserts that prior to Napoleon nobody thought war particularly unusual. Dynasties and empires waged war on other dynasties and empires using resources – men, munitions, logistical support, that were not necessarily subject to any democratic control. Napoleon, despite still being honoured in France, was responsible for the change and it was he who suborned the whole of the new French state to his purposes. He cared little for the French people and, at one stage, boasted to Metternich (Austrian statesman and diplomat) 'You cannot stop me … I can spend 30,000 men a month.' (Putin may feel the same.)

ANARCHY RULES

Anarchy is not saturnine men in cloaks hiding a bomb, as is often portrayed in entertainment. The nation-state (indeed, other non-state polities) lives in an anarchic world, where each nation-state is sovereign and can thus make its own independent decisions. There is no higher power, and the main legal remedies are through the community of other states – perhaps represented by the United Nations – imposing sanctions. There would also be reputational damage. Who would now trust Putin's word or treaties with the Russian Federation again?

ALTHOUGH THE *CHARACTER* OF WAR (ACTUALLY WARFARE) MAY CHANGE ITS *NATURE* WILL REMAIN THE SAME

There is a distinction to be made here between the *nature* of war and the *character* of war. The nature of war is the use of purposeful organised violence to change the political balance between two or more polities. The character of war can change and change rapidly. The spectrum of purposeful organised violence is wide, ranging from cyber-attacks to nuclear strikes and everything in between.

Perhaps the most prestigious organisation is The Changing Character of War Centre, part of the University of Oxford. They are an 'Interdisciplinary research centre for the study of change in armed conflict, with research into such subjects as Contractors And Contiguity: Assessing China's Private Security Presence In Kyrgyzstan or Reading The Wind: What Makes UN Special Political Missions Effective? or Strategy In The Peloponnesian War and Contemporary Military Strategy'. For those readers who have an interest in this subject, visiting the website is well worthwhile.

Although currently some 80 per cent of wars are intra-state, it would be foolish to ignore the possibility of interstate wars breaking out, such as happened in Ukraine.

WAR IS (NOT) GOOD FOR YOU

It is commonly thought that war is a bad idea, but this is a relatively recent concept. No one would dream of saying this today, but Field Marshal Helmuth Graf von Moltke, the victor in the wars of German unification famously said:

War is part of God's world order. War develops man's most noble virtues,
which otherwise would slumber and die out; courage, self-denial,
devotion to duty, and willingness to make sacrifices …

All very well for him, but, as a Field Marshall, he did not have to spend his time in trenches. Hitler thought the same; the nation 'cleansing itself in blood'. Or as we would say nowadays, a load of old bollocks.

There is however a rather bleak grain of value in the *War is good for you* idea. Many nation-states become more coherent, and their populations more nationalistic, after a war with another nation-state or after a civil war. Think of the United States 'war between the states' with its appalling casualties, France after the revolution, Germany after unification, Italy after the Risorgimento. And although the British nation resented having to go to war against Hitler, they now celebrate the whole idea of Dunkirk, rallying round while our 'backs against the wall'. What they choose to miss is the fact that Dunkirk was a resounding defeat.

THE SECURITY DILEMMA

The Security Dilemma is still as compelling as it ever was. The West was fully aware that Russia was transforming its armed forces and fully aware of Russian hegemonic intentions. The West would have been naïve to believe that this was all for defence. Yet it was inconvenient to imagine Russia's violent hegemonic intentions. After all, the West had done nothing about Chechnya, Georgia, etc. Why worry about Ukraine?

Winning the current security problem is necessary but the longer-term solution must be the ultimate gaol. Strategy is covered comprehensively in this trilogy: *strategy is everything about the future.* 'Strategy' now is largely how offensive methods of war – military, cyber, media are conducted with maybe less than a clearly defined overall objective.

Think of Hamas versus Israel. Both have clear short-term objectives, to defeat, or even destroy, the other side, but neither has a longer-term strategy.

INTELLIGENCE IS VITAL

Intelligence – military, economic, political and diplomatic – is of course vital in any country's dealing with any other. Yet, in the recent past, this seems to have been displaced by unreliable and in some cases fanciful intelligence, some even single source. Think of the rationale for joining in the invasion of Iraq in 2003: was it really credible that Saddam Hussein could launch an attack on the United Kingdom with forty-five minutes notice? Some commentators suggested that this was a rationale looking to support a decision already made.

Intelligence has been largely one-dimensional. For example, the Americans invaded Iraq with very little idea of the social conditions, norms or culture of the Iraqis. Libya was bombed in 2011 with little thought of what the effect of that might be.

For many years now under the Tory government, our overseas embassies have transformed themselves from diplomatic and political intelligence gathering into being salespeople for British exports. Cultural contacts seem to have suffered as well.

As any intelligence analyst will tell you, it's not so much the intelligence gathering that's important – OSINT is perhaps 90 per cent as effective – it's the interpretation and application that is important. Furthermore, any intelligence has to be politically neutral, something that may be disappearing from British and American discourse.

DETERRENCE

This is covered in some detail in this trilogy. It may be thought that deterrence did not work to deter Russia from invading Ukraine, but there are two snags with this opinion. The first is that deterrence was too focused on *nuclear deterrence* rather than *conventional deterrence*. The second is that once the invasion had taken place, the conventional deterrence was what is thought to be of limited value.

However, it was quite clear that air power was going to be very important to help Ukraine to defeat the Russians, and Ukraine, NATO and other European allies could have started constructing appropriate airfields in the east of Ukraine, but behind the front line.

Munitions were a key part of the West's support for Ukraine, but surely airfields would have been an equally powerful deterrent?

THE IMPORTANCE OF CIVILIAN RESOURCES

The importance of civil-military relations: as explained in the text, is vital. One is tempted to say that the most overwhelmingly vital, aspect of the conduct of war is the relationship between elected politicians, civil servants and the military. Recall the comments in *About War* about the invasion of Iraq: where was the political dimension? Recall also that there were maybe five locations for the generation and execution of strategy which was difficult to identify anyway. In the demotic: don't let the generals take over the whole war, but define their objectives carefully.

The United Kingdom has wealth of highly regarded institutions, scholars and other commentators, and more use should be made of this resource. The complete canon of deliberations about war, its conduct and causes, is vast. A lifetime of research would hardly scratch the surface. Artificial Intelligence might help but only leave the scholar with thorny problems of interpretation. It is true that *history is a constant dialogue*: whatever thesis is developed, there will always be a contrary one. This should not deter whatever government from seeking advice and counsel. One particularly explicit example of this might be that the

Versailles conference imposed to harsh a settlement on Germany after the First World War, but there are scholars who say that it wasn't harsh enough.

Some commentaries suggest that the actions of NATO and the West in general was the cause of Putin invading Ukraine, despite condemnations of Putin himself.

A common observation, particularly amongst journalists, is that generals fight the last war, as opposed to preparing for the next war. There might be some truth in this, but whereas journalists, scholars, and commentators in general can opine about all sorts of historic and current situations from the comfort of their offices, somebody, somewhere has to make decisions. No general could say that they cannot deploy to any particular theatre of war on the basis that they haven't planned for it.

DON'T FORGET MILITARY HISTORY

Military history is a very popular subject. Authors like Max Hastings or Anthony Beevor are almost bound to get a good audience for any book about a famous battle or campaign, often adding the subtitle 'with surprising new evidence' or 're-examined' or 'a new history'. As an aside, it is curious that the battles or campaigns covered in popular military history are relatively few compared with the number of battles fought. Trafalgar (1805) and Waterloo (1815) are great favourites; there are many books on the Somme, Operation Market Garden (Arnhem, 1944), Normandy (1944) and Dunkirk (1940). But who has heard of Battle of Attu (1943), the only World War II land battle fought on American soil, in which Japanese and American forces fought in snowy conditions, in contrast with the tropical climate in the rest of the Pacific.

The Ypres battles (1914 to 1918) in the First World War are well explored, but who now remembers the Battle of Tanga (November 1914), also known as the Battle of the Bees, in Tanzania? The point may be that these lesser-known battles are not as clear cut or interesting as the popular ones, but they are all part of the vast catalogue of military history, and could merit further research and incorporation into the whole canon.

My own nominee would be the reconquest of Burma, led by one of the greatest, if not *the* greatest Allied general in the Second World War, Bill Slim. The whole campaign lives up to its 'forgotten army' (XIV Army) name as a forgotten campaign.

Anyone reading a lot of military history is bound to come to the conclusion that some of it is well researched and enlightening, some less so. Nevertheless it's bound to occur to the enthusiastic reader to ask what the battle was about *politically*. Even Bill Slim's brilliant book on the reconquest of Burma, *Defeat into Victory* asks this question in the last chapter. Slim was triumphant, but he still wanted to know what the political context had been.

Throughout this trilogy, there have been many references to historical wars, and this represents a real conundrum for any commentator, journalist or scholar. On one hand, history is the only source of evidence that might contribute to a full comprehension of war and opinions about the future of war; on the other hand, every war is different, with different motivations on either side, means of fighting and outcome.

There are relatively few great writers on war. Frequently mentioned is Sun Tzu (c.544–c.496 BC), the Chinese military strategist and philosopher. His seminal work *The Art of War* is still read, though maybe not completely understood, today. His famous aphorism that 'There is no instance of a nation benefitting from prolonged warfare,' still has resonance. Some military historians are literally timeless: Thucydides' (c.460–c.400 BC) *fear, honour and interest* is still insightful.

Carl von Clausewitz (1780–1831) is perhaps the most well-known of past military writers, and his aphorism '... war is not merely an act of policy but a true political instrument, a continuation of political intercourse carried on with other means. What remains peculiar to war is simply the peculiar nature of its means.'

It contrasts with another well-known writer on war, although not for that subject. Niccolò Machiavelli, who thought that 'war becomes a continuation of politics', a subtle distinction between his and Clausewitz's concept.

Academics, think tanks and journalistic discourses on future war are popular, but one can read a lot without feeling much sense of satisfaction. There are, however, two modern writers who should be celebrated: one is the late Professor Sir Michael Howard, one-time head of War Studies at Kings College London, mentioned several times in the trilogy. Also, Professor Sir Lawrence Freedman, who held the same post.

BEWARE THE MILITARY-INDUSTRIAL COMPLEX!
The military-industrial complex is now even more influential than when President Eisenhower warned against it in 1961. It is appropriate at this stage to note that the most armed state in the world, the United States, also has the largest defence industry, largely in the private sector, with its obligation to turn in a profit.

Current political thinking is that privatised industry is more innovative, more effective and more efficient than government can possibly manage. Any debate on this could go on forever, but it's worth mentioning two points:

First, in looking at defence needs, whose interests are privatised industry considering? Although there is some grumbling in the press about, for example, Britain's privatised industries, there is no move to change the law. Which is ... Limited liability companies must act in the interest of their shareholders: not their customers, not the general public, not their employees, and although there are various laws constraining the environment, they don't have to take that much notice of that either.

Second, it may be that British politicians have been seduced by the American model where a good majority of defence work, development and manufacture is handled by the private sector. State representatives will lobby hard to make sure that they get their fair share of defence contracts. In fact, a cynic might say that this is one of the things that is holding the United States together. Any state seceding from the union would immediately lose its defence contracts. Indeed, defence contracts are sometimes described in the United States as 'defence welfare'.

Some years ago there was an attempt to privatise the maintenance for the London Underground. Yet when the limited liability vehicle which was put together by a number of larger contractors found that it was difficult for it to turn a good profit, they simply washed their hands of the whole thing. This might therefore not be the best model for defence equipment.

NEVER FORGET THAT WAR IS A HUMAN ACTIVITY ...

We cannot fail to emphasise here the overwhelming importance of the human factor. Clausewitz's theory of war emphasises the importance of moral factors: how the people who prosecute any war feel about it. This applies as much to the general public as much as those people in the front line. A famous line from Napoleon was, 'In war the moral is to the physical as three to one.' It's a curious saying, considering how little he cared for his troops ...

In 1939, there was a great feeling that 'Mr Hitler' had to be beaten, and morale was good. In 2003, where the then British Prime Minister Tony Blair decided (seemingly on his own) to support George Bush's invasion of Iraq, millions of people demonstrated against that deployment, with the protest 'not in my name'.

It is also people, politicians with their own foibles, weaknesses and short sightedness who decide about war. They can be strong, sensible and farsighted, but that is relatively rare. The UK prime minister at the time, Sir Anthony Eden decided on the Suez debacle (1956), partly because he couldn't stand the sight of Gamal Abdel Nasser, the Egyptian president. The feeling was mutual. One of the reasons advanced for George Bush's (junior) invasion of Iraq was because Saddam Hussein had attempted to assassinate his father. War can break out at any time, for a whole range of reasons.

PROMOTE ALLIANCES

Initiatives to proscribe, control, limit or regulate war by political or legal means are vital in reducing the likelihood of war. Detractors from this would point out that such alliances will always be friable, and vulnerable to being broken by the demands of a belligerent, such as happened with Russia when invading Ukraine.

Obviously the most successful example of these is first the United States of America, with its fifty states, under a federal system. Although their constitution has come under some criticism, they are unlikely to resort to armed conflict.

Another example is of course the European Union, now twenty-seven states strong. Though some of the eastern states take pleasure in challenging the overall consensus, they again are unlikely to resort to armed conflict.

24 CONCLUSIONS ABOUT WAR

The central question of this book is that having experienced Russia's invasion of Ukraine, what are the prospects for war? How can we forge all the concepts, questions and conundrums above to provide a framework to answer this vital question? We must start here with a disclaimer: there is no one definitive answer, but there are many things we can do to prepare ourselves for contingencies.

There are initiatives that can be undertaken with little extra budget, and without compromising our current posture or plans.

Let us focus even further, by taking it as accepted that the basis for military and offensive action is well understood and a continuous occupation for planners and the armed forces. These would include: the recruitment and training of personnel; the development of weaponry of all types – land, sea, air, and missiles; R&D into future technologies and various doctrines for handling whatever situations arise.

Here, we focus just on the *political* aspects for the United Kingdom. We also make some proposals for the International Community.

IMPERATIVE 1:

Democratise and professionalise foreign policy. This century alone has seen about fourteen foreign secretaries in the United Kingdom, few of whom have had any serious experience in foreign affairs. I say that because some of them hardly had time to find where the FCDO was. Contrast this with Anthony Blinken, the current Secretary of State in the United States, who has had some thirty years' diplomatic experience. Although there is a UK foreign policy committee, it is questionable what influence this has on cabinet's decisions.

Foreign policy should be determined by an executive committee, represented and informed by foreign policy experts from think tanks and universities both at home and abroad. This is not an isolated thought:

Policy Exchange, a British conservative think tank based in London, described by the *Daily Telegraph* as '*the largest, but also the most influential think tank on the right*', suggests that '*Parliament can play a greater role in foreign affairs, and urges enhanced roles for a reconstituted foreign affairs and defence select committee*'.

E-international Relations, an open-access website covering international relations and politics, suggests that '*... because the executive has held, and still holds, royal prerogative for foreign affairs matters, Parliament has been 'unusually limited' in its influence over the area. Scrutiny of foreign policy is unique because, unlike in other areas of governance, 'Parliament is in no sense a regular participant in the process, either by right or custom*'.

The United Kingdom's Institute for Government, commenting on the UK's exit from Afghanistan, observed that '*a real dispatch of this ugly episode will come only with a coherent foreign policy ... the report by the Foreign Affairs Committee into the UK's exit from Afghanistan is searing in its criticism of ministers and senior civil servants ...*' It goes on to say '*which is so scathing about government failures and devastating in its view of what that means for the UK's reputation in the world ...*'

Since security is the primary responsibility of any state, it is a dereliction of duty that the system for defining and setting foreign policy is inadequate to the task.

This could be facilitated by convening and holding a modern-day

Project Solarium. This is covered in *War in Context*, but was, briefly, Eisenhower's 1953 effort at achieving consensus amongst his cabinet and officials as to what to do about the Soviet Union. It is not well-known, reflecting that the output largely confirmed Harry Truman's (the previous US president) concept of 'containing' Russia.

The United Kingdom could benefit from such an exercise, not just for our relations with Russia and possibly China, but also for all autocracies and dictatorships around the world. It may also be expedient to carry out such an exercise in the light of a possible change of US president to Trump, but in any case, Britain's deliberations would contribute greatly to the relationship with the US anyway.

IMPERATIVE 2:

Where British armed forces are to be deployed anywhere in the world, this should be subject to members of Parliament being given access to intelligence briefings, and then a *free vote in the Commons* about the deployment. The monarchical powers to declare war, usurped by the Cabinet, actually the prime minister, must be stopped.

IMPERATIVE 3:

Although the concept of 'Global Britain' seems to have receded, we still need to recognise security threats and the *'arc of insecurity'* around Europe. To illustrate that, if and when the Russian Federation is thrown out of Ukraine, this could have very adverse effects on the countries surrounding the Black Sea. In fact Neal Ascherson believes that if Russia is defeated in Ukraine, it could cause a bloodbath in the surrounding countries. This represents a security risk to the European Union, and to the United Kingdom as well.

IMPERATIVE 4:

Recognise that **our current Armed Forces are inadequate to the task** of defending the United Kingdom, even in conjunction with NATO forces, and particularly in conjunction with NATO forces where the main contributor, the US, may be less than enthusiastic. This is what happened when the United Kingdom and France decided to bomb Libya. The then US president (Obama) was sceptical about the utility of such a move. Practically, the UK and France had to draw down on NATO weapons stocks to fulfil the mission. The tragedy of the bombing of Libya was that although it broke a state ruled by a brutal dictator, Muammar Gaddafi, Libya then descended into civil war with competing warlords, both attempting to monopolise the oil reserves.

With foreign policy a more democratic process, there could be recognition of the 'arc of insecurity' (see *War in Context*) and contingency plans drawn up. This would reveal the weakness in the British Armed Forces and there should be a demand for more and better resources and personnel.

At the moment, the United Kingdom has one of the smallest proportions of its population serving in the Armed Forces, including reserve (Territorial) personnel. Given the threat from Russia and the unlikelihood of this going away or being resolved, this should be addressed immediately.

IMPERATIVE 5:

Support and expand **cultural exchange**. The BBC and the British Council should be well funded to manage this, but it might be better to focus on one region as opposed to the whole world. As the continent with the greatest number of previous colonies which have been infiltrated by Russia's Wagner Group, it may be that Africa is a suitable candidate here. But that provision may need to be supported by a military presence, and the whole exercise coordinated.

IMPERATIVE 6:

All governments who commit to using purposeful, organised, violence should be obliged by the UN to present (a) the rationale behind their deployment, (b) their overall strategy and what end result is planned and (c) how this will contribute to a stable and lasting peace for all parties. This may seem wishful thinking with, in early days, many refusals from other states. But we could start with our own country. There would be no need to legislate, but the debate in whatever representative chamber was contemplating such action might expose the lack of any thought-through strategy.

IMPERATIVE 7:

Governments should recognise that now, although war will continue to be fought on the battlefield, this will require a long and high-capacity logistics tail, including manufacturing capacity.

And also ...

War will be fought on many more fronts: diplomatic, cyber and resource availability. For example, currently, it is reported that Ukrainian troops have deployed to Africa to prevent Russian forces (probably mercenaries) taking (stealing?) gold which is used to finance the war in Ukraine.

IMPERATIVE 8:

Rediscover Clausewitz: Many years ago, towards the end of the 20th century, the writings of Carl von Clausewitz were thought to be from 'just another' military commentator.

In the intervening years, the subtlety and percipience of what he has written has been recognised as valuable for all time. There have been some detractors: it is thought that the translation from the original German of *On War* (his classic masterpiece) to English might repay some revision.

It has been pointed out that previous writers on war (such as Antoine-Henri Jomini, Alfred Thayer Mahan and Immanuel Kant) contributed to Clausewitz's thinking, but this does not detract from the core message, which is that war is first, last and always a political act, and that all the actions in war should serve the political objective.

A seminal book on Clausewitz is *Reading Clausewitz* by Beatrice Heuser.

25 WHAT, THEN, IS THE FUTURE FOR WAR?

If we look at the incidence of war over the past century, each millennium, and indeed the whole of human existence, war has always been the main driver of relationships between groups, polities, nations and states. This has been independent of the size, nature or location of any polity, of whatever system of government the polity chooses or has thrust upon them or even their location on the historic scale – ancient prehistory to the modern day.

And here is the point: *history* is a reasonably good guide to the future for war. Tragic as it sounds, war will be a permanent feature of the international environment. War will always be political, in every sense of the word, and Thucydides' maxim about *fear, honour and interest* will endure. Sun Tzu, Machiavelli, Clausewitz will all contribute, as will Howard and Freedman in the modern era.

This trilogy has covered a long span of history, made examples of many different wars, contemplated many concepts and philosophies. It provides an invaluable basis for thinking about war, understanding the many aspects of strategy and may even point the way to a more peaceful future.

It's nothing of a surprise to learn that although many wars are necessary, the majority are not, and do not achieve their initial objectives.

Most of all, this trilogy has been understanding war as a way of achieving peace. One of the most famous aphorisms about war is 'if you want peace, prepare for war', suggested by Publius Flavius Vegetius Renatus's tract about war, written in the 4th or 5th century AD.

The phrase purports to present the idea that the conditions of peace are often maintained by a readiness and willingness to make war when necessary. Publius had obviously never heard of the Security Dilemma, and he clearly has the ring of the brutal Roman attitude to what they thought of as other, inferior races.

Perhaps readers might indulge an aphorism of my own: If you want peace, understand war, and understand it as a political act. Understand who wages it, who starts it, its provenance, its prosecution and resolution. And recall that war does not 'break out', as some past historians imagine. Somebody breaks it out. It is people who wage war; there is no place for the passive tense.

Most of all, and the one thing that stands out in this discourse, is that war is a paradox. Refer to the introduction to Chapter 17, quoting the journalist Simon Tisdall. Other paradoxes present themselves, such as:

o   Nuclear weapons too powerful to use.

o   The Security Dilemma.

o   Big wars, requiring mobilisation, require all ordinary citizens to 'join up' and become soldiers (sailors, aviators). When it's finished, they have to go back to civilian life and learn to be peaceful.

o   We take it for granted that civilian politicians should direct war. The paradox is civil-military relations: politicians have a little idea of what the military can achieve, and the military cannot understand the concept of political balance. What's more, military people are more likely to be right-wing than left-wing, with obvious implications for the conflict. The important lesson is that there should be a much better relationship between the military and politicians.

o   Even Churchill's dictum: 'in war, resolution; in defeat, defiance; in victory, magnanimity; in peace, goodwill' is paradox: magnanimity and goodwill to people we were trying to kill no so long ago.

Paradox here is not some philosophical or intellectual exercise: there are practical implications. We can easily assert that the only guide we have to the future is the past, and that somewhere, somehow, war will break out (or, *pace* the above, someone will break it out). And here we have the *ultimate* paradox of war. Even if we, as a state, a nation or any other polity are completely committed to peace in general, and to a peaceful resolution of any dispute, and if there is any possibility that someone – anyone – would use military force against us, then we have to invest in military power and, most of all, be good at using it to achieve our political goals. And as part of our political goal, the overwhelmingly important aspect is our security in every sense of the word.

In the ebb and flow of international affairs, understanding war is our best path to peace, recognising it not as an inevitability but a political choice shaped by human agency.

APPENDICES

Appendix A: What is 'Europe'? What is 'The West'?

Appendix B: Components of European security architecture within the European Union

Appendix C: Contributors to European security architecture – International Bodies

Appendix D: The Truman doctrine – Containing the Soviet Union

Appendix E: Previously independent Soviet republics

Appendix F: Some countries have forsaken nuclear weapons: what was their rationale?

APPENDIX A: WHAT IS 'EUROPE'? WHAT IS 'THE WEST'?

It's important to define exactly what countries make up 'Europe' and, complementarily, what 'The West' is. One might imagine that is simple question: on page 148 we quote that even *The Economist* cannot exactly define what a country is.

Searching the web comes up with between forty-five and fifty countries in Europe, but some of the lists include Russia and Turkey and some do not. Some include Kazakhstan, Georgia, Armenia and Cyprus, and so some even mention Transnistria, a breakaway region of Moldova which has Russian troops stationed there. Some lists also include Abkhazia, Nagorno-Karabakh, Kosovo, Northern Cyprus and South Ossetia.

Of these, thirty countries are members of NATO – this includes Sweden and Finland (only recently acceded) but excludes, for the purposes of this definition, the United States and Canada.

Of those, some twenty-seven countries are members of the European Union – the EU, one of the largest and most prosperous alliances in the world, second only, but only just, to the United States.

'The West' is used as a shorthand for those countries in Europe, the Americas and Australasia who share similar, or at least parallel, political, cultural and economic value systems. The West is sometimes called the Occident, to distinguish it from the Orient, the eastern world. Neither definition is permanent, and sometimes varies with context.

This may sound pedantic, but it is important to define exactly the area we are considering when talking about security and particularly security threats. At the time of writing, the Russian Federation has cancelled the Ukrainian wheat export deal which allowed ships to leave Odesa on their way to feed the world.

NATO talks of the 'North Atlantic Area', which is not defined (it may be 'obvious', but it still needs defining!). The Black Sea no longer enjoys freedom of navigation: is this a security concern for NATO? What are they doing about it?

APPENDIX B: COMPONENTS OF EUROPEAN SECURITY ARCHI-
TECTURE WITHIN THE EUROPEAN UNION AND NATO

The European Union (EU) was originally created to make war impossible within Europe, mainly between the two most powerful continental European countries, Germany and France. The original 'six' created the Council of Europe and then, in 1950, the European Coal and Steel Community. Inspired by the concept of 'ever closer union', the EU has developed into a major worldwide political player and now has some twenty-seven members. I repeat this here to recall that the *original* motivation was focussed on security and an avoidance of war. Over the past seventy years, the EU has also developed its own security and defence interests.

The main framework for managing security challenges – crisis management, conflict prevention, and capacity-building efforts – is the EU's Common Security and Defence Policy (CSDP). The EU also has the European External Action Service (EEAS), which coordinates and implements security policies. The CSDP is part of the EU's Common Foreign and Security Policy (CFSP) and involves the EU's security, defence diplomacy and implementation. In accordance with the principles of the United Nations Charter, the CSDP contributes military and civilian missions to preserve peace, prevent conflict and strengthen international security.

The CSDP also involves the Permanent Structured Cooperation (PESCO), under whose auspices the member countries' armed forces seek structural integration.

Supposedly vital to security considerations (particularly so after the Russian invasion of Ukraine), PESCO, was conceptualised by the Treaty of Lisbon in 2009. However, the 2010s saw the security environment in the EU's near abroad changing dramatically, with the Libyan Civil War, the Syrian Civil War and the rise of the Islamic State of Iraq and the

Levant, which caused an overwhelming migrant crisis.

PESCO got off the ground in 2017, with the Coordinated Annual Review on Defence (CARD), the Military Planning and Conduct Capability (MPCC) and finally the European Defence Fund in 2021. This was launched in 2021 to provide financial support to promote defence research, development and procurement projects within the EU. The blurb suggest that it addresses capability gaps, promotes 'disruptive technologies', and will, eventually, boost the EU's strategic defence autonomy.

Then there is the European Defence Agency (EDA), which coordinates defence capabilities among EU member states. Established in 2004, it acts as an executive agency of the EU's Common Security and Defence Policy (CSDP), promoting collaboration among EU member states, standardisation of military equipment and R&D.

The Organisation for Joint Armament Cooperation (OCCAR) has a similar role, but includes only Belgium, France, Germany, Italy, Spain and the United Kingdom, and focusses on efficiency and cost reduction through better procurement, cost sharing and, again, standardisation and interoperability.

After the Russian invasion of Ukraine 2022, a group of forty-four European countries (the EU has twenty-seven members) formed the European Political Community (EPC) as an intergovernmental assembly for strategic discussions about the future of Europe. It also includes Presidents of the European Council and the European Commission, both EU bodies.

Inspired by President Emmanuel Macron of France, the concept was to provide a facility for democratic European nations with 'shared core values' to find space for cooperation. Macron suggested political coordination, security cooperation, energy and the free movement of people, particularly young people, already a realty in the EU.

The group first met in October 2022 in Prague. It comprises twenty-seven EU Member States, the Western Balkan States, Albania, Northern Macedonia, Kosovo, Serbia, Bosnia and Herzegovina and Montenegro. All of these have been identified by the EU as candidates or potential candidates for membership. Also included are Georgia, Moldova, Ukraine, all of which applied to join the EU following Russia's invasion of Ukraine in February 2022, with Armenia, Azerbaijan and Turkey.

Finally, there is the European Peace Facility. Not part of the main EU budget or budgetary cycle, it was set up in March 2021 to deliver military aid to partner countries and the funding the EU military missions abroad under the Common Foreign and Security Policy.

Partly NATO, partly EU, partly other countries, the Ukraine Defense Contact Group, also known as the Ramstein Group pulls together an alliance of fifty-four countries, being all thirty-one NATO members plus twenty-three other countries. The focus is on sending military resources to Ukraine in their hour of need. The group escalated the overall contribution to Ukraine, though the supply of tanks was somewhat contentious. Germany eventually announced it would provide some of its own Leopard 2A6 tanks, but only in tandem with the United States who provided thirty-one M1 Abrams tanks. Other countries followed suit.

One body that gets very little publicity is the North Atlantic Council, which is the political decision-making body within NATO, serving as a forum for coordination and decision-making within NATO and its strategic direction. It comprises ambassadors, permanently nominated from each of the thirty-one NATO members. The NAC, responsible for political and strategic decisions, formulates policies, strategic concepts and ultimately action plans. It also has a role in crisis response and subsequent consequent decision-making.

There are a number of bodies that are subsidiary to the organisations listed above. For example in 2022, Defence Ministers from fifteen NATO

Allies agreed to the development of a 'European Sky Shield Initiative', led by Germany. It aims to create a European air and missile defence system through the common acquisition of air defence equipment and missiles by European nations. This will strengthen NATO's Integrated Air and Missile Defence.

APPENDIX C: CONTRIBUTORS TO EUROPEAN SECURITY AR-
CHITECTURE: INTERNATIONAL BODIES

The Organisation for Security and Cooperation in Europe (OSCE) is the world's largest regional security organisation and comprises some fifty-seven states across Europe, central Asia and North America. Its role covers security issues, arms control, human rights and democracy, and it handled various initiatives to promote security, conflict resolution and cooperation amongst states on shared problems.

As well as its security function, the OSCE focuses on a variety of 'good purposes', such as sustainable development and environmental issues. It also promotes good governance, anti-corruption measures, deals with people trafficking and transnational threats such as organised crime and terrorism. For good measure, throw in conflict mediation, election monitoring and capacity-building too.

For the sake of completeness, the **Council of Europe** is an international organisation that promotes human rights, democracy and the rule of law. It is not primarily a security organisation, nor is it part of the European Union, though there are many common members.

The European Court of Human Rights (ECHR)is part of the **Council of Europe,** and also known as the Strasbourg Court. This court interprets the **European Convention on Human Rights**.

Perhaps the most important contributor to world peace is, and has been the **United Nations**. This is covered adequately in other volumes and is not expanded here.

APPENDIX D: THE TRUMAN DOCTRINE – CONTAINING THE
SOVIET UNION

The Truman Doctrine, announced in March 1947, promised support for
'democracies against authoritarian threats', a consequence of wishing to
contain Soviet geopolitical expansion during the Cold War.

Over the following twenty years, deterrence theory, or more
particularly nuclear deterrence theory was developed on the basis of
MAD (Mutual Assured Destruction), and that in turn was based on
second strike capability.

This is explained in detail in *About War* and *War in Context*.

The point is that it doesn't look as if American/Western/NATO
thinking has moved very much beyond this. Although this may be an
entirely appropriate response to the Russian bear, we're still wishing to
'contain' the threat, and to deter Russia, although that does not seem
to have worked very well with this war. The West should never make
the mistake of assuming rationality in opponents. It made no sense for
Putin to invade Ukraine. But that did not stop him.

Whatever the present outcome, Russia, a nuclear power, remains
the largest country by land area in the world with considerable natural
resources. Russia is bitter about its loss of empire and status. James
Nixey, the Russian expert at Chatham House, argues that we must learn
to live without Russia. That they have no interest in consensus and
respect no agreement. If we no longer sit at tables with them, like the
G8, and accept that we should not, we must adopt a consistent policy of
defensive quarantine.

APPENDIX E: PREVIOUSLY INDEPENDENT SOVIET REPUBLICS
The Soviet Union dissolved in 1991, and the Russian Federation was declared. This led to the independence of several former Soviet Republics, but these are distinct from the Russian Federation.

Some former Soviet Republics gained independence from the Soviet Union in 1991 and are no longer part of the Russian Federation itself. The Russian Federation, most often referred to as Russia, was itself one of the fifteen Republics of the Soviet Union.

Although several other former Soviet Republics became independent, Russia continued as an independent state, retained most of the Soviet Union's territory and reclaimed its nuclear weapons.

The former Soviet republics that gained independence in 1991 and are now fully independent countries are listed below:

- Ukraine
- Belarus
- Armenia
- Azerbaijan
- Georgia
- Kazakhstan
- Uzbekistan
- Turkmenistan
- Tajikistan
- Kyrgyzstan
- Moldova
- Estonia
- Latvia
- Lithuania

These countries are recognised as independent sovereign states. However, they may have a variety of political, economic, and security relationships with Russia and neighbouring countries.

APPENDIX F: SOME COUNTRIES HAVE FORSAKEN NUCLEAR
WEAPONS. WHAT WAS THEIR RATIONALE?

The following countries have forsaken their nuclear weapons in one way
or another:

South Africa is the only country known to have voluntarily dismantled
its nuclear weapons programme. In the early 1990s, negotiations were
underway to transition South Africa to majority rule and democracy,
and to abolish apartheid. As part of this, the white leadership decided
to dismantle its nuclear weapons programme. Between 1991 and 1993,
South Africa cooperated with the International Atomic Energy Agency
(IAEA), to verify the dismantlement of its nuclear weapons, and in
March 1993 signed the Treaty on the Non-Proliferation of Nuclear
Weapons (NPT) as a non-nuclear-weapon state. South Africa set an
example for other nations and contributed to international efforts to
prevent the spread of nuclear weapons.

Belarus, Kazakhstan and Ukraine are three former Soviet Republics
who inherited nuclear weapons from the Soviet Union. By 1996, all the
weapons had been transferred to Russia.

Libya abandoned its nuclear weapons programme in the early 2000s.
This was a noteworthy success for non-proliferation.

Iraq: Following the First Gulf War in 1991, Iraq's nuclear programmes
were largely eliminated as a result of UN supervision.

Both **Argentina and Brazil** have had nuclear weapons programmes,
but eventually abandoned them. They both signed the Treaty of
Tlatelolco, originally conceived in 1968, which established a nuclear-
weapon-free zone in Latin America and the Caribbean.

Although **Sweden** never developed nuclear weapons, it explored the
possibility in the early stages of the Cold War, although until the Russian
invasion of Ukraine, Sweden had always safeguarded their neutrality.
They have subsequently consistently supported disarmament efforts.

In all these cases, there were varying degrees of international diplomacy, inspections and cooperation. We can assume that there was some coercion. About 5 per cent of states in the world by number are nuclear armed. All in all, although the number of nuclear weapons states has increased, it is to the credit of the non-proliferation act, its implementation and the United Nations that there are not more in the world.

INDEX

Inevitably, in a discourse about Russia's attack on Ukraine, the words 'Russia', 'Ukraine' and several other topics come up on every page. These are therefore not indexed, providing a more focused and useful reference.